The World's Longest Climb

DEAD SEA TO EVEREST SUMMIT

PAULINE SANDERSON

Enjoy!
Pauline Sanderson

50% of all profits from this book will be donated to
SOS Children's Villages and Practical Action

Dedicated to my mum - Nora Cooney

I have dedicated this book to Mum. Nobody can meet her without commenting what a genuinely kind, fun and loving person she is. She is the rock I have built my life upon. I know whatever I do, she will be there for me. She is my perfect Mum and friend.

Credits

All the Everestmax expedition photos were taken by the team: Dominic Faulkner, Nic Clarke, Sarah Lyle, Richard Walters, Rowena Wright, Jamie Rouen, Pauline and Phil Sanderson. The front cover shot is my favourite and merits special thanks to Richard Walters, aka Dickie. The maps were very kindly created by Martyn Mills (route map) and Alan Arnette (Mt Everest photo map).

The facts and figures about each country featured at the start of each chapter from Chapter 7 to 14 were researched from various sources and are not to be taken as official figures. It is intended to add some interesting background.

First published by Grafika in July 2011

ISBN: 978-0-9541089-4-6 (sc)

This book is printed on wood free, environmentally friendly paper.

Published by Grafika Ltd.
Riverside Studio, Riverside Business Park,
Buxton Road, Bakewell, Derbyshire DE45 1GS.
Tel: 01629 813300 Fax: 01629 815783
www.grafika-uk.com

Contents

Foreword

I'd like to introduce you to my friend Pauline. Perhaps it's unfair of me but I feel she needs an introduction, a form of warning, to steel yourself for what you are about to experience.

Pauline is without doubt the most exuberant person I have ever met. I feel slightly exhausted even thinking about her. She describes herself as "average"; she could not be more wrong. It's true I would never have predicted that she'd climb Everest but she is remarkable, and that's because of her approach to life.

We met as teenagers when we were both at the same strict convent school in Guernsey. We were a small happy gang of girls discovering smoking, drinking and boys together. Not that Pauline cared about any of that, she just wanted to have fun and our more typical teenage activities involved too much angst. I have a vivid memory of a group of us squeezed into a tiny Fiat 126 car with her dog, a Great Dane, squashed in too, hurtling down a Guernsey lane to a beach and Pauline's laugh ringing out. She is always laughing.

One of my favourite lines in this book is her husband Phil's comment, "Pauline! You don't have to be happy all the time, give your other emotions a chance." Not surprisingly, as she recounts, her reaction is to burst into laughter. That's why I give the word of caution. It can take a moment to adjust to Pauline's world.

On one of the first trips she ever took, her fellow travellers in the truck in Africa admitted that they nearly pulled out when they first met her. She can be very excitable. But they, like almost everyone else I know who's met her, soon realises what a wonderful character she is and falls for her.

Her constant happy, enthusiastic style should be maddening but there's something about Pauline that makes it only engaging. Perhaps because she is also extremely kind-hearted. In all the years I've known her I don't think I've heard her say a bad word about anyone, even when I know she doesn't like something they've done.

Unlike the rest of us Pauline feels no need to conform to any of society's expectations. While her friends were taking out mortgages and having children she was converting a transit van to live in. Years ago when she told me about some life-changing plan, I can remember voicing my concern about whether it would make her happy, she blithely replied, 'well then I'll do something else'. Since then she's had so many life-changing adventures and I can no longer imagine being surprised, or doubting, any plan she came up with. Life, for Pauline, should always be challenging and exciting and if it's not then you should be thinking about how to make it so.

That enthusiasm for life combined with her dogged determination makes her a remarkable and inspiring character. I also know that if she's coming over for supper I'll spend most of the evening laughing.

That's why I am confident that like me you will end up loving her.

Sarah Montague
BBC Radio 4 Today Presenter

A note from the Author

The bulk of this book is about the Everestmax Expedition, a journey that seems to have captured the imagination of everybody we speak to. But I think what will make the book even more interesting is the fact that I am not a professional adventurer or your average world record holder. I am actually a very ordinary person, who was lucky enough to take part in this extraordinary journey.

I am not brilliant at anything; I just don't mind failing or being average at something as long as I am enjoying it. However, I do have an almost warped sense of pleasure when it comes to endurance and enjoying uncomfortable situations. My goal was to enjoy the journey and all the successes of firsts and summits were a bonus, not a necessity. I would like this book to be an inspiration to fellow normal folk to give things a go and have a laugh along the way.

I can't write a book like this without thanking my husband for being my soul mate, play mate and personal adventure bodyguard. He is, without question, the reason I am still here today. He kept me safe, not just on Everest, but through so many of the adventures we have had. We still have many more to come, so his job is not over yet. In addition, my family and friends are fundamental to all I have done and do. I hope this comes across loud and clear. If not, I am shouting it now!

This amazing journey couldn't have happened without the belief and support of companies giving us generators, bikes, tents and much, much more. I want to give particular thanks to Marmot and Tiso, who came in at the last minute with so much enthusiasm and generous backing for Phil and I. Glenmore Lodge was also key to our decision to take part for giving us unpaid leave; this meant we didn't have to leave great jobs to chase a dream or lie too much to our bank to get a loan.

The Everestmax team was exceptional. I didn't know any of them before we left for Jordan and now I have six life-long friends. We shared adversity and elation as a team rather than as individuals. We also shared too many of each other's personal habits which I've tried to forget!

I would like to thank Mark Ramsden and his team at Grafika for rescuing me from drowning in the world of self-publishing. Writing the book seemed easy, publishing it made Everest look easy until Mark got his hands on it. They helped me bring the book alive so even if you don't like the read - it looks good!

We were all inspired by the warmth and hospitality we were shown throughout our journey. Media, generalisations and hearsay about cultures influence all of us. We expected more hostility from countries earmarked as unfriendly to westerners, especially during turbulent political times. Yet we saw none of it. As a result, I will never form an opinion about a culture based solely on general perception. The only generalisation I make is that people are kind all over the world - and politicians, religious leaders and extremists are not representative of a country's people just because they get more air time on the news.

I hope you enjoy the stories as much as I enjoyed writing them. I have several mantras, one of which is 'enjoy the journey'. So in that context... enjoy the read!

Happy days.
Pauline Sanderson

CHAPTER **ONE**

Cheap Underwear

Mum was 50 years of age and I was 18. We were having a chat in the kitchen with a cup of tea. You can't chat with an Irish mother without a cup of tea, it just doesn't feel right. She was trying to explain how time had flown by so fast and she couldn't believe her baby (I was the youngest of three) was leaving home. Just then, Terry Wogan on Radio 2 stopped us in our tracks with: "Age is like cheap underwear... it creeps up on you." Mum burst out laughing: "That's it! It's like cheap underwear!" Well, I don't know about you, but I have had lots of cheap underwear and every time it rides up I now think of my age. I mention this as my story with Everestmax came about largely because I see life racing by. I can't say no to a good opportunity as you never know if the chance will come around again. I have never been scared of failure. However, I am scared of missing out or not living life to the fullest. Life seems to speed up with every year that goes by while my body seems to be slowing down! I needed to do the Everestmax expedition because I knew there would never be another opportunity.

I was 41 when I heard about Everestmax and had the perfect job working with my gorgeous husband in a lovely home. How could I risk it all to go on a six-month expedition with people I had never met to do the biggest overland adventure I had ever heard of? The answer comes from my background and the people and places that have influenced me. That is why I am inviting you to come back with me in time and share my journey from the start...

My tale is that of a classic working class girl who, thanks to parental sacrifice, great brothers, friends and timely opportunities, has a book in her. You could sum me up by saying I have had a fantastic life tinged with an average dose of tragedy. My parents were hard working Irish immigrants who met while working on the buses in Leicester. They saved hard and bought their own petrol station and then removal firm. My childhood saw the transition from working class to middle class in the space of about 10 years.

My mum on our wedding day. She is the best!

I loved school: on my first day, aged five and a half, I jumped onto a rocking horse and thought I'd been transported to heaven.

A family shot at the petrol station. David and I are the kids, mum with her arm around me then my two aunts and gran

Until then, I had stayed with Mum while she served on the petrol station. At eight, I was sent to St Paul's Convent Primary School in Leicester. My biggest memory of getting ready is the big brown, almost furry, regulation knickers. Even at that tender age, I knew they weren't cool. School was playtime interrupted by study. I loved being with friends and, whilst I was always average or lower in the class throughout my academic life, not being number one didn't worry me as it was never on my agenda. As long as school was fun and I didn't let my parents down by being lazy, I didn't mind.

I was a weekly boarder at my senior school, Loughborough Convent. I came armed with my posters and things to decorate my dormitory cubicle. Other girls promoted pop stars or even their horses; I, being a devout Catholic, unveiled pictures of Jesus and Our Lady, which was another mark for the 'uncool' chart. Nobody was nasty about it; instead it was a source of lots of amusement, even with the head of dormitory Sister Mary Celine. I never minded being the victim of ridicule as long as it wasn't malicious. Maybe, my over inflated ego allows me to believe taking the mickey shows people are comfortable enough to have a joke with me. I have never looked for trouble but always for the positive. It drives my poor husband nuts; he calls it my 'fluffy Pauline world'. Bless!

I was in the best class in the school, complete with an upbeat approach and loads of great characters. I was never one for 'best friends', preferring to be my own person. Why have the same best mate when you can be friends with all? This is a characteristic that has helped me deal with so many career changes, going off on solo adventures and having a distinct lack of boyfriends in my twenties!

Seeing my parents physically work so hard from a very early age produced a very strong work ethic in me. It must be hard for children when they see a very smart office with a nice desk and lots of people chatting to understand that work is actually stressful and hard. Mum laboured at petrol stations in the days when they served the petrol, checked the oil and sold coal in all weathers. Dad would come back from long days doing removals absolutely exhausted.

When we sold the petrol station, Dad continued with the removals and invested in property. They would buy flats, do them up and rent them out. By the time I was 16, they had more than

Me aged 12. A good convent girl

20 flats and houses. I would help Mum clean them every week during the holidays; it wasn't exactly fun work but we managed to have a laugh all the same. Being with Mum was always positive. She was and still is a walking angel. My opinion on childhood is that spending time with somebody is what really counts. Shopping for food, visiting launderettes and cleaning flats didn't exactly add up to the ideal modern entertainment schedule, but we enjoyed each other's company and giggled over folding sheets and hoovering. I never expected to be entertained.

When I was 16, a family friend died of a heart attack at the age of 44. Dad was so scared by this he decided to sell up, chill out, pay less tax and move to Guernsey. He spent a couple of years finishing business off in Leicester while Mum and I lived in Guernsey. Thank God for that as he changed the whole ambiance of the house when he was there. He had turned into an angry bully of a man, who cared little about any opinion other than his own; if you didn't agree with him or pump his ego, you were 'out'. We were allowed to be happy, but only on his terms. This didn't sit well with me as my driver in life was to be happy. Why should he ruin it for me and those I loved? My respect for him changed dramatically over the next few years as I became more and more aware of what a Draconian existence he had started to impose on us. He wasn't going to bully me even though I tried to believe deep down he was a good person doing his best. I didn't respect or like him. He was obviously going through a mid-life crisis but it wasn't a temporary condition. I like to create a happy world around me; I try to avoid confrontation and talk up the situation, but will not tolerate injustice and he was constantly dishing out injustices to our family. He is why I have never chased money as it became his social medal of success. He surrounded himself with sycophants; the only people he would tolerate. I am not anti rich people. Indeed, far from it. I enjoy money as much as the next person but it doesn't stand alone as a symbol of success. It needs to be matched with equal amounts of good personality and good values.

The positive parenting in my life came from Mum. She told me what her mother told her: "If you haven't got something good to say about somebody, don't say it at all." A great philosophy, but absolutely impossible to live up to. She taught me so much without even knowing. She has a lovely Irish lilt and smiley face; all my friends tell me I had the luck of the Irish in having a great mother.

There is one aspect of her Irish culture we don't completely see eye-to-eye on: she was a complete product of Irish Catholic indoctrination, treating men of the cloth with real respect as God's representatives. One day, I tried on a new dress and she said what a great figure it gave me. I brushed the compliment off by saying every mother thinks their daughter looks great in a paper bag. Our local priest was in the lounge, so she asked him what he thought and he very kindly replied that he, too, thought it gave me a great figure. Suitably reassured, she said: "See, Father thinks the same as me - and he can't lie!" I managed to bottle the laughter until I got back to my room.

We all questioned the Catholic religion when the old man was behaving badly and there was negative press about the Church being involved in awful things. I asked her if she was still a Catholic or just a Christian? She replied: "I just want to be good and I don't know what they call it any more." That says it all. Without even trying, she became my role model for life. She never let trivia bother her or got stressed about anything unless it was protecting us from Dad's bad moods or very rare bouts of illness. Mum never felt educated enough to help us get on and voiced her feelings of inadequacy. All I could do was reassure her she offered so much more than facts and figures: unconditional love, support and total belief we could be anything we wanted was worth more than any degree.

I was so naïve about boys. Yes, I had two brothers, including Robert, who was seven years older with fun and 'fancyable' friends, but I would always be 'little sis'. Shame! David was 18 months older and we always got on really well, offering plenty of scope for socialising. But I never fancied any of his friends (or maybe it was the other way around and my ego is ruling my memory). The time we could have helped each other with dates was when I moved to Guernsey and he went to college in the UK. Bad timing.

Despite being on an island only nine miles by five, Dad insisted I went weekly boarding in Guernsey. This was a tad ridiculous but at least I got to fast track new friends. The first girl I met was Sarah Ratigan or, as I knew her, Grey. She was stunning, incredibly cool with black nail varnish. Radical! It took milliseconds to place her in the cool gang, who hated Catholicism and had attitude. She was very entertaining, adored by her juniors, and a good egg. Socially, I was a ticking time bomb - loud, excitable and able to put people off within seconds. I had just left a fantastic school with amazing friends whose love was mutual and was oblivious to the fact this would take time to redevelop. Pauline does instant – instant everything, not just coffee – and retrospective wisdom has to be learned in hindsight! Grey did very well to take her time and be nice to a juvenile nutter on springs.

Next day, I met the rest of my 11 classmates. Everyone got on well but there was one academic who was going to Oxford - I will call her Miss X, for sake of discretion. She was never nasty but, let's just say, she only spoke to us when necessary as I was her idea of a juvenile delinquent with no serious ambition. Little did she know I was to meet her in a later life and cause her jaw to drop…

Most of my class had boarded because their folks lived abroad but had convinced their parents to get them digs in town with relations or friends for sixth form. Among them was Maxine, who had been raised in Tanzania with her two sisters Sam and Terri, and became the most exciting person I had ever met. She lived in Africa, for God's sake, with beach huts and safaris on her CV. My dreams and impressions of Africa were limited to Tarzan (yes, I know I was a bit out of date!). Max and I started talking and laughing and our friendship was instantly based on the strongest grounds of all: chemistry and respect. She was loved by the rest and considered mature. She had shouldered more responsibility than most - looking after her sisters on international flights between her Mum in America and Dad in Tanzania from the age of 12.

Max and I became a team and she was part of my family. Her younger sister Terri, aged 12 at the time, was a complete rebel, who hated wearing shoes and anything resembling a rule. She wanted to be in Africa and found convent life as a boarder both stifling and boring. Keeping me entertained with her stories and rebellious streak and attitude, Terri was to have a huge impact on my life over the next few years.

Meanwhile, the 'cool gang' accepted me for what I was: a harmless fun character and a willing, if slow, pupil in the all-important art of becoming a social diva. They were a great bunch, many of whom are still great friends today. The disco scene rotated around the island; I loved dancing and was a sweaty mess by the time the slow dances came on – I had more chance of pulling a muscle than a decent bloke!

I remain convinced that having a great time did me more good than dating as I had no emotional stresses and was never in tears because someone had let me down or didn't understand. Who needs all that stuff? Of course, I was jealous of those with boys but not to a great extent. Max and I used to go to jumble sales, buy funky clothes and always turn up in alternative outfits. I looked like anything from an Oxfam Manikin to a fancy dress guest at the wrong party, yet Max was always stunning. I really didn't mind not being taken too seriously because, when I did get it right, it was always noticed. Again, not too much has changed on that front.

The thing I loved most about Guernsey (apart from the palm tree in our garden) was living by the sea as there are some stunning beaches. We had a gorgeous grey Great Dane dog, the classic gentle giant. I would go for regular runs on the beach before school with her. The outdoors had always stimulated me and made me feel alive despite having had relatively little exposure to it at this stage. We used to camp in the garden and climb trees. I was introduced to the countryside in earnest when I went on my first school trip to an Outward Bound experience in the Lake District when I was 15. I had never asked to go on a school trip before but just reading about it gave me sleepless nights.

My parents said 'yes' and I had such a great holiday. We went climbing, kayaking and camping and I was so consumed by it all. I didn't want to sleep in case I missed a single second. I never realised then that these sports could be hobbies rather than one-off experiences as nobody in my family had done anything similar. My parents were never raised with this kind of exposure to the outdoors, although Mum was brought up in the remote hills of Ireland. Her life had been about survival rather than adventure sports. They both left school at 13 able to read, write, perform basic maths and knowing the Catechism. After that, Mum worked in a local house until she left at 20 and came to England; Dad came over on the ferry to England at the age of 15 with £5 in his pocket and made his way. They had never been entertained as kids and didn't know anything about the outdoor adventure world. Thankfully, I found my own way there through school and friends.

My travels took a huge leap forward when Max asked me to come and spend my summer holidays with them in Tanzania… yes, please! Dad said 'no' without drawing breath and I hadn't a leg to stand on. Why did I deserve a holiday? But Max, being Max, grew a set of very large balls and came to the house to convince him it was the right thing to do and would cost just the price of a ticket. I loved her! He agreed and I was off for the best summer ever. I was just about to turn 18 and it was my first time on a plane. The girls watched in amazement as I screeched and twitched and babbled onto the plane from Guernsey to England. Onboard was a boy I'd fancied for ages, but I didn't care…I was on a plane and being cool wasn't part of the game plan. My next flight on Aeroflot to Tanzania via Moscow (who did the route planning for that one?) soon calmed me down into an average excitable flyer.

My other family the Hayward Shotts. Terri, Max, me and Sam after camping in a storm on an island in Tanzania

Africa offered adventure in a way I had no idea existed. It opened up a side of me that has since developed into a large part of my raison d'être: a thirst for experiencing and learning from different cultures and geography. The girls amazed themselves with how much they knew about their country as they hadn't had anybody to show it off to before. I was a sponge for information and soaked up every single moment. They adopted me as an extra sister and I became an honorary Hayward Shot. Their father Baz was a white African with a larger-than-life physical presence to match his personality. He had three other gorgeous half-African little girls whom he adored. On my return, I was brown, slim, exhilarated and buzzing. However a quick dose of cerebral malaria cured that and I was sent to hospital for a week. I found it all rather exciting and exotic, especially when 18 doctors came to see me as a novelty case. Some were quite cute!

Back at school, I had been voted head of house in my absence. This was the first year the school wasn't allowed to choose the head girl as there were too many who were disapproved of – yours truly included! How do I know that? She, the headmistress, told me. I am sure she was a witch cunningly disguised as a nun. All the nuns I had known before her were kind, fun and wonderful people; she was everything religion shouldn't be: unforgiving, opinionated and miserable, She ordered me to her room to explain why I thought I had the right to apply for university and laughed at me because my attitude wasn't that of a serious student. Hers was a sad world in which success comes from hard work, a somber approach to life and Mass on Sundays. Fortunately, I choose whose opinions I respect and react to. I neither liked nor respected her; so her comments meant nothing. This is still my philosophy. I went home and told Mum; she laughed a lot, mostly at my bad impression of an Irish nun, but also because she didn't agree. As far as she was concerned, it was my 'attitude' that was going to get me just where I wanted. Just to make the 'witch' nun happy that Christmas, I arranged for the whole school to do a conga procession with tinsel headdresses. She did her nut and called me into her office again. Whatever!

Next life-changing stage for me was Finishing School in Switzerland. Yes, I was sent off to become a proper little madam. Dad's bank manager said it was a 'must do' for young ladies trying to mix with the right sort. I obviously disagreed, but was ordered to find one, book it and fly. When something is compulsory you either get the most out of it or begrudge it all the way - I chose the former. The school I selected, Videmanette in Rougement, Switzerland, had the most skiing, the most French and was one of the cheapest. I was told it would be full of Sloane

Rangers as well as aristocrats and rich foreigners. What would I have in common with them? The answer was lots because they were human just like me. It was a fantastic year in which I lost that inverted snob chip on my shoulder and gained another valuable lesson: there are good and bad in this world, wealth and status has nothing to do with it.

Learning to ski was the most exciting sport I had ever tackled. I laughed solidly, often with tears in my eyes during my first few weeks on the slopes. I was only 19, had no fear and knew of no consequences. Never worried about being the best, I just wanted to enjoy the journey of learning something new and fun. My great friends Bones and Scotty (aka Amanda Hope Kibble and Claire Gell) were my partners in crime as we skied as much as humanly possible. Bones and I, in particular, got to know that mountain inside out and backwards. We would ski from the first lift to the last on our days off. This was my first real taste of mountains and what they could offer; I had no idea mountains were to become a much bigger part of my life, but the seed was well and truly sewn. I just felt so energized; loving nothing more than having the slope to ourselves and going as fast as possible. We screamed and whooped with sheer exhilaration at the scenery and fresh air. Nothing could top it.

Skiing gave me the chance to fall in love with the mountains and opened up a new playground I never knew existed

A predictable scenario was our constant battle with the teachers. We were a bunch of young women confined to quarters after 11pm; little wonder we tried to escape and leave body-shaped pillows in our beds as the world of men and bars was out there and calling. One Saturday night I was hanging from the first floor window when I heard in mid-stretch: "Pauline, qu'est-ce que vous faites?" (Pauline, what are you doing?). Even when in trouble we had to speak in French so, hanging precariously from the sill, I shouted back: "J'ai besoin de l'air frais" (I need some fresh air). Funnily enough, I was grounded whilst the others scuttled back to bed laughing their posh little socks off. At least, I left with some wonderful memories and great friends who are still an important part of my life.

That summer was my last before starting at Leicester University. Max, by now living in Virginia in the USA with her mum studying physiotherapy, said I just needed my flight fare and I could hang out there for the summer. Spoilt brat springs to

David my brother visited me in Switzerland. We make great 80's models. Check out those straight skis!

mind but, hey, if you don't ask, you don't get. Dad had been told travelling was an important element to any young lady's prospects... I loved whoever was educating our family into the nouveau riche ways of life as I was benefiting tremendously! That summer was spent with Max and Terri, who had rebelled out of Guernsey and had been studying in Tanzania for three years. She had grown into an absolutely beautiful young lady with a figure to die for, yet remained a rebel and hugely entertaining. Jude and Bill, their mum and stepdad, hosted us with incredible generosity and made me feel at home very quickly. They were as much a part of our social life as any of the young people.

Terri and I washed cars for pocket money, so we could go out and explore America. One of many trips saw the three of us driving down in Max's beat-up car to Florida and onto Disney World and Epcot. We had such a ball, having fun as only girls on tour can and creating perfect teenage memories. Another superb trip was into the Blue Ridged Mountains with Debbie, a family friend who had become a mum at 15! I was in shock as she was now only 35 and had two grown-up sons: a huge insight for me about America. Something else that shocked me was that they were still racist, not just in the hills, but in Virginia too. Max had a gorgeous black boyfriend who looked like Eddie Murphy, but had to be discreet for fear of the grief it would cause her family. Was this really America, the land of the free?

Terri and I had never had as much as a cross word in all the time we knew each other. Yet, on the plane on the way back to England, she was getting annoyed about her parents and seemingly everyone else. They were telling her to grow up because she was 17 with virtually no qualifications after not working hard enough at school. She had also fallen out big time with her father and I saw her and Jude have moments as Terri dug her heals in. Now I found myself doing the same thing and I will always remember her saying: "Not you, too, Pauline; I never expected it of you." We didn't fall out, but this was the nearest we had come to having a heated discussion. Her flight transfer took her from Heathrow to Tanzania and I continued home.

Six months later, I got a great letter from Terri. She was getting on great with her Dad, had got her life sorted and all was good. I was so happy for her but the next communication from Max brought the most awful shock - Terri had died suddenly in hospital! Nobody knew exactly what happened. Nothing had impacted my life like this dreadful news; she was just 17 with all her life ahead of her. Max, Jude, Bill and I missed the funeral as she was buried on an open pyre in Tanzania. Apparently, she looked beautiful and at peace. It took me years to come to terms with losing her and I really believe a lot of that was due to not being at the funeral. Terri was a fun and light-hearted person, who didn't want to take life seriously. Many of us spend too much time worrying about tomorrow instead of living for today and a disproportionate amount of time was spent nagging instead of just enjoying her. Now she was gone and qualifications and career plans meant nothing; I am not encouraging a reckless approach to life but, from then on, I decided to live for the day, taking any opportunity if it felt right. My gut reactions rule... one such instinct led me onto the Everestmax expedition, despite the obstacles that needed to be overcome. Life isn't a dress rehearsal and the one thing that scares me is dying with regrets associated with relationships or missed opportunities. From then on, too, I have always tried to resolve any argument with somebody I cared and/or respected before going to sleep. Terri and I didn't have an argument as such, but I regret our last flight together causing a strained parting instead of being in keeping with our regular relationship. Our letters had remedied this but still...

CHAPTER **TWO**

Legalities

Would you trust this woman to represent you in court?

FROM THE AGE OF 12, I was going to be the most famous judge in the world. I watched my big brother Robert become a barrister and very cool he looked too. My naïve thinking went like this: he was a fantastic big brother and a barrister, so the law must be a good profession. Get it? So I signed up for law without really knowing a great deal, other than I'd need to wear a wig and gown and go to court. Needless to say, I kept the fact I went to a finishing school secret from everybody when I went to Leicester University. The reputation of law students was pompous enough without adding fuel to the fire.

Robert said I could move in with him. He had a small terraced cottage in a place called Wistow. Living with Robert was fantastic because we became friends rather than a brother and sister who saw each other now and again. He taught me how to be a good housemate and was always there for me as I went through the disappointments of not being a babe and pulling at Fresher Week (the first week of parties in your first year). Everyone pulls then, so what about me? I went to every party and befriended people in all five halls of residence without even a sniff of a snog after two full weeks of letting rip on the dance floor... maybe the sweaty look didn't help? However, a few tears and big brother words later, I settled into being Pauline again and life took a big upward turn. I was in my element being single and invited to all the parties. A few of the halls actually thought I belonged there and I would often go for dinner and breakfast without being questioned. Then I pushed my luck too far; our table got a bit out of control at our Christmas dinner at Stamford Hall and we were reported. When they took names, I came fatally unstuck – mine wasn't on the list and all my mates were with me, so I couldn't adopt one of theirs. I was banned for the next term. Oops, but good party!

One of the best things about uni was 'OTC'. It stood for Officer Training Corps, part of the Territorial Army and a way of recruiting young officers. Jo Pawley, one of my best friends, had started uni at Nottingham the year before and rightly promised me I'd love it. It was the best social club ever and we even got paid. Every Wednesday, we dressed up in our green kit, got picked up by a coach and met up in Nottingham along with students from Loughborough and Nottingham unis. We played soldiers all afternoon and ended up in the mess at night with cheap drinks and chat to consolidate the day's flirting into a couple of hours.

Hormones were rife but, yet again, I somehow got passed by. Instead I became everybody's understudy for partners for balls, parties or the alternative role of 'sister' which suited me just fine: I met some of my best mates this way; people I'm still close to

My platoon in the OTC. I am the one on my knees trying to look hard while they look cool

today. I have crashed over and slept with more men than any girl I know… I mean just slept! I did manage to get a fantastic boyfriend, Will, at the end of my second year, but felt claustrophobic after six months and needed to be single again. A little bit ironic, don't you think?

The OTC also gave me more opportunities to get into the outdoors. We went on trips to Ardintigh in Scotland where we went kayaking, walking and camping in the remote islands; we went to Denmark for summer camp and, although I missed several other camps because I had to go home and work at a new family business, I did enough to be part of the gang in a big way. By pure chance, I managed to get roped into taking drill in the yard outside the Colonel's office. He noticed my dulcet tones and earmarked me for promotion to platoon sergeant. Great, I was about to have 24 people under my command… power! It was a huge stepping-stone in learning how to become part of an effective team.

Although I treated our combat exercises like a game, we really wanted to do it well and I watched how the other platoon sergeants and commanders got the most from their teams. There were some amazing natural leaders among the gang and I learned from them first hand. I remember when we were out on exercise during a three-week summer camp to Inverness; I had been put in as platoon commander, having to make all the decisions both tactically and team-wise for three sections, each of which included seven people. Pressure on! I had three other platoon commanders to call upon - all with loads more experience and intending to go full time into the real army. They knew I was there by default yet took me under their wings and never once made me feel inadequate. We got a good job done because we worked so well as a team. There were no egos, lots of hard work and morale was high. This was to be my teamwork formula for a long time to come.

I learned a lot about how important morale is whether for a military exercise, preparing a party or just working in an office. We took pride in making sure our teams oozed morale and, when they finally picked us up from the field after 10 days of midges and camping and no showers, none of us were ready to come in. A case perhaps of 'I'm not a celebrity keep us in here!' We teamed up with my mate Dave Wilson and his platoon. Every time somebody said the word 'barracks' we all did a fake spit to demonstrate our disdain for leaving the harder life for the soft option. Attitude is contagious and there was no better example than this. It was about maintaining the balance of being professional and having fun.

Again, I could go on and on about all the anecdotes and characters. Suffice to say, a good percentage of my closest friends nearly 30 years later are from the OTC. We shared more fulfilling experiences in three years than many friends can boast over a lifetime. Being thrown together into that environment means you have to rise to the challenge and fit in. Playing and working hard was worth the effort as these experiences laid good foundations for my future Everestmax expedition.

Back at uni, I was coming to terms with the law Pauline-style. I really wasn't that interested in the detail; going to every lecture and taking notes, but finding it hard to prepare for the tutorials. You could blend in with lectures as you were just one in a crowd of several hundred; in tutorials it was just the professor and six of us. Once I lapsed into daydream world and completely missed what we were talking about. I usually managed to say nothing, but the professor put a question to the group and then turned to me and asked: "What do you think Pauline?' I was clueless and just replied: "Well, it is the law, isn't it?" My friends and legal support team, Tony and Dean, couldn't contain themselves. They laughed so much the professor couldn't help but see the funny side. Has there ever been a more useless answer?

Dean of the Faculty Professor Grew called me into his office at just the wrong moment: I was in a gorilla's outfit walking through the law library and hadn't been to bed the night before. "Miss Cooney, give me the name of one professor who could give you a reference as a good student? Your attitude towards this profession is far from appropriate blah, blah, blah..." I gave him what he wanted: an apology and a promise to change my attitude. In truth, the last thing on earth I wanted was to be like him. I joined the rag parade in my gorilla's outfit and life moved on.

I was off to London next to train to be a barrister at Bar School. Once you have a law degree, you need to do one year at Bar School, climaxed by a hideous set of exams. You need to join one of the four Inns of Court in London and I followed in Robert's footsteps by joining Middle Temple. Merely walking around the Inns takes you back to Dickensian times, particularly at night. I sat on a bench and watched as barristers walked briskly past gowns flowing in the wind, followed by a subservient or a solicitor... not that there is much difference ha, ha. I felt very privileged to be part of this living history, even as a student. Going into the Great Hall, I was in awe of how many famous folk had dined and been party to the formal and informal events there. To help you visualize the Great Hall, it is the dining and presentation hall featured in Harry Potter. It certainly cast a spell on me.

Bar school offered me yet another bunch of great people, including Patrick Davenport who made law seem so easy. He never did any work and still passed first time with flying colours. It was so easy he didn't bother to stay at the bar; he now lives in LA and works in TV, being a judge for some of the BAFTA awards (I knew he was going to be a judge one day!). Don't let people brainwash you into thinking a barrister qualification is super hard and only for serious academics. Some, like Patrick, found it easy; just a pity I wasn't one of them! Academic snobbery still surrounds it however: for example, one of the first people who stopped me in the lecture theatre was Miss X, from Guernsey, now an Oxford graduate. I distinctly remember her jaw dropping and saying: "Pauline, what are you doing here?" I replied with a suitably sarcastic reply, given the fact she obviously thought there must be some mistake on the intake list: "Yes, I managed 'A' levels, then a degree and now I'm at the same academic institution as you! Oh, and yes, I haven't changed. I still prefer life to strife, and, judging from the look of you, you haven't changed either!"

In the early stages of Bar School, you need to apply for pupilage; an apprentice barrister position which is compulsory for one year. Perhaps it was my average degree or complete lack of interview technique that was responsible for me getting rejected by more than 20 sets of chambers. I look back and realise I was far too casual, confident and lacking in professional subservience to get past such an obstacle. I didn't worry about it for long; I might have to make it happen in a different way.

I was convinced a year at Bar School would be the same as a year at uni, so I got involved with the Middle Temple Social committee, socialised for two thirds of the year and was ready to study really, really hard for the last third. Oops! I was putting in an average of 14 hours a day just to go through the syllabus rather than revise it - needless to say I failed with drooping colours. I didn't take it as seriously as some; one girl on the same exam table collapsed and got carried out on the second day of a five-day stretch of exams. She wasn't alone. We could retake our exams within three months, so no sooner had I finished failing exams than I was back to revising. Freddie Talberg, one of my best mates from OTC days, was living round the corner from me. He came and visited with sustaining comfort food in the form of cream cakes (he had no idea what a morale booster he was).

I was a surprise pass; so got my CV typed up and door knocked on nearly every chambers in Middle Temple, telling them I was ready to start straightaway as a pupil. Loads of people had failed and there were bound to be some barristers in desperate need of a young skivvy (aka pupil). Bingo! It only took two days and, on the third, I started at 2 Crown Office Row, a highly prestigious commercial chambers that wouldn't have looked at me but for the fact their 'chosen one' had failed. I may not have got a great pass and plead guilty to having been a very average student throughout my academic career but, hey, I was where I wanted to be and had enjoyed a great journey getting there. I was more chuffed than a chuffed thing on a chuffed day! My friend took me shopping to get me a black suit, overcoat and, just to be a bit radical, I bought a hat too. Doesn't take much to stand out in the legal world.

The night I was 'Called to the Bar' my mum, brothers and London gang came to help me celebrate.

My pupil master was Richard Perkoff – a very serious man in his early 40s, but with a good heart and sense of humour once you found it. It didn't take him long to discover I needed a lot of nurturing to get excited by commercial law. I'd thought I'd go to a common law practice and do crime and general stuff rather than be part of a high-powered commercial academic bunch. Having said that, I was off to the Royal Courts of Justice and part of the system for real - something I had dreamed about when we walked past this great place as a student. I was well and truly in. Ok, I was only carrying books and papers and wasn't allowed to open my mouth, but I was in.

My co-pupil was a big black happy fellow called Orial, a great guy with a fabulous sense of humour. We would cross in the corridor en-route to making tea and coffee for the bosses or doing their copying. We were both there by default and felt frauds, yet loved it all the more as a result. We were like big kids having the giggles in an almost monastic environment. Our roles were boring and insignificant; a necessary evil. Again, circumstances were outside our control but our attitude made each day a good one.

Richard was a great guy, too, but I couldn't take anybody so serious too seriously. I was curious about a fun-loving guy trapped in a straight-laced body. He would only have two weeks holiday a year, plus Christmas, Boxing and New Year's Day; the type of guy who would say good night to his kids over the phone but obviously adored them. As a young 23-year-old, I went into maternal mode by nagging him to go home and play. So he came over all paternal, advising me to follow my dreams and beware of falling for law, mortgages and family commitments too young. He wanted to be an archaeologist but had dug himself a hole and was now committed to a future he had created by accident. I felt kind of sorry for such a nice guy although he loved his family. I thank Richard for being a big influence on my desire to avoid the career trap.

My favourite memory with Richard was when he took me to Simpson's on he Strand for a lunchtime treat. I had never seen anything like Simpsons; it was grand, ostentatious and simply oozing with people who wanted to be seen (or not, as the case may be) and those so comfortable with the status they had become part of the wallpaper. We were waited on by a very subservient waiter, who made me feel like a princess. Richard recommended the beef. It was delivered on a trolley with a huge silver dome on top. My face and gasps spoke volumes… cor blimey! Along with that went the traditional tip of £1 to the waiter, something inflation will never keep up with and tradition never kill.

By the end, we had sampled several glasses of wine and Richard had let slip that he had always wanted to wear a trilby hat. Perfect. As we poured ourselves out of the front doors, behold on the opposite side of the street was a gentleman's outfitter. "Richard, you are coming with me!" I took his hand and we went shopping. He tried on several trilbies until his face lit up. I'm not sure when I have enjoyed shopping so much. We walked back into chambers and Richard and I laughed heartily as he walked up to the clerks' office, took off his new hat and threw it James Bond-style onto the hat stand. It was one of those jaw-dropping moments. The secretaries and chief clerk looked in wonder; what had happened to Richard? Nothing whatsoever, folks, he was just being himself.

I saw an advert in Middle Temple from Customs and Excise, who were now able to offer the second sixth month pupilage and a salary of £11,000 pro rata per year. The idea of having a salary was fantastic as I had never earned proper money before. Holidays between uni terms had often been spent back in Guernsey working for the latest family business; totally reasonable given the education and international trips I had enjoyed. The Irish philosophy was that you work hard for the family: you don't get paid but you get life paid for! This was fine, but I was now in debt and ready to take control of my life. So I went for the job, got an interview and, blow me down, I got it. I was now officially independent. This job meant I never needed to ask for money from my family again. I was in a position to start paying back my debt and save some for travel. I still get a thrill from saving: when you know you've earned something rather than just been given it, it means so much more.

Customs and Excise was a great move as I loved the work, the people and the lifestyle. My new boss Derek was like a surrogate father and the team believed in a 5.30pm work curfew. In other areas of law, solicitors firms or chambers, it was snubbed at if you left before your boss and you shouldn't expect that to happen before 7pm. No thanks. On top of that, I had my own office, phone (social hotline) and support team to type up my documents and help with all I needed to know. I had arrived; closing the door behind Derek, I just squealed and span around in my chair half a dozen times before calling every friend I could.

I was in the VAT department, going to tribunals all over the country and representing government against individuals, accountants and lawyers. I loved having to present a case. That was what I'd trained for but it still scared the **** out of me. I could guarantee loose bowl syndrome every time before I went into court but that youthful hunger for exposure makes you a masochist. Secretly I loved it. I was never a brilliant lawyer; good at saving court time by sorting things out in advance yet hopeless at examining witnesses. It always looks so easy on the TV where lawyers somehow catch out witnesses by getting them to say things that confirm your case. Instead judges constantly had me for 'leading the witness' by giving the answer I wanted in the question. I never really mastered it, but they got used to me and never lost their rag.

I also have quite a poor vocabulary for a lawyer. Once a judge asked me a question using a word I had never heard of, but fundamental to its comprehension. I asked for time to confer and confessed to my instructing officer I had no idea what he meant. Neither did he! I humbly asked the judge to rephrase the question in simple English: a sense of humour is often more use than an ego. I then got my own back when I made an analogy in the case of an appellant actor claiming his health club expenses as part of his VAT allowance; saying it would be appropriate if he was playing the part of Rambo, but not the sedentary role he was in. The judge stopped me in my tracks: "Miss Cooney, who is this Rambo you refer to?" I smiled and suggested his generation might consider Tarzan a better analogy. Humour won the day as we then debated the joys of old fashioned films.

My star role came presenting in Bristol Magistrates Court. I was more used to formal tribunal centres with chairs and desks; this was an old fashioned court with the judge high up on an elevated platform and us down in the dark wood bench-like arrangement. I finished presenting my case and went to sit down; getting lower and lower before it was too late...I had completely forgotten the seats flipped up and hadn't pulled it down. I fell unceremoniously below the table, much to the concern of the old judge. As I pulled my head up over the bench, I said 'hello!' with a big smile and he stood up and asked whether I was alright in that grandfatherly kind of way. My opponent somehow just moved on, without as much as an acknowledgement - a great mickey-taking opportunity missed. It was too funny for me to be embarrassed and I wasn't after a date, so it was his loss.

Life at the office was a blast. I made great friends with the lawyers and support team. We also had a tiny gym in the basement for £6 per year and just big enough for about six machines. I worked out with two of the support team, John and Jan, preparing for sports days and events against other offices all over the country. I ran in cross-country, 800m and 1500m track races and loved it. I got hooked on training and swore never to leave until I had won a medal. One gold, one silver and one bronze later meant total fulfillment. I ran about 30 races to get them but they were well worth the effort.

Lawyers ranged from hard-nosed academics to those like me who had just passed the exams but were quite practical; a fascinating mix. I entertained the intellectuals with my irreverent approach to life and hierarchy and they entertained me with genuine wit and rapport. I needed to share this with the whole office, especially the support teams so they could see that lawyers do have funny bones in their bodies. There were about 500 people in the office and about 100 lawyers. Geoff Tack, my number one pal, and I got another eight lawyers together for a Christmas show with comedy sketches, songs and dances that brought the

Sue, Nicky, Chris, Geoff and Nancy showed how lawyers have a sense of humour by putting on a great show

house down. The finale was a version of Grease's *You're the one that I want*, with words taking the mickey out of the senior lawyers and culminating in a raunchy dance routine in which I straddled Les, until then a respectable lawyer. This one show did more for office morale than any party or pay rise had done in a long time. Lawyers weren't only human; they were funny!

Life in London is really what you make it. I was lucky having a ready-made social club at Middle Temple and also as most of my mates had got their first job in London. None of us had loads of money, but we did have time and relatively little stress… party time! Each weekend saw a gathering, often at the coast and normally in fancy dress. I had very creative influences in my life such as Simon Ratigan. We had cocktail parties in Hyde Park on roller skates and dinner parties followed by casino nights. We dressed according to the film we were going to see – you ought to have seen my catwoman outfit! Simon and Stuart, another creative, disappeared for a couple of weekends and turned up at a fancy dress party in a car converted into a tiger called Fang: it literally had fangs and every part had been painted or ornamented to look like a tiger, even down to the sound system being wired to roar. Simon let me use it when he went travelling; imagine my street cred for not only having an unconventional car but one that was both fur-lined and roaring! I felt like the young folk in a Coca Cola advert, having fun with a bunch of great people.

Another aspect of London was the myriad of posh yet affordable parties organised by our friends. Dressing up was always a great excuse for our wee girl band to get the evening off to a good start. My great friend Elaine Binks, a talented song writer and guitarist, wrote satirical songs about subjects such as dieting, pmt,

Fang, the roaring car that helped to give me the ultimate street cred as a lawyer

spinsters, the list goes on - shame on all talent scouts for missing her. I was one of her co-stars and jumped at any chance to perform. Our home-grown audience never failed to make us feel special and pump our ego. For her 40th, Jo Pawley used her connections to organise for us to cut a CD of all her best songs. We recorded in a proper studio with ear phones, big microphones et al. I felt like Kylie Minogue, but without the figure, or money. All you need is a taste of these things that seem a sacrosanct place for the talented - or not so talented in the case of Jordan!

I saved up enough money working at Customs for three years to fund the year out travelling I had always promised myself. Rent was cheap, my wardrobe not a priority (still did Oxfam), entertainment creative and a dinner party for six cost me a tenner, complete with cheap plonk. Entertainment is about whom you are with rather than how much it cost That's been my line for years... I still get away with it.

I was 27 and was due to leave on March 10 1991: time for the best Valentine's Day, bar none. Any female between 14 and marriage or commitment has mixed emotions about February 14. For years 'ego rescue' friends sent me cards to ensure rejection came with a laugh. This year I had 10 and a bunch of roses! What was going on? Easy, I was going away, so people could be brave or foolish enough to declare minimal interest with little chance of commitment. Who needs analysis anyway? I had 10! Bloody marvellous.

I did have a proper date with Dave Wilson, my OTC mate. It was all a bit bizarre as we had been good mates for years without even a flirt; perhaps the heels and black suit did it. I was on a real date with a hunk and he was paying! It was a great night but where was it leading? I was off for a year. Should I abandon my travels as it felt special? My gut instinct said: don't risk my travel dream for a love dream, regardless of how good his pecs are!

My employers were very supportive of my travel plans but, as it was a government set-up, I had to resign rather than have a sabbatical. So I did! When making big decisions, I put all my thoughts down on paper and list the pros and cons. Seeing it all on paper seems to help me view things more clearly. Going travelling for a year would mean leaving my well paid job, with no guarantee of getting it back. Was it worth the risk? Of course it was. Alternative was to scrap my dream, so it was an easy decision after all.

I got leaving presents and a big party with many admitting they wished they could do the same thing. Mum had reservations. Her best and most memorable comment was: "Don't you go falling in love with any Australian farmers... I've seen the Thornbirds!" Believe it or not, that came back to haunt me. Being sentimental and soppy, I hate saying goodbye to anybody for a long time, especially family. Dad wasn't interested, so no problem there; but my brothers and Mum were very hard.

CHAPTER **THREE**

Have Dream, Will Travel

Our truck had some sensational bridges and obstacles to negotiate

ANNA HARDY, an OTC friend, was my first travel buddy. We signed up for Truck Africa, the cheapest company to get us over land in a truck from England through Africa, along with another 20 would-be adventurers. We met fellow members of the team over a few drinks at the company home. I later found out I was the reason why a few people nearly pulled off the trip as my excitable nature reared its ugly head far too early. I think even I would have been put off by me! I was loud; thought I was funny and loved everybody totally oblivious to the fact they couldn't love me. Fortunately, it was only a couple of weeks before we realised we were the best group ever. The banter and rapport was relentless.

West Africa was a hard place to travel independently with relatively little experience. Things like the Sahara and parts of Africa such as Zaire were just a bit too unknown for someone without a huge amount of independent travelling experience in Third World countries. Not only did we get to see amazing areas hard to access without independent transport, we had a ball as a team!

We had such a range of people - a doctor, cockney dance instructor, 'ozzy' traveller, couple of post grads, plus a sprinkling of eccentrics. We enjoyed barn dancing in the desserts, football matches, sing-a-longs, juggling shows and more. We shared the kitchen, cooking and shopping duties with nobody wanting to slack. Hard work, no egos and good morale were keys to our successful team. It was a fantastic way to learn how to handle borders, police and travelling in general as well as great preparation for facing adverse weather and comfort challenges. We spent hours/days digging our four ton truck out of sand in the dessert and mud in Zaire, as well as rebuilding certain dodgy bridges that were hard for a Land Rover never mind our truck.

Anna, Adam and I enjoying some monsoon cooking

I loved the mud; the rawer the situation, the happier I was. Solid foundations indeed for my Everestmax experience.

Anna had a couple of unfortunate incidents, including having her passport stolen in Bakino Faso. Best thing was to get her to the nearest British Embassy in the Ivory Coast. Anna and I left the truck for two weeks before re-joining the team. We took the local train for three days - fantastic. We decided to jump into the empty cargo carriage as the seats looked a bit full and just enjoy the view from the open door. Every time the train stopped (which was quite often) more women joined us with baskets of mangos. We couldn't speak a word to each other but that never stopped us. Body language is great and, before long, they had adopted us. They were doing our hair and we were helping them sell their mangos as each stop further down the line became a market place. It was a superb experience and one to treasure.

The Sahara was vast and a great place for a bonfire and barn dancing

The truck often needed digging out. Dave Green and I enjoying a successful mud fest

Meeting up again with the gang, we couldn't wait to exchange stories. Our short stint convinced me I was ready to go it alone when the time was right. Meanwhile, there was too much fun to be had and Zaire was the biggest physical challenge, both for the truck and us. It was also where Anna had her second incident: having got stuck for a couple of days due to the road/ mud track, Anna, a hardy sort and not one to fain illness, started to have the shakes, fever and general discomfort at regular intervals. We knew we had a case of advanced malaria on our hands and no way of getting her to the hospital in our truck in time. Then, with the aid I am sure of Mum's hotline to God, a Land Rover came by with two people offering help. A one-day journey would have taken us five in the truck and Anna was on her way out when we got her there. Yet, despite the very rudimentary level of the hospital, it had the right drugs, nursing staff and doctors to help

24 great people in a truck going through Africa

her make a very fast recovery. I remember walking her to the toilet carrying her drip and watching a rat run through the gutter. Amazing how your environment dictates the norm - we both laughed, just glad she was getting well. What's a rat between friends, even in a hospital?

By the time we got to Uganda, I felt it was time to leave the gang and go solo as they were continuing to Zimbabwe. We had been together for nearly three months and it's always good to leave wanting more. Another fine reason was that I had received a letter from Dave about a month before saying he was going to try and meet me in Tanzania. We said our goodbyes and I got the train to the border town into Kenya. The windows were covered in bullet holes, a harsh reminder of the Idi Amin days when they were ruled by fear and torture. It was dark by the time I got to the border town which, like nearly all border towns, was the worst of all things - dirty, smelly and over-populated with drunks and weirdoes. Best place to look for refuge was the police station as

Music is always a great way to interact with kids.
Even my efforts seemed welcome

the places that could have passed as hotels or houses with rooms would have complemented a horror movie. I explained I was too scared to wait for the border to open and asked to use one of their cells. Startled, shocked and incredulous, they said they were dirty and not right for me. I insisted I trusted them more than the street, so they gave in, said I could sleep between the cells and became protective towards me. I put down my sleep mat, tied my mosquito net to the cell and slept like a baby: gut instincts have often proved to be accurate when judging people, helped by a huge dose of luck.

Next bus journey took me to Nairobi and into backpacker paradise with bunkhouses and cheap accommodation everywhere. There were tours and excursions and more. Only negative was there was no water for showers due to engineering problems in Nairobi. I'd have to rely on personality! I met a great Scottish guy called Richard in my bunkhouse and we shared a couple of excursions together. Then I called my old housemate in England, Jonny Hardy, to find out whether Dave was coming. I went out for the morning with Richard and when I got back there was a message for me: 'Dave arrives at 2pm tomorrow in Arusha.' I was shocked. He was actually coming; he must like me! One small issue to overcome was that I was in Nairobi in Kenya and he was arriving at Arusha in Tanzania in less than 24 hours. Off I went on a local bus to the border. I arrived late that night where I managed to blag a lift to Arusha, arriving in the middle of the night. No buses were going to the airport until morning but I spotted a guard outside a building with steps and, more importantly, a stairwell. I asked him to guard me until morning as I pitched my sleep mat and bag there. We had a bit of chat and he woke me up with a smile, pointing me in the direction of a café and the bus stop. I made it to the airport with 20 minutes to spare. For the ladies out there, I was in a bit of a dilemma with regard to looking 'haveable'. No proper wash for a week had done little for my greasy hair and travelling for more than 24 hours on dusty roads even less for my skin. Despite wearing my cleanest set of trousers and top, I looked a bag of ****. This will test him! I remember standing on the balcony watching all these very clean people walk off the plane and one stood out in bright orange trousers and a sun hat. It was Dave. He greeted me with the enthusiasm of a long-lost lover, which automatically made me forget what I looked like. But he didn't object to us checking into a hotel and having a bath before we got up close and personal.

We went on Safari in Ongorogoro Crater with a really cheap outfit - hardly classic 'out of Africa' but did the job - and we had a great laugh together before going off to climb Mt Kilimonjaro. I had convinced Richard while in Kenya he should join us and, again to my surprise, he did. He had never really done anything like this and wasn't sure what the big deal was about. In Tanzania, it's compulsory to go through a company to climb the mountain which means you get your food and accommodation and porters. How easy is that? Richard kept saying "this is a breeze". Indeed it was for the first three days when the scenery and chat was great. Then came summit day and, as we set off in the early hours, I remember hearing a strong Scottish accent repeating the phrase: "this is a nightmare; a bloody nightmare!" We approached the top at dawn… how romantic. I turned to Dave for a momentous snog at the top of the African plateau at sunrise just as he was turning away to throw up. He was an army boy trained not to show fallibility, so posed for photos and smiles as if all was well. The summit isn't typical as it is a huge expanse rather than a defined top but nonetheless felt great. The route down offered the option of a scree run (masses of small rocks that allow you to take a fast line down if you run at them). Altitude feels better as soon as you start going down so we both threw ourselves down at high speed, much to the amusement of our guide. I love the mountains!

Our next stop was Malawi to go and stay with my mate Max, who had married a farmer, Ian, out there the year before. Best way there was on one of those lovely slow trains with open doors and fantastic views. A couple of days went very fast as we watched Africa slip by before we stopped very dramatically several miles from the border with no local transport. We hitched a lift on some bicycles with some kids and had to stay the night at the border in what could only be described as cement boxes with an excuse for a bed. It was all part of the adventure and the joy of Dave was the way he rose to adversity ...he laughed and, as long as we were safe and not ill, all was good in the world. At dawn and after a phenomenally good sleep (I jest), I pinned down what looked like the only truck going into Malawi and got a lift all the way to Lilongwe where we found Max and Ian ready and waiting with top notch African farmer hospitality.

We spent time at Lake Malawi; then Dave flew back to his world and I carried on with mine by going to Zimbabwe with Max and Ian where we rafted the Zambezi together, my first big river experience. It was fantastic. I was so impressed with Zimbabwe, the nearest I saw to real cosmopolitan services and facilities in Africa. There seemed to be a very healthy balance of wealth between the black and white populations and to see it today with all its poverty, famine and injustice is a tragedy. It was hard saying goodbye to Max as deep down I knew she wanted to come with me. She had introduced me to wanderlust and we always planned to go and travel together. Our time will come.

Next stop was Australia, where I planned to catch up with my friends Tor and Mike Torrento for a couple of weeks and go onto South America. Little did I know I would stay with them in Sydney for a few days, take a weekend trip to Burke for the annual horse races and not return for another four months.

Burke is known as the Gateway to the Outback and it was at the races that I heard about Kakadoo. It sounded great. I only had a weekend bag; but who needs more? I told Tor I wouldn't go back with her to Sydney but come and get my kit in a few weeks. I started to hitch north; I remember sitting on the side of a deserted road opposite a loan store with doors banging in the wind and the occasional tumbleweed flying past - another horror film setting sprang to mind. I said I would give myself a couple of hours and be very selective whom I went with. It wasn't exactly the M4, so the choice was non-existent. After nearly an hour, a pick-up went straight past; then stopped, waited a few minutes and reversed. One dark haired skinny-booted man got out and the other cute outback-looking kind of guy was leaning out the window to see if I needed a lift. I have always trusted my gut instincts about people and these two looked just fine. I jumped in the third seat in the front and within minutes the banter was there. We had nothing in common other than humour, yet I relaxed very quickly as I could tell they probably picked me up to protect a lone woman.

I struck gold getting a lift with Carl

They were good country folk having their first holiday in several years from running a farm in Picola. They took to the road and stopped at places along the way, including the museum of farming. Talk about a busman's holiday. You couldn't get two more different people: Bob wasn't exactly simple, but not totally firing on all cylinders; he was genuine, funny but a bit quirky. Carl was initially shy, but possessed a smile to melt any woman's heart. I ended up spending three days with them and sleeping in the back of the pick up. They were such gentlemen and, when it came to finding my next lift because our destinations didn't match, they asked around the coffee shop at the trucker stops for advice. They vetted the drivers and came up with Bob, who was driving his road train (really, really long truck) to Darwin. We said our goodbyes and exchanged addresses in case I happened to pass through Picola on my way back to Sydney (slightly indirect route by about 1,000km, but watch this space).

Bob had been a driver for about 20 years and never picked up hitch hikers. He liked his own company and told me so, so the first day wasn't that chatty as he listened to the radio all the time. Current affairs was his pet love judging from the proportion of news we consumed. Slowly, slowly I started to drip feed him my points of view and he couldn't help himself; he shared his opinions and, before he knew it, we were solving the political situations of the world. Our rapport grew and we ended up sharing personal stories and dreams. We got on so well he even let me use his bed while he drove. Apparently, this is sacrosanct, so I was really honored. Best bit was when we had a flat tyre; I was helping where I could and he looked at me and said: "Who'd have thought it? A bloody pommy lawyer and an outback trucker making such a good team!" That was a good moment. As we approached Darwin, he invited me to go for a drink and meet some of his buddies at the sailing club who could help me arrange things in Kakadoo. He introduced me to a character called Dan, a former oilrigger who was going to sail his yacht to Indonesia. By the end of the night, he offered me the opportunity to crew on it. He was leaving in 10 days which was just perfect.

I saw a whole new side of Australia thanks to Bob and his road train

I spent that time doing the backpacker excursions, which were fun, fascinating and really easy. As a backpacker, you don't even need a pack; as soon as your transport stops, they take your bag from you and put it onto another bus for your backpacker hostel which organises all your excursions. From there, you're put on another bus before unloading at the campsite and going off for your mini-adventures. Phew, got it? I'm not knocking it; safe, affordable, great views of nature and just a bit more convenient than I had become used to.

I left for Indonesia with Dan and two other packers he picked up as crew. They were a lovely couple from the UK. It took five days and my best memory was hanging over the bow with dolphins playing up close. Superb. I was the luckiest person in the world; except in the movies there's always a hunk with an adorable smile and knowing look. Ah well, dolphins and a weirdo captain was a good alternative. Weirdo is a bit of an understatement actually; he was obviously used to buying his way into several female beds as he wasn't exactly an oil painting and four missing digits on his left hand didn't help. If I'm building a hostile picture, it's because he turned a beautiful journey on a small yacht into a game of verbal ping pong. He made rude suggestions and I batted them back at him. He couldn't get that all I wanted was company and an adventure sailing to Indonesia. Sex wasn't on my agenda; however rich he was. I was working my passage by cooking and being a first mate (but not in the Biblical sense). Can't blame him for trying but tenacity isn't an attractive quality in a dirty old man. Next stop and I was off.

I had bought a rough guide to Indonesia and read about Borneo, the ultimate Indiana Jones venue. It said: 'Anybody attempting to cross Pontianak to Samarinda through the river networks and jungle will be one of the few people to have crossed the west to the east Borneo.' Red rag to a bull! Loads of us crave the experience that 'few have done' so you can wallow in the raw pleasure of seeing unexplored worlds minus guides, backpackers and excursions. I made my way to the capital Jakata, where I went down to the harbour to ask around for a cargo ship to take me to Pontianak. Luckily, one was leaving in a couple of days. I turned up early with a few luxuries from the food stores I thought might be in short supply in Borneo. I had also invested in an Indonesian dictionary as there would be nobody to talk to in English. I was welcomed by the crew on board and shown my bunk in the crew area. There were a few other women on board a working cargo ship which lacked refinement but was very hospitable.

Chess was a great communication tool as everybody plays in this country. The captain invited this white westerner to the upper deck to play him. The crowd gathered and I rose to the challenge with the body language of an undefeated champion. Unsurprisingly, I got absolutely slaughtered. The crowd loved it; the captain's ego was magnified and I avoided becoming the hate figure of a foreign conqueror.

When we arrived in Pontianak a few days later, I booked onto a river boat using my best Indonesian. This was like the main bus at peak hour in central London as it was the only way people could access the villages that go inland. We started with several hundred people. I spent five days playing dominos, talking,

Commuting in Borneo on a 5 day river boat. It got cosy

singing and washing with the friendliest bunch of commuters in the world. There was only minimal space to sit; usually it was on our bags. Food was served from the kitchen and everyone was ordered to wash at least three times a day. This consisted of grabbing a bucket of river water and doing your thing in the back cupboard. It broke up the routine and was good excuse for a stretch.

The river boat life was never boring or lonely

More and more people left until life became almost luxurious on a fast flowing but calm river. By the end, it had narrowed and wasn't navigable by your average people carrier.
My Indonesian was coming on a bundle, so when thrown out into the last village before the real jungle I was able to ask around for a bed and a guide to get me through the next stage of the journey on water and land. This was when I met a man called Tama, who became the best part of this journey. By the end of five days going through the deepest and most dense jungle of Borneo, my respect for him knew no bounds. He had tattoos around his neck and looked very native and uncorrupted by western materialism; being shoeless and sporting a backpack made of wickerwork. Tama agreed to take me as long as he could bring his mate to go hunting. His mate Lujah was raw and less endearing but with equally impressive jungle survival skills.
The first part of our journey was in a dug out boat with an outboard motor going upstream (against the flow of a river in rapids that in England would be classed as a three).
People pay good money in our country for this kind of adrenalin fix. I shared the journey with a mother and baby who needed to get to their village upstream. I found myself staring at her red gums from chewing beetle nut, but her spitting ensured it was never for long.

As we left the final 'normal' village, we were already in the

Going upstream in Borneo was an adventure in itself

heart of Borneo and it would take another five days walking through the jungle before we would reach the river to take us on to Samarinda. Our supplies were minimal; I had bought food that didn't need cooking from Jakarta, but Tama and Lujah had other ideas.

We walked through swamp-like terrain mixed with crossing rivers up to our thighs and meeting snakes and creatures I'd never seen before. Although our route didn't vaguely resemble a trail, I never doubted Tama, who always made sure I was within sight. I got my first experience of a leech within minutes and Lujah just laughed at my girly reaction to it. Tama explained how to pull them off and it wasn't long before leeches were part of my wardrobe. I took off my boots and 'deleeched' at each stop. Just part of jungle life, I suppose. We stopped to camp and Lujah took out his knife and made string from the bark of a tree. Tama caught some fresh fish in the streams which the men proceeded to cook over an open fire with rice. I was well fed and contributed condensed milk for the rice pudding… not their favorite, but I loved it. They made me a shelter with tarpaulin and Banu's string! I was as safe and snug as a bug in a rug, thanks to two jungle experts. I had a set of dry clothes for each night as my day clothes were totally drenched in sweat or swamp water. The heat meant I woke to discover my wet clothes were covered in jungle ants and bugs. I was living the Indiana Jones adventure... I love a bit of rough!

Tama my hero in Borneo

Beetle nut smiles from ladies of the jungle

We communicated well enough to have a laugh and share thoughts. It was quite an experience and feels as unique now as when it happened nearly 20 years ago.

One day we came across a stilted village with a long house. All the women had red teeth and were chewing beetle nut and looking happy with life and their animals. It is such a simple, primitive and forgotten world. It was a hard life but they had all they needed - home, animals, jungle food, water, men and beetle nut! I never dwelt on the saying that jungle people are still cannibals. White meat would have been bad for their constitution anyway!

I had seen and learnt a great deal in the five days in the jungle and, when it came to saying goodbye before I got on the next river boat, I found myself choking. Tama had somehow touched my world without ever seeing it. He was a strong individual both mentally and physically who had taken a total stranger under his care in a way a westerner, who knew our culture, would find hard to do.The next four days saw me back to riverboat life. More lovely people and Samarindar was a great ending to my Borneo adventure.

Indonesia offered all the trappings of western tourism perks and I felt compelled to try to some of them out. I went scuba diving with an instructor called James. I'd spent nearly three weeks without speaking a word of English and was desperate to talk at my normal level. Despite knowing this, he still took me on as his only student without wearing ear plugs. What a stunning place to dive; I highly recommend it.

I spent two months in all enjoying Indonesia before flying back to Australia. I found my way back to Carl's farm in a very small town called Picola. I did a surprise visit on my way back to Sydney. Not exactly en route, but how could I refuse an invitation to stay on an outback farm particularly when the man who invited me was the personification of 'sexy'? I spent more than a few days and, before I knew it, was invited for Christmas. It must be love! They weren't a rich family and, apart from a big dinner, I knew Christmas would be a humble affair. I had never met a family where mum goes out to get the boys their annual pair of jeans in time for the Christmas dance in town. So you can imagine how surprised I was to open a present that was so special. They had bought me my very own acubra hat which moved me to tears as I know they weren't cheap. It fitted me so perfectly; I lived in it from that day on.

I loved working on the farm with the boys. It was hard labour with old-fashioned machinery I'm sure only otherwise existed in John Wayne films. Throwing bails of hay onto a slow moving truck was their job and arranging them on the truck was mine. This was followed by loading them onto a conveyer belt into the barn one by one. We all worked so well together and I was part of a team having a good time. I remember one night, we went into town. As we approached, I heard the laughter and noise of a regular bar. Then we walked in. It was one of those moments where everything stops; drinks were held mid-swig, even the resident spiders on the walls stopped and stared! Then I realised I was the problem. Carl just said: "It's ok; she's a good Sheila." It was like somebody released the pause button and all was back to normal. I had passed the initiation test and that was that. Men in these parts were far from chauvinist; they were chivalrous, but only if they respected you. I never did find out what they were like if they didn't.

Carl had a superb horse - a 16ft stallion – and let me ride it. Being a Brit, I ride like a Brit. As I proudly trotted down the drive - straight back, rising trot, head up - all I heard from behind was Carl shouting: "Remove the poker from up your backside." Just another cultural difference, I suppose. We rode for a couple of days with a 'swag pack' and I did manage to remove the said 'poker'. I slouched and used one hand on the reins... yee bloody ha!

Time came to make a decision: continue on my travels or I would never leave. I was starting to feel far too much for Carl and becoming part of the family. His parents wanted

Jude and Dan showing me what to do with the bales.... hundreds of them!

me to stay as long as possible as they had never seen Carl talk and laugh so much. We had a natural chemistry and were in big danger of falling in love…help! The words of my mother came rushing back to me:"Don't fall in love with an Australian farmer!" I said I was going to leave and, although he was agitated, he didn't talk me out of it.

Picture a hot day in the middle of an Australian outback town: Carl, rugged and farmer-like with his hat tilted back, rolled up shirt sleeves, leaning against his pick-up trying not to cry; me, in my travel dress, trying to look cute and in control. The bus turned up and forced us to say goodbye; potentially forever… I hope you are crying now! I bawled my eyes out all the way to Melbourne, which is a long way. Wow, that was a hard call; being a practical person can be overwhelmingly emotional.

Fast track forward and Carl called me when I got back to England. He had tried to find me in Melbourne to catch me before I left Oz. His folks had told him to propose, but it was too late; he had missed me and I couldn't go back. He visited me in later years and we remain good friends to this day. He is married with three kids and still farming.

So, after leaving for a weekend trip more than four months previously, I returned to Sydney to catch my flight out to Easter Islands and on to Chile. Trekking around Torres del Paine was amazing; I teamed up with a Dutch guy who made me laugh most of the long way round. It was on this trek I first realised the potential of rock climbing and I was lucky enough to have a clear day when looking over to the three Torres: three huge granite pillars in the park and about one km high. They stood out in the distance like three purpose-built natural features in a theme park. I fine tuned my binoculars and couldn't believe what I saw tiny but clear – climbers! I really wanted a bit of that.

The rest of my travel time in Chile was spent hiking and hitching a lift on a navel ship to the Antarctic before completely running out of money. There were many more great stories from this year but I have been selective. I learned so much, met so many wonderful people and fulfilled a dream.

When I flew into London, I had just enough money to get me to Clapham station. I hailed a taxi and was greeted at the house by an overwhelmingly excited girl gang, who gladly paid for my taxi. I had been away for over a year so picture the scene... half a dozen girls, high pitched voices, all wanting to talk and no time to breathe. Fantastic!

Next stop was Guernsey to see the family. Bob and his wife Ju had had Olivia, a gorgeous baby girl. They, along with Mum and David, were all there to meet me at the airport. I love travelling and I love coming home. Dad couldn't be bothered to come to the airport. Need I say more?

Me standing with the amazing Torres del Paine in Chile.

CHAPTER **FOUR**

Dave and I after climbing Snake Dyke on Half Dome Yosemite

Peak Time - Discovering Climbing

IT'S AMAZING how quickly we slip back to the norm and within two weeks I was back at Customs and Excise, this time in drugs and porn... lucky me! Although I'd resigned, they hadn't rushed to fill my post and my boss wrote to me in Chile to offer me my job back if I was there by April.

Dave and I behaved like we had been an item for years and I was off to Plymouth most weekends to stay in the officers' mess in Seaton. This was my first proper grown up long term relationship. Dave was the reason I enjoyed trying to become more lady-like. I bought nice underwear and dabbled in make-up, yet we were also playmates, so rough and ready was part of the package. It was only a couple of months before Dave was posted out to Belize. We decided to meet up after three months in California to go climbing in Yosemite National Park. We said our goodbyes (I did the drama queen girlfriend version). I decided to learn to climb before we had a holiday in one of the climbing Meccas of the world. I found a 'learn to rock climb' course in Sennen in Cornwall for a week and was totally hooked. It was a five-day course and we were doing multi-pitch routes by the end of the week. More, more, more!

My next climbing experience was based from Camp 4 in Yosemite and included climbing Snake Dike on Half Dome and some of the lower graded classics. Camp 4 had its fair share of bargain basement, scabby climbers (not a derogatory term, just a common one), who made life look cool by a rough sleeper's norm with their ripped muscles, chalk covered clothing and heaps of passion for analysing 'moves'. Little wonder my first three weeks of climbing meant I was hooked for life.

Dave introduced me to mountaineering in an equally superb venue, namely, the Alpine peaks of the Monch and Jungfrau in Switzerland by the Eiger. Wow! We spent half a day on the snow bank outside the mountain hut learning how to ice axe arrest[3], walk in crampons[4] and rope up[5] etc. All we had to do was pray I never had to use any of these emergency skills in anger... oops. The Monch was a straightforward plod: nothing technical or challenging but a really great start. Then we went to an old and gorgeous mountain hut made in classic wood with a log burning stove and had it to ourselves... how romantic! Dave looked a tad distracted most of the time and, despite numerous attempts at frivolity, sensible was the order of the day. This was my introduction to 'mountain responsibility syndrome'. I had never really thought about mountains as dangerous and avalanches only happen in the movies but Dave knew better. After a night of heavy snow, he decided we needed to rope up and then he started to belay[6] me to the top of a slope to the main area again. It all felt quite involved to me and a very long winded way of getting up a steady slope I would sledge down in the valley. However, I was enjoying playing at being a mountaineer and looking cool until a couple of blokes came from nowhere and casually walked straight past us in the opposite direction with no ropes on. Without much ado, Dave untied us and decided to walk back to the world of looking cool.

Next day, we were off to do the Jung Frau: a lovely climb with one steep wall before the final summit ridge. We got to the top and it was a perfect day. All was well. On the way down, Dave went behind with the heavy bag. We were roped together but with quite a lot of rope between us. I started off down the steep snow wall that was just ok to walk down facing out. In my head, I was going steady, slow and sure. I had joked about it being a perfect face to bomb down on a sledge as it had a natural run out at the end. My inclination was about to come true; in the corner of my eye, I saw a fast moving object go flying by.

Apparently I looked quite cool on the Junfrau mountain... for the 80s!

It was big, with legs, arms and a rucksack. It was Dave! He had slipped and was going at the rate of knots down the mountain. I instinctively turned into the mountain to do an ice axe arrest but he had picked up too much speed and both the axe and I were ripped off the face - and we were off too. Before I knew it, we were at the bottom. I sat up, looked at the 70ft plus drop and said: "What a rush!" That was, of course, the comment of a naïve and clueless student with no idea of consequences. Dave meanwhile looked a tad shaken but not stirred and we both commented on the fact we must have been going really fast as we had both flown over a crevasse[7] halfway up. All in all, I loved the whole adventure side of mountaineering. It would still be a while before I really got to grips with how much decision making is involved in being safe.

Life back in London was fast, fun and fulfilling. I was sent on a training course for five days to Wales with the legal team. We did what is now considered predictable: built rafts, orienteering and chat. What a great industry! By the end of the week, individuals in our team had either confirmed they were weirdoes or created new and much better relationships. I went back to the office knocking on doors that may have otherwise appeared closed for legal advice. I wanted more of this.

Dave and I hatched a plan for me to train as an outdoor instructor and for him to leave the army. We would start a business as we both loved the outdoors and he seemed to be choosing civvy life as a future option. We found a one-year course for me in Llanberis North Wales. It was £5,000 for the year and I would get all my basic training and qualifications as well as trips to the Alps and Scotland with loads of work experience i.e. cheap labour for a business run on the back of our training. Perfect. I just needed to save enough money and a little extra and I could start in 18 months. Saving cash meant I was back to a dinner party for six, including wine for £10. My mates were ace and, as I never really drank loads, they never made me buy rounds. It felt normal again. I had basically only had six months when I wasn't saving for some big project - just as well I bought a nice range of underwear when I did!

Six months before I was due to leave the law and start in Wales, Dave dropped a bombshell. He called me on the phone and said we needed to split up as he didn't know if he would marry me. He wanted to do the SAS, so it wouldn't be fair on me. WHATEVER! It would probably be wrong not to be heartbroken at least once in your life. Otherwise, how on earth can you relate to all those movies dedicated to broken hearts? Just then I could relate a little more than I would have wished - but that's life.

My brother Robert, always first port of call at point for elation or tragedy, gave me the best advice I could have wished for: don't meet up or talk to each other for at least six months. Apart from making him tell me face-to-face he wanted to split up (not very brave these hard men), I banned him from calling or seeing me. This was made much easier as he had a posting in Canada but in my world I was laying down the law. I created a complete lie to get me through and lived it for months. Apart from the odd infrequent yet dramatic breakdown, I did just fine. Why do we insist on putting on Greatest Love Songs when what you really need is *Bob the Builder... yes we can!?*

Despite our split, I decided to continue my outdoor dream and start my own outdoor company, Jo helped name it Peak Time and I called some of my more affluent friends to see if they wanted to invest. Dave Collinson didn't hesitate and just said: "Tell me how much and when and we will make it happen." I never asked him if he really meant it, but it didn't matter; the fact he said it when I needed him to was the important thing. I was on the road to recovery thanks to a strong support team of family and friends and belief in myself. In fact, I had one of the best weekends of my life six months later, coinciding nicely with my deadline to get over Dave. Due to a combination of leaving London and my 30th birthday party, I invited about 40 of my best mates to Llanberis. Dave called after finishing his posting and I said we should meet up the weekend before my party to see if I got upset. Well, blow me down, I was so in control. So, ironically, he was my right hand man at my party weekend. I had moved on; I still loved him but, to his surprise, didn't need him. I honestly didn't need him.

My 30th birthday weekend was a blast. We took over a hotel/bunkhouse in Llanberis and spent the weekend doing obstacle courses, races, dancing and staying up around a camp fire by the lake singing songs till 4am. Afterwards I drove away in my van and burst into tears of happiness, thinking I had the best mates and life in the world. I was ready for the next stage knowing they would always be part of my life wherever I went.

One month later on Friday, September 30 1994, I left a great job at Customs and Excise, complete with £36,000 salary, gorgeous Chiswick flat and fabulous social network, and jumped in my red ex-post office van (called Mutley), with a range of outdoor gear and £3,000 cash. I stopped off at Elaine's place for the Saturday night and drove into Mountain Ventures next day to meet the other 17 people who had signed up to do the same thing. As you can imagine, I was a mix of nerves and excitement. If I hated it, I could always go back... couldn't I?

The official meet and greet was in the dining room before lunch. A tall blonde, bright- eyed and bushy-tailed, fleece-covered man walked in laughing with a long-haired hippy-looking younger man. They sat opposite me and carried on their chat before, eventually, I couldn't cope with being left out any longer. Well, talk about hormones at first sight. My blonde 'Adonis' was called Phil Sanderson: confident, funny and very, very cute. Last thing I was looking for was a relationship after what I had just gone through, so I put this down to pure lust and fun.

From day one, I knew I was going to love this whole experience. As a year to get an insight into the outdoors industry, it was hard to top. The company was called Mountain Ventures. Ok, it didn't always spend money on kit, we had to fight for our rights and were definitely cheap labour, yet the scheme worked. We got our training (not the best), food and accommodation (not the best), worked on youth groups and corporate groups (you've guessed it) and got loads of opportunity to play (simply the best).I love the old adage 'what you put in is what you get out'. We didn't wait to be spoon-fed opportunities and experience. We had a mixture of mature students, of which I was the oldest, and freshers straight from school who had never worked before.
Between us all, we had a recipe to max on the experience.

I shared a room with Lorraine McCall, who was also 30 and the best possible room mate: contagious laugh, endless enthusiasm for the outdoors and just a lovely, lovely person. We had a bunkbed in a room 10ft long by 6ft wide and there wasn't one cross word the whole year. Lorraine and I shared our terraced cottage with four blokes and, yes, one of them was Phil. How convenient. I saw the house list and convinced a naive 18-year-old to change places with me as sometimes fate needs a gentle hand. Steve English was an 18 year old who, judging from his array of green kit, seemed like he was on the wrong course and meant to sign up for the army. It didn't take long to discover that he was less of a soldier and more like a Cadburys Cream egg, hard on the outside and incredibly soft on the inside. His sense of humour ranged from obscene to childlike and he continues to make us laugh today as he lives around the corner and

Leading my first HVS in Llanberis

continues to be special. John, a 26-year-old, had made the very brave leap from the army institution into civvy street. His eyes looked like a bunny in lights and he was an easy victim of pranks as he would get so angry and then laugh… most of the time. Last, but not least, was Yoz, our resident long-haired free love hippy, who was actually a 10-year-old trapped in a 24-year-old body. We had the perfect house!

People maketh the journey and this journey was great. The year was a rollercoaster of outdoor experiences from sea level traverses where I got swept off; an intro to Scottish winter

Mountain Ventures team on a sea kayaking course in Wales

River kayaking in the Alps during my Mountain Ventures year

mountaineering, kayaking through ice, leading my first HVS[8] , the list goes on. The fact that Phil was really good at everything made him even sexier and suddenly I found myself being a super keen river kayaker. I bought Phil flapjacks if he looked after me on the river. He taught me to roll a kayak in a pool in about 40 minutes and I followed him down every river and rolled myself out of trouble. I was never a particularly good technical kayaker but, boy, was my roll a goody. From never having been on a river before, I was doing grade four and the occasional grade five rapids in Wales, Scotland and then on a 10 day trip in the Alps. By day eight, I had run out of adrenalin and become a bank bimbo doing the shuttles[2]. How much of a good time can a girl take? It was like being back at uni again. Focus was on having fun, but with a serious agenda. Recipe for success was hard work, lots of fun and sharing strengths with no egos. We needed to put in the time to ensure we had enough experience in all disciplines to be assessed at the end of the year.

Phil and I walking toward Cosmic Arrete on our first Alpine trip together

We worked as instructors on weekend and five-day kids' programmes. The children were mostly from Liverpool and came complete with attitude, strong accents and great senses of humour. I put everything into the courses and hated to see them go. This experience made me feel I wasn't meant to be an outdoor instructor. I really enjoyed teaching kids though, so the long-term solution was to be a teacher where I'd have the opportunity to really make a difference…watch this space!

I still had a few months of the course left when a friend called Ian Roberts (Robbo) turned up. He had left the army to work in Nepal for a rafting and kayaking company called Equator Expeditions and had brought a Nepalese Sherpa called Purna back to England for the experience. They stayed with us and Robbo talked about life in the outdoor industry in Nepal. Before I knew it, I had planned to go to Nepal, spend a few months out there to learn the territory then sell myself as a leader to trekking companies. This would use the last of my savings. I had no responsibilities to anybody, so my ideas could be limitless.

I finished the course at Mountain Ventures at the end of September 1995, flew out to Nepal on October 1 and came back at Christmas. This was to be a life-changing journey; I flew out on my own and thought I could team up with another mountaineer in Kathmandu to do a peak – a slight presumption using the word 'another' there. Little Miss Naïve was wrong. After pacing for hours/days through Thamel, the tourist nucleus in Kathmandu, talking to loads of Nepalese agencies to get a permit and find a buddy, I found I could share a permit with two other climbers but they would be climbing separately. I needed a guide as part of the permit and this was to be a lovely man called Sunir. He would not need to climb but would walk in with me. He would help me to interact with locals, tell me history and make life so much more interesting. Never having been to Nepal, I expected everything to be much harder than it actually was. Navigating my way to a mountain in the Everest region seemed daunting but it proved much easier with Nepalese bed and breakfasts, called tea houses, all the way. They varied in style from places to roll your mat out in front of their dung fire to quite well presented private rooms in mini-hotels. Given I have the navigational skills of a compass without a needle, I was pleased to discover the only time you would need a compass would be in a white out[9].

We took a local bus from Kathmandu for a nice long ride to a place called Jiri, the starting point for a trek into the Everest region. You could fly in and save up to a week's walking but time was my friend not my enemy. I sat on top of the bus with the luggage and a few other Nepalese people. If it does crash, you can at least jump clear. Inside, you could get crushed with a chicken in your face to add further fowl insult to injury. In true Asian local bus style, it was overcrowded with people, food, luggage and animals, so a blonde, blue-eyed white man really stood out. His name was Paul, a tank driver in the Danish army, who joined me on the roof. He also had a guide and was planning on spending three weeks trekking around the Everest region. We hit it off straightaway and so did our guides as we became a pack of four and the journey changed complexion into a banter-packed, cultural adventure. By the time we reached Namche, the market town in the Everest region where you can get just about anything, Paul had agreed to come and climb Island Peak with me. There was no way to get his name on the permit but it was either now or never; I had a rope and kit for me and we hired a tent and kit for him in Namche. It was all basic and, given my 'extensive experience', it was ridiculous I nominated myself as experienced enough to lead. We got to base camp, put up our makeshift tent – the zips nearly worked – with only apple turnovers from the last tea house and noodles as food.

We camped next to a very posh outfit bedecked with tables, chairs, table cloths and three-course meals. Being a compulsive social animal, I felt obliged to make their acquaintance and forced myself to have a few cups of tea and a piece of cake. The posh crew moved to make another camp higher up the next day. Very early the next morning, we set off with our apple turnovers and bottle of water, plus as much kit as we thought we'd need to attempt our first Himalayan peak. Only Sunir had come with us to base camp; Paul's guide had sensibly stayed at the last tea house. Sunir had the look of a worried parent watching his children go off to their first day at school - except this school was 6,119m high and a highly dangerous commute for novice mountaineers.

We walked into the night and got to the posh team's higher camp. A kindly-looking Sherpa had obviously just finished making tea and breakfast for his clients. We acknowledged each other with smiles and heavy breathing and walked on. It was dark and the approach was becoming steep up a scrambling rock face. I felt sick and dizzy and turned to Paul who was feeling rough too. We didn't hesitate in turning back: it was only a peak and being ill wasn't part of the 'enjoy the journey and live' game plan. People have died from altitude sickness at much lower levels than this as it can kick in over 3,000m. After that, your approach has to be calculated and reactive. Your brain and lungs are vulnerable to the lack of water and oxygen in the air and the air pressure. Cerebral oedema[10] and pulmory oedema[11] are common causes of sickness or death if left unchecked.

Paul and I on the summit of our first Himalayan mountain, Island Peak Nepal

Paul and I went down to the friendly Sherpa at high camp who sat us down and gave us some soup. We recovered quickly and felt so recharged just by descending a few hundred meters that we both agreed to try again. Maybe logic flies out of the window above 5,000m! A member of the posh team had come down on his own and jumped at our offer to go to rejoin his group. We moved as a threesome and reached the snowline and glacier around dawn. The posh team was only 100m away and we waved to say we had one of their team with us. They refused to wait, a reaction that still stuns me. We roped up together and the three of us walked across the glacier; not entirely sensible as, if one went, did the other two know what to do? We had a chat, but it was all I could do to remember the right knots. This isn't a role model approach to climbing your first Himalayan mountain… don't do it at home!

We went slowly, yet surely, across the glacier until we reached the 100ft snow wall. The posh team had a fixed line* on it which was great for us. However, they had clients at the base of the rope who had obviously completely forgotten how to tie on their prussic loop (piece of thin rope that when tied on to the fixed line acts as a brake in the event of a fall). I helped the last three and our extra new team mate by tying them on and we followed a bit later to distance ourselves from them. We were also absolutely knackered and the break was a good excuse to enjoy the spectacular views. Paul and I got to the summit along a narrow ridge and felt very, very chuffed with ourselves.

We continued our trek together around the Everest region. There is a mountain called Ama Dablam (6,812m), the Materhorn of the region. It is a chocolate box mountain and I knew I would climb it one day. Mt Everest was always there, but didn't look as impressive as Ama Dablam. Almost merging into the skyline with Nuptse and Lhotse, it was unspectacular in its own right. No seeds were sewn to bag the big one, just the sexy one.

Paul and I said our goodbyes. He went back to Denmark and I continued my adventure exploring the rivers. I met up with Robbo who was still working with Equator Expeditions. He got me a cheap deal to go kayaking with a couple of Equator's commercial rafting trips – three days on the River Seti and the Kali Gandaki for a further five. On the later journey, I met another river leader called Jon Fauver, a chisel-jawed blue-eyed blonde American dude. Both trips were amazing; the white sandy beaches, camping every night with fabulous food and having an outstanding social time with folk amid the big volume waves. I always had a dedicated Nepalese kayaker with me to make sure I was ok. Any chance to play on a wave, do a spin or show off their limitless skills and there they were. Their primary role was safety kayaking for the rafters, but who said you can't enjoy your job and provide entertainment at the same time?

I went back into Pokhara, a very mellow version of Thamel on the shores of a beautiful lake overlooked by the sacred mountain of Machupacharu (Fish Tail). Festooned with bakeries, bars, cheap hippy clothing and lakeside eating places that carry the scent of the 60s, it also has a touch of the 80s thrown in to make it all the more commercially viable. Robbo introduced me to Gerry Moffat, co-founder and one of the three owners of Equator. He was a Scot whose American lilt owed much to spending so much time in Sun Valley Idaho. Before we knew it, we were talking business. I loved the product so much and had many ideas to help them in their offices and business. We came to an arrangement over a bottle of rum. I would go home as planned in a couple of days and then return in eight weeks to work for a season in the office. I would get bed and board, free trips on the river, a return flight to the UK and $1,000 for three months. Ok, so I wasn't in it for the money.

Going back to Kathmandu next day, I was told to go to the Equator office and ask for Mahendra Thapa, Gerry's Nepalese business partner. I was very surprised to find Mahendra was over 6ft, well built with black Ray-Bans and dressed more like a businessman than anyone I had seen in months. Looking nothing like your regular Nepalese man, he had a calm disposition but with a loud and contagious laugh. We didn't spend long together but he obviously trusted his partner's judgement and we agreed a loose arrangement for me to turn up near the end of February.

I flew back to England and was met by Dave. Oh, I forgot to mention Dave and I had kind of got back together in-between Phil and me kind of getting together. Anyway, he was finishing off selection for the SAS. I had been back a day when he decided I wasn't the officer wife for him, so we split up again. No worries, by this time I wasn't convinced either. I had spent more than two months in Nepal and was missing Phil who had been my main playmate, housemate, personal comedian and occasional lovemate for a whole year.

I drove back to my new digs in Llanberis. Apparently, Phil had driven by four times the previous day to see if I'd got back (mobiles weren't yet in). I had popped round to the centre where he was working but he wasn't there. Then pouring a cup of tea to calm myself down, I saw his car pull into the drive. Quick dash to the mirror to check I possessed the travelled-yet-cool look he found so sexy and there he was. He hugged me like I'd never been hugged before; long and powerful. I found enough air to say "you missed me then?" Holding me in an even tighter grip, he replied: "You have no idea how much." Well, that was good enough for me - the rest, as they say, is history.

Despite the love tie with Phil, I still went out to Nepal for the season, as planned. This was pretty normal as the outdoor industry is full of nomadic existences with temporary homes and flexible relationships. Mind you, I've never looked into the divorce rates to decide whether it should be encouraged. I flew out to Kathmandu and checked into a cheap hotel as it was late. It had all been so exciting until then but, as I lay on a less than comfy bed with the noises and smells of Asia through my window, I had an 'I hope they remember I'm coming!' moment. Insecurity flooded me for a few minutes until a wave of excitement usurped it, sending me into a deep sleep.

I went to the Equator office next day and Mahendra welcomed me like a long-lost friend. He arranged for me and my bags to be taken to his home. I was to live with his family for the next few years. His wife Rashmi, was a long suffering raft guide/company director wife who juggled rafts, guides, porters and more during season time. That's besides the three lovely children Manish, Manisha and Kanchu. Season one was a riot. Thamel was full of backpacking travellers and holidaymakers determined to experience what Nepal had to offer. Hundreds of businesses offer rafting, trekking and safari tours and I took to sales like a duck to water in an uncomplicated fashion. I went onto the streets of Thamel, next to the street kids selling tiger balm, force-feeding flyers into the hands of innocent passing tourists to entice them to a promotional slide show with free rum and coke. We tried to get Gerry, Jon or Robbo to do the show as they were macho enough for men and sexy enough for women - it really was that vulgar. The most popular river was the Kali Gandaki, so that was the name the street boys gave me. 'How are you Kali Gandaki didi?' (didi is a common term meaning elder sister). I was finding my new world fun, exciting and not too sophisticated.

As a team we were unstoppable. We all had ideas and the passion to make them happen. All wanted the business to be a success but none needed to be rich; just 'wealthy' enough to sustain a lifestyle. All that is except Mahendra who, unlike us westerners, had a family. He had come from a very poor childhood in the foothills and wanted to give his children everything. He never hid the fact he would love to be rich, but would never put money before safety or friendship. He was respected and loved by everyone in the industry and was the 'wise one'.

Robbo and I wanted to expand the company into the mountains. We both knew so many people just wanted the opportunity to climb a mountain while trekking in the Everest region. Thousands of people go trekking each year and Nepal, with its equivalent of bed and breakfasts all the way around the routes, is totally trekker-friendly. We had a team chat and, by the end of that season, opened two more companies, Equator Trekking and Equator Tours and Travels. This meant we could organise anything for visitors to Nepal and start a climbing school on Island Peak. I became a director and partner in the company.

I was fully committed to Equator and the life in Nepal but the season was coming to a close in May and I'd heard nothing from Phil. I called him to see whether we were still an item. The answer was a resounding 'yes' but he was really unhappy in his position in Wales. The solution was simple, leave his job, come out here and let's make Equator work together. I had no idea what a big deal this would be for him. Phil had been confident living in a stable environment where we played and worked hard in familiar territory, now I was asking him to up sticks and live in Asia – unknown territory. No longer the one to turn to and not knowing the locals, he would feel like he was starting again. Knowing him as I do now, I am even more impressed he did it.

Phil came out in time to catch two river trips on the Kali Gandaki and the Sun Kosi to give him a flavour of what we were doing. Then we took off to India for the summer break between May and late August. We went by bus and train to Manali, but not alone. We had agreed to take an 80kg raft along to Mahendra's friend who needed it to run rafting trips. Poor old Phil was not only introduced to Third World public transport over long distances but had this huge raft to manage over four days between one border, two buses and two trains, including a second class sleeper. He really thanked me for it! But we got there, delivered the goods and spent the rest of the summer trying to climb mountains with one rope, a basic rack and no maps.

In the bank in Manali, I saw another white man with a mountain-look about him. I asked if he knew anything about mountaineering in these ranges and he replied that he would be happy to help. Phil pulled me aside and said: "Have you any idea who that is? He is John Barry!" I was still clueless but apparently he is a pretty well traveled mountain guide. My immediate response was "Great, he can help us then. Let's go buy him a drink." We spent the night being highly entertained by John and his old RSM (Sergeant) with some of the rudest stories I've ever heard.

Phil and I spent the summer in the mountains trying to climb Menthosa and Phabrang but unable to top out on either of them. We were camped only 200m from the summit of Menthosa in perfect conditions; then it snowed all night making the whole place avalanche prone. We walked back out despite being tantalisingly close to a summit where we would have been the first or second British ascent, according to John. We were trapped for three days on Phabrang in our tent in bad weather. Thank God for cards! We eventually got a weather window and had been going for an hour or two when we heard loose rocks falling at such a rate they sounded like bullets. If one hit, we were history. Phil and I turned around and burst into tears of relief back in the tent. We were a three-day walk from the village and were on our own if trouble occurred. This was all good experience. Turning back is part of mountaineering; if you haven't got the ability to make a judgement call not to summit, you shouldn't go up a mountain. Once you have done it a few times, it becomes part of your mountaineering emotional toolbox - an essential tool, in my opinion.

That summer had still been a great time for exploring. Roof top rides on buses had drivers with death wishes on the route between Manali and Ladak. Let's just say, the gorges are very, very steep and the buses go very, very close to the edge. It feels very, very fast. You really feel alive once you've reassured yourself you're not dead. We made it back to Kathmandu ready for the start of the next season. We always had a start-of-season party, so Mahendra could round up the troops and we got to be known as the Equator Family. Mahendra promised to look after all the families of the guides while they were out working and was true to his word. These parties often ended with rickshaw races to the casinos and maybe the odd bet or two to finish the night off.

Mahendra was a very positive influence on my approach to management and being part of a team. I may have been to university and worked in London with professionals and even been on management training, but getting results is what really counts. I talked fast, walked fast, thought fast, and reacted fast. Passion from running my own business made me hungry for success and gave me a sixth sense to see and do things everyone else missed. When I walked into a room, I would automatically see something that needed doing. Why couldn't my staff see it too? This made me frustrated and occasionally impatient. It wasn't long before the team read me very quickly and I got the reputation of being a scary woman. Whenever I got too uptight, Mahendra walked in, had a big laugh, placed his hand on my shoulder and said in a very slow, soft voice: "Pauline, be mellow!" Not sure if it was how he said it or just his timing, but it always worked. He made me mellow, the team chatted and we moved on. We had a bit of a good cop, bad cop role. I had never been the boss before and was suddenly on a steep learning curve in a different work culture. Nepalese folk love to please and tell you what you want to hear, not out of deception but to make your life easier before they go and sort things out. Fortunately, tense times were few and laughter was more the norm. The thought of my angry face was obviously enough to make everybody perform or hide. I now have great empathy for leaders and people running their own business. That sixth sense brings with it good and bad characteristics and being aware of that has helped me a lot.

How success is defined is always a good moot point. To me, it was a real mix of happy clients and an office atmosphere I wanted to run into. Oh and making money helped too. Our clients always came back happy and the numbers looked great. Robbo and John were very much a part of the development of the company, but were out on the rivers most of the time. The whole season felt like one long party with friends of friends always arriving in need of a night out. I got to know the regulars in Nepal and ended up socialising with climbers I had only read about like Alan Burgess and Jo Simpson. I chatted over expeditions with Simon Yates and Henry Todd; I felt part of a world I had always regarded as glamorous in an adventure context but, as ever, they were all just regular folk. In Nepal, the major players mixed in with travellers and novices. It was no big deal – and I loved it. I had no idea what a living legend Gerry was: he is one of the world's best expedition kayakers leading many first descents in Asia, yet when we did self support[1] on small rivers he made me feel as if it was as special as any river he had done. This was the joy of Nepal - no hierarchy, just good experiences in the Himalayas. I was buzzing the whole

Gerry and I using local transport in Nepal to get to a river

time and never ran out of energy which was just as well as the hours were long and the workload grew with the business.

Phil was still adjusting to being nominated as the first instructor to work on the Equator Climbing schools on Island Peak. He had never been up there, unlike Robbo and me. I'm sure knowing I'd led the mountain route on Island Peak saved him from being intimidated as he knew it really couldn't have been that difficult. I knew Phil would have no problems with the mountain itself. Possessing a gift to make people feel calm and secure, he was born to be an instructor and is also one of the safest mountaineers I have ever met. He needs to be properly prepared and ready for any eventuality.

Our approach to work was very different and we clashed. I had to cope with Phil hating anything to do with logistics and getting stressed to the eyeballs; he had to cope with me wanting everything done now and oversimplifying things he saw as important. I often took tasks off him just to get them done which undermined him and meant he never gained the confidence to tackle the same things next time. We were both extreme in our own approach. Despite some tense times, I waved Phil off to Lukla airport with a huge hug and love oozing. He was off to lead his first Himalayan peak with one client and another five to follow afterwards. The climbing clinic consisted of letting clients make their own way to the last tea house before the mountain and then joining the team at base camp for three days as Phil taught them about crampons, jumars[12], ropes and general mountaineering skills before they spent two days climbing Island Peak. Phil had Purna Sherpa, who had visited us in Wales, and a cook, Pemba, with him. This was a fast track introduction and proved to be a very successful formula that is still operating successfully today.

I was back down in Kathmandu working and playing like a crazy thing. Henry Todd, who leads commercial climbs, asked if we knew of anybody who wanted to climb Ama Dablam as he had a couple of places left on his permit. I just about bit his hand off and, once I got the ok from Mahendra to go missing for three weeks, I was away. This was love-at-first-sight-mountain and only two days walk from where Phil was based. I sent up another set of climbing clients but missed them leaving so had no way of warning Phil that we were now both on our way to do Ama Dablam. I took the normal six days to walk in to Chukung, the last tea house before base camp for Island Peak.

I was chatting with a couple of Sherpas on my walk towards Chukung when I turned to see Phil looking like the man from the Milk Tray advert - black duvet top, black trousers, the works. I cut my conversation short and ran up to him. Giving me one of those special Phil-style hugs that make me feel all warm inside

Ama Dablam stole my heart and appropriately was the place Phil proposed

he kept holding on and said: "I have been thinking…" I got the distinct impression he was about to finish with me as his face didn't suggest great happiness. He explained he had seen a man die and get carried off Island Peak and it had really made him reassess his life (my untypical negative thoughts seemed confirmed as he was still looking vexed). Then he said: "I want you. Will you marry me?" I wasn't expecting that but then he wasn't expecting my answer: "Of course I will, you silly sod!" He had expected everything except a straight 'yes', so was completely thrown. We walked along hand in hand with cheesy grins on our faces all the way to Chukung with Ama Dablam as our backdrop. Can you hear the violins as I type away? I made him ask me again just to make sure he wasn't suffering from altitude sickness. It was true… hooray!

I joined Phil and his team to climb Island Peak as an acclimatisation exercise. Phil had already done it twice so was already deluxe acclimatised and fit. Office woman here seemed to be remarkably fit considering all I did all day was push flyers around coffee shops, talk to clients and be the bossy office manager.

So next stop was Ama Dablam; what an absolutely lovely climb for our first contact with independent mountaineering teams on the same mountain i.e. not commercial teams. We had a great rapport at camp one with a team of four French climbers through our tent walls. The weather wasn't perfect, so all banter was done through canvas. They had a great sense of humour, a good thing in the mountains as when things go wrong, they go big time wrong. One of their team dropped a rucksack irretrievably down the mountain, halting their attempt to summit. They refused to be disheartened and went back down to base camp, to get all the spares and kit they could beg or borrow and come up a few days later. That's the spirit I admire; no blame culture just mutual support and a 'can do' attitude. They saw me later in the Equator shop in Kathmandu and were all clean and washed. I didn't recognise them until they laughed and that was enough. How could I forget their laughter? Phil and I really enjoyed Ama Dablam as a climb, standing on the summit looking over at Everest and drinking in the best view in the whole region. Also, although I didn't know it at the time, I was just the third British woman to summit Ama Dablam. Nice bonus.

At the end of that season (December 2006), Phil and I officially announced our engagement back in London when I hijacked Jonny and Anna Hardy's Christmas drinks party. I stood on a chair, banged a glass for everybody's attention and announced to a very shocked crowd that I had found a man who wanted to spend the rest of his life with me. I knew about 80 per cent really well but Phil hadn't met any of them. I was floating on air with all my mates hugging and congratulating me and wanting to meet this amazing man.

Poor old Phil got whiplash from being introduced to everybody. We went out for lunch and dinner over the next three days to meet as many of my great friends as we could, so Phil got to taste a little of my previous life – a life he had no reason to relate to. He had been an engineer in Edinburgh for five years, so was used to having an office job, but London and my gang was a different breed. He was surprised he liked them all so much and got rid of some of his inverted snobbery. Then on our last night, just as we were going to sleep, he went for a long walk. He came back in, took my hand and looked deeply into my eyes with one of those 'this could change everything' looks. I had a nervous moment. He loved me - and that hadn't changed - but in those three days not one person had congratulated him.

The 'brave man' jibe may have been meant in jest but had almost been translated into a warning through constant repetition. I laughed my socks off, reassured him they were all joking and we were back on track.

I went back to Nepal the following February for another season while Phil got a job at Outward Bound in Ullswater so he could continue his progression as an instructor in the UK system. He enjoyed the team there although we were again separated for four months. I got back six weeks before the wedding. Life had been too busy for both of us to be too worried about the formal details. We had booked the venue and sent the invitations; so that was the important bits done!

Both our families were fantastic at supporting our marriage in their own ways. Maureen, my mother-in-law, is a very elegant and etiquette-driven lady: everything in her life is well organised and looks perfect. When I arrived back from Nepal - six weeks before the wedding with four weeks of work lined up with Phil at Outward Bound - she asked me about the wedding arrangements without a hint of panic. Inside, she must have been screaming with anxiety, as I waxed lyrical about how casual everything was going to be. When she asked about my dress, I excitedly opened my smelly rucksack and pulled everything out in the kitchen – the dress was in a black bin liner at the bottom. Looking like a startled bunny as her eyes opened wider and wider, she laughed out loud before giving me all the support I needed to hear: "That is such a beautiful colour and look at the material and... it's squashed in a bin liner! How novel dear!" The dress looked like a bundle of gold rags (Phil still insists it was orange but I assure you it was gold). She never let on if she disliked the dress and was just keen to get it ironed and tweaked to its optimum.

My father and I hadn't been in contact for several years. I did ring him to see if he wanted to meet Phil, but he didn't. When he heard I was marrying a Protestant in a non-Catholic Scottish castle, he refused to help with the cost of the wedding. But, just so he could feel involved, he threatened to come and smash it up. Without going into gory details, he was capable of doing so but I really didn't worry about it too much. I told my father-in-law John, so he could be on standby and co-ordinate a counter attack if necessary. John, who has been a surrogate father almost since we met, turned to me and said in that warm and reassuringly Cumbrian accent: "Don't you worry pet, I've dealt with more nutters than I care to mention. I won't let anybody ruin your day." Only John and I knew about this; the fewer the better as Phil had enough on his plate marrying me. I felt obliged to tell the venue to call the police if a short Irish man with a grudge turned up alone or with a posse looking a tad aggressive. As far as I was concerned, that box had been ticked and there was no more need to worry. My brother Robert was also threatened by the old man: if he went to the wedding, Dad was going to make business in Guernsey harder for him. Robert never told me this until much later as he wanted me to enjoy the day. Courage paid off and he came with wife Julia and daughter Olivia, who was one of my bridesmaids. Fortunately, Robert is not only a great brother and wonderful person, but an astonishingly good business man, so Dad's threats never became reality.

This was the closing chapter for my father and me. I had tried to understand him and suggest he got help but could only try so hard for so long before it became destructive to my world. If there was a remote chance of anything positive happening on either side, I would never have given up - but even the optimist

Phil and I with mum and Robert either side, David, Angie and Julia behind with Jeb and Olivia at the front stealing the show

in me was beaten. Family can produce the most stressful relationships in your life as you are thrown together by genes rather than choice. David and I have had our moments (as normal families do) but we have both put effort and understanding into getting where we are today (which is a great place) based on the fact we love each other. In Dad's case, any effort and emotion I put into him would be thrown back. I had stopped loving him long before. What was the benefit in even trying to have a relationship? He only gave pain, hurt and distress. I have never seen him again and my life feels sweeter for it. I see myself as having a fantastic family, having great relationships with my Mum and brothers and their families as well as Phil's family. Who needs more?

Phil and I got married in July. It was a perfect weekend, complete with sunshine, best friends, family and volleyball matches on the lawn before and after the ceremony. On the morning of the wedding, I lost track of time and had just an hour to get ready for the ceremony after playing volleyball in a heatwave. I was so excited and hot, not even a cold shower could cool me down. I had my bridesmaids Olivia and Goddaughter Jeb, aged five and eight respectively, dashing around like little princesses. Meanwhile Max, over from Africa, had the huge role of making me look radiant... I still have no idea how she did my hair so well! Mum was as gorgeous as ever, trying not to interfere but desperately sad I wasn't wearing a meringue bridal gown rather than a gold cross between a saree and Maid Marion. I was still glowing (a polite version of overheating) before Robert called me from my room to lead me off with a piper. The ceremony was in a small chamber in the castle keep with a large open fire. Funny enough, I remained 'glowing' throughout the service. I managed to blub my way through the vows and take half the congregation with me... I always cry if I'm happy. It didn't help that the Vicar was my great friend, Johnathan Wilkes, who'd known me since uni days and shared a house in London. Every parish needs a Johnathan as their vicar. Having somebody so special in such an important role made me even more emotional even if it played havoc with my 'radiant' look! The wedding lasted the whole weekend and included lunch

I asked Robert to give me away at the wedding. He looked a little too happy about it!

back at Wamphray Gate Farm where Phil's family ran a dairy herd. The weather, people and simplicity of the whole weekend was perfect.

Phil and I spent our four-day honeymoon in Skye in Scotland. As anybody knows who has been married, it is exhausting! So our first night was spent in the youth hostel in Portree in bunk beds, so we could get a good night's sleep. We had fish and chips on the dock of the bay and then spent the next three days camping at Glen Brittle and climbing. Room service was lacking but we made up for it in views! That was the perfect honeymoon for us. It was almost fate we didn't have any money as we may have done something different and that would have been a shame.

We spent the summer in Wales as Phil needed to pass an important qualification to get him up the outdoors ladder (his MIA[14] for those in the know). He went back to Ullswater and I went back to Nepal for another full season. The next year was spent between the UK and Nepal. Phil came out to Nepal in 1998 a couple of times and we enjoyed some great trips thanks to our travel agency status allowing us to 'try the goods'. This included a week in Bhutan and self support river trips down the Lower Bheri landing at the 'five star' Tiger Tops Bardia resort where we were greeted from our kayaks by porters dressed in whites and offering us a cup of tea from a silver tray before we had even got out of our wetsuits.

Living in Nepal presented limitless opportunities to go off on adventures. One such opportunity was to kayak the Tamur river with Whit Deschner, an incredibly well respected veteran within the river world and a very funny and able expedition kayaker. He came into the Equator office looking to find a companion with whom to kayak the Tamur. This was one river I had wanted to do even though it had been kayaked less than a dozen times and required a special permit. I was the most average of average kayakers but he agreed to take me despite the fact I was everything he was not. Instinct served him well and we had an incredible trip, so much so that, when asked to contribute a story to a book collated by another veteran Dave Manby of some of the best river trips by the best kayakers, Whit chose to write about ours. How ironic is that? Here was I a class four cling-on kayaker immortalised with the heroes of kayaking in a book called *Many Rivers Run.*

One feature of our journey epitomised our approach. Whit describes our seats on the local overnight bus as being on the front row in a horror movie: the driver behaved as if he was in a race whilst trying to stay awake at the wheel. At one point, Whit was the only person awake on the bus – and that included the driver. Someone had to be conscious to see our bus career off the road and stop dead in a swamp! In typical Nepalese fashion, there was no panic or anger. People grabbed their things and walked along a wooden bench, acting as a bridge between the bus and the road. Only problem was the road was about 10 meters away and the bench ended after three, so we had to get dirty in the swamp up to our thighs and calmly wait for another passing bus in the middle of nowhere and in the dead of night. We also had the task of getting our kayaks off the roof. I had been thrown forward onto the driver cage,

Whit showing his calm approach at the thought of going down the Tamur river with me

Whit and I took 2 days on a bus and 3 days walking with porters to get to the amazing Tamur river

so had a gash on my head, but nothing life threatening. Whit and I found the casual approach almost hilarious as this would have been considered a dramatic situation in the west. We knew we would have a good trip together after this.

We had a three day walk into the Kanchanjunga area with two porters, then an amazing five-day river journey down the Tamur river, totally at my top end of kayaking ability. If we lost a boat or had an accident we were days from anywhere. These adventures gave me so much great experience to deal with difficult situations. I learnt loads from Whit as he was incredibly experienced on remote expeditions and his relaxed attitude and humour was contagious, even in stressful scenarios. Whit has also written a book Travels with a Kayak providing superb insight into his humour and approach to life. It is hilarious and kept me laughing out loud on a long haul flight. A very talented, funny and kind man, Whit is still a great friend.

This is a typical camp on the Tamur river. Perfect

Phil came out for another season in the autumn of 1998. Unfortunately, whilst I'd felt important as a director of a great company in Kathmandu, Phil felt trapped and undervalued in the city. Our unspoken tensions eventually erupted into a cracker of a row – net result we couldn't just carry on and expect our marriage to get better. So we finished the season and flew to Thailand to rethink. The outcome was we both needed to go back to the UK and make a life together. Nepal was an amazing experience for me but the business was starting to need me more and more as Equator was full-on work during the season. I learned so much and achieved so much both in terms of how to run a business, manage people and have adventures. Mahendra and I could talk about nothing else. The team was amazing; we had parties and adventures together and I had an insatiable passion for making it a success. We had 30 families who depended on it, morale was always high and, if it wasn't, Mahendra sorted it out. He was like a wise old man knowing exactly what to say to make people feel valued or guilty if they screwed up. There is nothing worse than when someone you respect is disappointed in you. He had this impact on the office team, mountain team but especially the river team. Mahendra had been a cook, porter, raft guide and now he was a director of his own company. He didn't need me...

Leaving this environment was huge for me. We had developed this company over the last four years to an unforeseeable extent. Gerry Moffat wasn't there for much of the time but still inspired us all; especially on the river where he never stopped developing the Nepalese team. Seeing Gerry in action as a river leader was an experience worth having. He was able to take the team and the clients with him and make them feel it was a truly special time whether it was a drink in the bar, a two-day low level river trip or an incredibly hard expedition. That is a gift. Jon Fauver and Robbo were also an important part of this. The goal was for all the river trips to be led by the Nepalese team as this was their life and their country.

Gerry, Mahendra and Guy Robins had done all the hard work starting Equator Expeditions several years before I arrived. Then, Jon, Robbo and I were a huge part of the transition to the next stage of the business with Mahendra at the helm. We had been part of the golden time of change and I loved it. I loved the rickshaw races to the casinos; spontaneous parties, the local bus ride to work, festivals, talking to the street boys; Rashmi and kids making me at home, the smells, chaos and excitement. It was like living in an adventure book I wanted to read as a kid and gave me insatiable energy. However, it was now taking more of me than it should. Unless I left to try and give more to my marriage, I would lose the thing I most treasured in my life, Phil.

I called Mahendra from Scotland to say I couldn't come back. He took it well on the phone although he told me later he shut himself in his room for three hours to wonder how to handle the next season. We had become a working partnership and I was one half of the daily workings. I had dropped him in it but knew all the systems were in place and that nobody is indispensable. I was right to an almost disappointing degree!

CHAPTER **FIVE**

Phil and I loved living in the Lakes.
It is a great playground with great people.

We lived with Phil's parents for the first few weeks we were back in the UK while we tried to find jobs. It was large and very homely and a great place to get grounded with the positive aspects of family life. We knew we would be happy to live in The Lakes as Phil had friends there and would easily find a job as an instructor. I focused on looking for work there, starting by calling Guy Baker, a VIP client on one of our Bhutan river trips with Equator. We had hit it off over welcome and goodbye drinks; he was an adventurer and a successful businessman who was also fascinating to talk to as, like me, he had an opinion on almost everything. I asked if he knew anybody in The Lakes who needed someone like me and he paused for a second and said: "What are you like at sales?" Before I knew it, I was into a self sales pitch declaring that was what I had done in Nepal for the last four years. He got me an interview with his directors and three weeks later I was driving a Peugeot 405, complete with mobile phone, desk and a great salary.

I was a sales rep for Catalyst Events, a company started by Guy and his best friend David Ruby to do fun challenges for corporate events. Their philosophy was to create a business fun for people to work at and meaning they didn't have to toil when the sun was shining. He was almost there. Walking into the office, the first thing I saw was a huge 12ft multi-coloured dragon on the ceiling. There was such a positive energy in the place; creativity oozed out of the people, the walls, computers, even the stairwell. Yet again, I'd found a team I could really relate to. I loved what they did and how they did it. They were fantastic and had a good time together. I found a chat mate in bookkeeper Pam Purcell. She was from California but had been in the UK for years and was convinced she no longer had an accent. Let's just say that instead of a coffee, she'd ask you for a 'kwaffee' - yeah you have really lost the accent, Pam! It was open plan so they were worried about putting us together in case we talked too much yet we had a great time and worked more productively as a consequence... well, they bought that line anyway. Catalyst was also flexible about taking extended time off as the directors knew how much time off meant to them. They were always off to foreign places doing exciting things so they could totally relate to our need for time to play. Phil and I took advantage of this on a few occasions. They recognised early on that, when recharged by having time off, I perform better.

Phil got a great job as an outdoor technician at Brathay, based in a superb setting in Ambleside. He had regular hours, people he could go off climbing with after work and was very happy. I took out a loan for the deposit for a cheap terraced cottage and we spent the next couple of years doing it up. It was in a small hamlet of about 20 houses next to the industrial estate where Catalyst was based. This meant we lived in the countryside yet I had to walk less than three minutes to get to work. Best thing of all was that it was next to Penny and Martyn Mills, young, fun and our best mates over the next four years. Our houses became a bit of a social scene and soon other friends were moving to the area. Kendal is a great place with a great balance of town and country and full of real people rather than being a tourist haven. I feel you belong when you can go to a bar and almost guarantee to meet someone you know and The Brewery Arts Centre in Kendal and Wilf's in Staveley are those kind of places...

Louise Burner, another good friend, lived in Staveley village and I always remember her saying: "You can't be bored in Staveley, no matter how young or old you are." Mum was alone now and I had the idea of getting her up to Staveley to see if she liked it. She rented for six months and then the perfect bungalow came up next to Joyce, now her best friend. The place needed gutting but that was fine and The Lakes became Mum's home too. Good jobs, great friends, lovely home, Phil's family only an hour away and Mum down the road. What more could we want? Answer nothing – for three years anyway!

Phil wasn't fulfilling his potential at Brathay. His work needed only low level skills and he needed to move on in his career. He had worked to gain his next winter qualification at Glenmore Lodge, Scotland's National Outdoor Training Centre, but wasn't being stretched in his current position and had so much more to give and the ambition, hunger and talent to get it. He had spent the winter training for his MIC[15] assessment in Scotland on extended leave from Brathay. He passed with flying colours and knew that, should a position come up at Glenmore Lodge, he would be eligible. Working at the Lodge is a skills instructor's dream as it is one of only three national centers in the UK, the others being in Wales and Northern Ireland. Phil, being Scottish, obviously favoured Glenmore. An opportunity came up but he didn't get the job so, as compensation and a timely break from routine, we planned a six-month trip in our van around Europe. This also meant I needed to leave Catalyst as six months off was too much to ask for and I had plans to fulfill another goal of training to be a teacher after our travels. We saved hard and lived with Mum as we rented out our house to save more money for our trip. How she put up with us I have no idea. Phil converted our Ford Transit long wheel base van in her driveway and all our friends used her house as a coffee shop between bike rides. Plus she had to tolerate me and Phil having domestics over what colour to paint the interiors of the van. Yet she loved it and the more bacon butties she could make everybody the better. What a star!

Phil and I in our converted van which was home for 6 months

Living in the van and climbing around Europe was fantastic. We got back to where we started together - in the outdoors, enjoying adventures, no responsibilities and no agenda. Rock climbing presented the perfect reason to go somewhere. We avoided cities and found Europe fascinating both culturally and geographically. As with any couple, we took a bit of time to adjust being together 24/7. Phil tolerated me being positive about everything - there is nothing more irritating than a positive person with a big smile saying nothing is a problem when all you want to do is hit the table and shout 'f**k it!' One particular incident on Christmas Eve made me laugh: we were in the car park in Chamonix along with loads of other vans, with freezing temperatures, great skiing and our friends in town. All was good until the clutch cable broke. Phil was stressed as we knew we wouldn't be able to fix it for days due to the holiday season.

Phil climbing in Italy overlooking Lake Garda

As for me, death and destruction weren't involved and anyway we were within walking distance of shops, ski slopes and bars. Phil burst out with: "Pauline! You don't have to be happy all the time... give your other emotions a chance." I burst into hysterical laughter at such a fantastic comment and the whole thing diffused. Being opposite in a relationship is fantastic once you get the tolerance balance right.

I wonder now what we talked about as the longer we were on our own the more we babbled on and on. We loved it. One topic that did come up a few times was: did we want kids? This is the million dollar question for any couple in their late thirties, who have not already done the deed. Society expects you to have them if you are in a good marriage or partnership and it was a regular topic of conversation among our friends. We decided to have a week to consider the positives and negatives. Logic never overrides emotion, otherwise we wouldn't have had some of the greatest/disastrous love stories in history like Anthony and Cleopatra, Helen of Troy or Angelina and Brad! If you have the emotion to have a child, it is really easy; if you don't, like us, it is really tricky. You then have to weigh all the emotional arguments like 'you will never experience giving and receiving unconditional love like you do with a child'; then logical arguments kick in like 'they curtail your playtime', 'cost a fortune', 'all parents seem exhausted' and 'they limit your social life'. Then we had to ask ourselves whether the reason we weren't giving emotions a chance was because we were happy with how we were and had lots of plans that didn't include children. If neither of us had an urge to have one, why have one? Ignorance is bliss; you don't miss what you don't have. Phil and I agreed that, if either of us wanted one, we would go ahead. Yet we loved our lifestyle and each other so much we really didn't want anything else. I love kids, having five godchildren I adore and six nieces and a nephew I would do anything for. However, I really have no maternal instinct. Was that guaranteed to come as soon as the hormones kicked in? What if it didn't? Of course, I would still love and adore the child but would I begrudge other things? If we were happy, why change anything? This was an irreversible decision and probably the only occasion I have gone against my life inclination to 'give everything a go regardless of potential failure'. The future will tell if we made the right decision. I may have had lots of adventures, careers and amazing times but could feel something is missing by the time I am 60. All I can report is it's a case of so far so good!

Six months flew by and reality kicked back in when we went home so Phil could do another winter season at the Lodge and keep his name in the loop for any future contract. He fitted in very well and loved the team and the work. I meanwhile had got into Lancaster Uni for a PGCE course to become a teacher. This would start in eight months so I did all sorts of odds and sods to make money such as working for Wilf's café in Staveley, serving drinks and food from a mobile unit at outdoor events. They are a great team at Wilf's and hard work was fun. I also did youth training for Brathay and Fairbridge which was particularly fulfilling as I seemed to have a natural rapport with inner city or underprivileged kids. You never know what difference you can make but it was great thinking that maybe you could. It is also a good way to remind yourself how lucky you are. Some people start life without any help and need to battle to get out of their world; it would be easier for them to just accept they will never get a job as nobody tells them they are good enough.

Can you imagine feeling you are good for nothing?

I also learned how to stain and polish furniture for my friend John Purcell at Out of the Woods, a furniture makers' outfit in Staveley. Working with John was the first time I had been in a trade/workman environment: you stopped at 10.30am for a brew, 12.30pm for lunch and 3pm for a brew and that happened every day. There was young John, the boss who was in his forties; old John, his father-in-law and in his 70s; and me. Young John and I went off to fit a kitchen one day and realised he had cut the sink area on the wrong section of wood. We came back to the workshop and explained to old John who looked exasperated at young John and burst out: "This is due to the f**k up of impetuous youth!" Forty-something is a youth compared to 70-something... hooray! I loved working with these two. They were talented, hard working and made time to have a laugh. A great combination.

I used my free time to go off on a trip to Mongolia. I had read an article in National Geographic about nomads. It got me so unsettled that I got that sleepless night and funny tummy thing going on. When this happens, I know the decision to go is non-negotiable. I saved up and Phil said: "Off you go." It was an amazing trip and I have decided to include an article I wrote when I got back to share my experience

Nomad to Notting Hill

A lot of us think we are really brave and radical to make a career change. I certainly did. However, those who fall into this bracket may choose to eat a slice of humble pie when they hear Enke's story.

I had been reading about the nomads of Mongolia: despite a 70-year Russian intervention between the 1920's and 1990's, they continue to live and love nomadic traditions going back hundreds of years. Being a bit of a culture vulture, and completely hooked on the outdoor life, I decided to experience this 'land without fences' for myself. I wanted to be part of a migration, which happens twice or four times a year depending on where you live in Mongolia; I wanted to meet people who had never been to the city and lived from the land, each other and their religion. I had travelled extensively in Asia and lived in Nepal for four years. Could this journey be that much different? Oh yes!

Good old Aeroflot, cheap cheerful and, believe it or not, very reliable. I ended up having a bit of a banter with a few young Mongolian policemen who had good enough English to make me laugh. It ended with Enke coming and sitting next to me. He was living in Notting Hill with his wife and worked in a hotel while studying for accountancy exams. His eight-year old daughter was being looked after in Ulan Bator by his wife's parents as family seems a much more flexible institution there. Providing a member of your family is living with another part of the family, they are at home; his daughter wasn't considered to be short changed because she was loved and looked after full time by family, other than her parents. The fact I was married and 39 yet had no children was a bit outside his scope of understanding. 'Why not? Who will look after you when you are old?' Mate, I don't have a pension and I live for the day. The thought of being 80 is as far removed from my planning as former President Bush is from reality.

I explained my Mongolian mission was to experience nomadic life. He casually mentioned that he had lived as a nomad until he was 18 and was happy to take me to visit his old camps in the west. I hesitated... well actually, I didn't, but I told my husband I did! Within an hour of meeting, our flight landed in Ulan Bator and he had taken responsibility for me from the moment I said 'yes' - getting through customs, carrying my bag, everything. His family was there to meet him and didn't bat an eyelid at his extra baggage and the fact I took them completely out of their way to find this cheap little hotel I had earmarked from my Lonely Planet Guide. They took me to a nicer place as he wanted to show his country off at a good standard, so I paid more than I had budgeted for - but a nice bathroom was a good way to start.

Only an hour after being dropped off, I got a call to say there was a family picnic and he would be picking me up in an hour. Great! His younger brother was the chauffeur; he said nothing, drove well, didn't smile much but seemed ready and willing to drop anything for any of us at any time. Then there were the three kids, including Enke's daughter Onka. We tried to teach each other our languages for the hour or so we travelled around various districts, collecting and dropping off people and goods. Enke was very proud of his daughter and encouraged her to speak English with me as he believed her future depended on it.

We passed the suburbs of Ulan Bator; a stark contrast to the Russian heritage of the city centre, with its stone buildings mixed with wooden shacks and felt gers (nomadic tent made of felt). As we left the built up areas behind us, we moved into real Mongolia with its wide open spaces, no fences and lush pastures. We crossed fields and rivers to end up at a small family homestay where we met the rest of Enke's family for a welcome home party. The kids and I jumped out of the jeep and ran straight to a small enclosure where their aunt was clipping cashmere from a goat. Then we raced to the river, skimmed stones and played tig, communicating in that unfailing international jargon of body language.

I got summoned to the grown-up area to meet the folks over some tea, meat and bread. His father held pride of place and I was made to feel incredibly welcome as all caught up on each other's news. Next was a Mongolian detox special… fresh goat's blood! Big brother number two got the knife with us all gathered around, slit the goat's neck, caught the blood in the bowl and offered it around: cue a vegetarian moment. The only way I like blood is in black pudding. I felt less of a wimp when a couple of the others declined too. Enke hated it but apparently it does you good, so went for it. Yuk! Stage two was the skinning and chopping of the goat which happened in the ger with a herder who looks after their homestay. They keep this place to stay in touch with their roots and Enke took great pride in explaining the traditions and history of the process.

The afternoon was spent, eating, and drinking traditional Mongolian food and drink. The kids did lots of running races with us as the audience. It felt like one big happy family as total harmony over three generations of this family hit home. It deserves its very own book as all have come from the far west and created their own success stories including four brothers and one sister. The sister still lives out in the west and we soon met her too. What a wonderful introduction to Mongolia: the modern Mongolian family still proud to practice the traditions of their heritage.

Next day, I entertained myself by trying to find my way around Ulan Bator where nobody speaks English and the street signs are in Mongolian script. Even with my 'Mongolian for idiots' guide it was tough, but I felt very safe and had a great day. My bus journeys were helped by friendly clippie conductors; I pointed to the map, they pointed me in the right direction. After finding a very nourishing German bakery and letting Phil know I was in safe hands via one of several internet sites, I ended up going to an art gallery and saw Giselle, the ballet, at a theatre not dissimilar to The Old Vic in London. The dancing and the theatre were absolutely stunning. What a treat. I was hardly roughing it in Outer Mongolia.

I felt like a VIP as Enke and his brother Jaga chauffeured us around in his even bigger four wheel drive. We booked and paid for our flight tickets which cost me $300 and Enke $100 – logical enough to me. I wasn't quite sure exactly what or where we were off to experience but my gut instinct had always served me well in the past and this was no exception. We popped in to see a friend of Jaga, who happens to be the head of the National Assembly of Mongolia. Good job I was wearing my best rucksack!

Next morning, I had an early wake-up call for a pick-up to an incredibly busy airport. Rumours of overbooking and bad weather left us with the possibility of not flying and only Enke's connections got us on this flight at such short notice. Stay flexible in Asia and leave all the stress and deadlines back at your office and you won't go far wrong. Our final destination was Bulgan, a four hour flight west of Ulan Bator. Flying over Mongolia in a small plane was a great way to really get a grip on the vast and predominantly unpopulated landscape. Considering its size (1,566,500 sq km), there are only two and a half million people living there. No wonder it is the land without fences....

We finally flew into Bulgan after a couple of stop offs – not so much an airport but a flat piece of land and a small office. Enke hadn't been back for 10 years and I thought a lot may have changed, but apparently not. He saw his sister Monke, and I was surprised at the lack of hugs but took my western hat off and recognised this was just the way. They are not a huggy nation; when they say hello or goodbye, just an acknowledgement is enough. She had her eight-year-old son Dalek with her and I wasn't quite sure how to take her so held back on being pally, pally. Naturally she proved to be exceptional and so welcoming I couldn't fault her hospitality. As we were waiting for the jeep (great Russian number that seems to go on for ever), a few people recognised Enke. He was wearing pinstriped trousers, very smart shoes, crisp white shirt and tank top; very much the gentleman making the statement 'I have moved on from here!' One older gentleman came to Enke and stared at me: he apparently had not seen a tourist before and was interested. I hope I lived up to expectations.

We drove a short distance home to Monke's flat. The town was another throwback to Russia. - characterless brick but functional buildings with communal shack toilets in the square (conveniently only 150m from our place). The flat was simple, clean and compact and typical of all in the blocks. It had a living room turning into a bedroom at night, a kitchen area without the mod cons of running water or a cooker, a bedroom and an outside hand basin so you never felt less than fresh after you washed.

We ate drank and talked as Enke got into full flow about his childhood. He seemed stimulated by being back here and having somebody from his new world (England) experience the world he had come from. I was a sponge and listened with fascination as he told stories I had been dying to hear; his childhood wasn't easy as he stayed with his grandparents living in a ger, herding the goats and living a classic, but very lonely, existence. His father was secretary of the co-op and lived in town with the rest of the family. Enke was needed on the land and led a very typical life - up early, his day consisted of making or collecting food and herding the goats. He can't remember having a bath before the age of nine when he started school. He loved school so much in town but had to return to his grandparents during the holidays. As I say, there is a book in his story and I am currently trying to get him to write one; so watch this space for the adventures of a nomad.

Bulgan town is a throwback to a rundown wild west set with horses and camels tied up to various poles and trees with sand-based dusty streets. I caught the local butcher with his back-of-a-truck shop. You could get the joint you wanted as he cut the requested appendage off the animal there and then - 'Is that with or without the hoof madam?' Lots of square and bland clay coloured shops next to each other all sold the same things. The population of this whole area is 10,000, just enough to keep everyone ticking in business if you spread it around. We visited several friends in gers and in flats in the town, being greeted in each with tea and various forms of food from biscuits to boiled mutton. The odd vodka helped to keep the flow going. Enke explained that in this area the nomadic people moved four times a year, always to the same places. He was about to take me to his old patch 10 miles out of town. It was an off-road trip in a jeep we would pay for in the UK. Hang on and enjoy the ride!

It had been 10 years since Enke had visited his old ger camp. There were four gers and one brick building with four families. Again, we were met and ushered in for the traditional tea, cheese and bread. Men handed around the snuff and made polite conversation without any of the 'wow, how the hell are you?' kind of feeling. The banter grew and grew as Enke keenly explained how far he had come from here and was apologetic for the basic level of life. He didn't have to apologise for anything as I respected and admired the way they continued to live. The green-eyed west envies the simple life without modern trappings. We spend so much time chasing a materialistic dream we miss the beauty of the biggest gift of all... time to enjoy our natural environment and each other.

We all went outside and I became the entertainment as I attempted to ride one of their horses, a small but powerful beast. I rode off from the main camp and couldn't flaunt my riding skills as my four legged friend obviously had a language problem with me. My audience was very entertained and Imagay, a lovely 16-year-old herder, gave me some great tips: 'choo choo' and a good slap. Bingo, off I went, not with the stylish laid back style of Mongolian herdsmen, but it worked. Enke visited some ill friends and body language was my communication tool. We had a great time! Imagay and I went off on horses and herded up the goats from across the river. I was in heaven in the land with no fences;

My milking teacher in Mongolia

I was in the dream I had come to experience, with nomads on horseback herding goats in a vast landscape. We had a really good time as we laughed at my attempts to copy his style and language for herding. As we came triumphantly back to base with all the goats, I got involved with the next stage... milking.

Grandma took me under her wing. They tie the goats in long lines, get two lines to face each other and tie them in a 'lockheads' position – sort of a rugby scrum for goats! Then she got her first goat and talked to me in fluent Mongolian about how to squeeze the teat to the very end. I explained in fluent English I wasn't quite getting it and could she give me a few more tips. We didn't understand a word of each other's, yet somehow totally understood what we meant and I got it!
A dozen goats later I had a decent amount of milk: a proud moment. The three women were milking with the men, laughing and joking with us all the time. It was a surreal

Enke and his nomadic family. They all look proud of what their clothing represents.

Enke's nomadic home has not changed a lot since he left

experience to feel like I fitted in so well to a lifestyle culturally and geographically light years away from my home in The Lakes. I felt incredibly comfortable and so happy to be there.

Next it was time to release the baby goats to get the leftovers - a case of mob control. I had brought a Polaroid camera so I could give people photos there and then and took a picture of Patamesurum and her little boy. She loved it and soon it was a line up and I ended up shooting nearly a whole film of them all. It was great fun taking photos and I was able to see them as great characters, enjoying each other and the moment. Patamesurum and I bonded over more tea and then Imagay taught me to dance Mongolian style (waltz with a funny bit in the middle). The time seemed appropriate to dress me up in her traditional dress to look the part. I felt like we were playing at dressing up and being adults; it was great fun. Then Imagay and his mate demonstrated some Mongolian wrestling and naturally won. I was suitably impressed and, if ever I had a daughter and Imagay was the boy she brought home, I would be very happy! He was polite, great fun and a real gentleman. Patamesurum enjoyed having somebody new around and they made my stay a complete and inspirational experience. Imagay and I went out for another ride to enjoy the sunset and freedom. Enke returned in time for us to take time to have tea/vodka with the older couple of the camp who watched him grow up. He translated for me and related some of their memories of him with pride. Maybe, he was remembering the good parts of his nomad life now? We said our goodbyes and I left feeling the luckiest person in the world. I really want to come back and do the migration with them one day. It takes about four days in June. They can take down a ger in about 40 minutes; it takes me that much time to pack to go away for a weekend! I went to sleep dreaming of the land with no fences.

A Kazak eagle hunter showing off his pride and joy

My experience in the west continued to inspire me as we went looking for and found Kazak eagle hunters and a major off-road experience to Khovd. However, that's for another story.
This is about Enke and his amazing transition from nomad to Notting Hill. He gave me first hand insight into a special world and I would like to thank him and his family for looking after me from the moment I arrived to the moment I left... literally!
I was their first guest but hopefully not their last. When Enke finishes studying in London for his accountancy exams, he will be back in Mongolia. He may even start his own travel company now he knows how enthralled foreigners are by his old world.

On my return from Mongolia, Phil was freelancing in The Lakes and at Glenmore Lodge. I was due to start my next challenge of becoming a primary teacher starting in September 2004 at Lancaster Uni. I was in the middle aged, mid-life, need to put something back into society stage. I got on really well with kids

There is always a warm welcome and tea in the pot in a nomadic Mongolian yurt

and got them excited and charged; surely I would be a great teacher? It is such a worthwhile profession in which you can have more of a positive influence on a child's life than any other.
My stomach and body told me this wasn't a guaranteed success; my family knew, too, but humoured me through it. I'd always wanted to do something worthwhile and this could just be it.

Student life was fantastic with five-a-side football and a fun class of students. I got on really well with a funny guy called Ian, who made me laugh so much we got separated in our English lesson. I couldn't believe it; I was 40 years of age and had been

A Kazak grandmother spinning goats wool

separated in class! However, the work experience section of the course made me realise I was as natural a primary school teacher as King Kong was born to dance ballet. I took a class of year one kids for phonics, with all 25 of the little darlings sitting on the carpet while I used a hand puppet to try and demonstrate the phonic 'ch'. By the end of the session, nearly all 25 of them were on my lap; the puppet was being treated like a pop idol and the noise level was challenging the sanity threshold. The 'real' teacher stepped in and within one minute had them sitting quietly at their desks. She took me aside and, in a very diplomatic way, said: "Pauline, I think they had a wonderful time... but do you think they learnt anything?"

The fact I didn't have the vocation for teaching became apparent when I started to clock watch; something I'd never done before. I knew that, if I carried on with the course, it would take me at least three years to get the skills to start enjoying my job - and I'm more of a quick fix person. So I told Phil I really had discovered teaching wasn't for me. He had never really thought it was, but had kindly let me carry on. My revelation coincided with Phil being called up for another interview at Glenmore Lodge and this time we knew he stood a very good chance. This was his dream job and the tension around the house couldn't be displaced even by my most irritable level of positivity. The interview went well but each day afterwards we waited for the call. Then it came and Phil's face said it all: he got the job!

The move to Scotland brought mixed emotions. You can never feel glad about leaving such good friends and, of course, Mum. We had the best social scene and were living the real life version of Friends, the TV series. I liked to think of myself as Rachel - only not as naive, slim or as good at fashion. Come to think of it, the only thing we had in common, apart from good friends, was an inability to cook. Anyway, another phrase I like to live by is 'leave wanting more'; I'd left London and Nepal and now I could leave The Lakes feeling I still loved it there. Fortunately, Mum was as supportive as ever - as long as I was happy, she was happy. Phil went ahead and was living at the Lodge by December and I came up for three days and managed to find a cheap flat in Grantown to buy. Impulsive is in my nature and poor old Phil was just trying to get settled into a job as his Mrs kept firing new ideas at him and committing him to a nice big debt; 'yes dear' was the easiest answer as he had no head space to really discuss. Fortunately, it was the right decision. I came up for good in February, we lived in at the Lodge for a few weeks and then moved into our new home in March 1995.

CHAPTER **SIX**

Phil and I on a perfect Scottish winter day.
Why did I need more?

Everestmax – To Go or Not To Go?

I managed to get the job as marketing manager at Glenmore Lodge. This was one of those right time, right place episodes in my life as the boss team at Glenmore Lodge, Tim Walker and Nigel Williams, heard about me from a mutual friend. They asked me in for a chat the day after I arrived in February and I started the following day! I had done the marketing for Equator in Nepal, including the website and flyers etc, but that was a much rawer product. Now, I was given a budget, title and a sophisticated western company with more rules and less scope for error. I was so excited as I saw there was so much to do and was hungry to do it. I love the industry and really believed in the Lodge as I'd been a student there myself. I would do the best I could and in a year we would all know whether I was a good investment. I was happy to review and so were they. The other huge positive of taking the job was that this was how I got to know about the Everestmax expedition.

It happened one day in August when I opened the mail and found another flyer someone wanted me to put up on our notice board. It read: 'Wanted, somebody to cycle over 5,000 miles from the Dead Sea to Mt Everest and then climb to the summit. 6 months. Please call Dom Faulkner on...' There was also a picture of a cyclist in Pakistan looking tiny next to this amazing backdrop of mountains and a rough road. I put one flyer up on the board and kept the other one for myself. I couldn't stop thinking about it and just had to call Dom to ask whether he would consider me before I even got back to my work. It was an answer machine and I became more excited with each hour waiting for a reply. I knew that 'let's do it' was never going to be Phil's first response as he likes to think about things and review the pros and cons. I needed more information before I could even tell him about it. It seemed pie in the sky, but there was no harm in doing the research and finding out as much as possible before dismissing it out of hand. The trip was due to leave on December 6, only four months away, so decisions had to be made and fast.

Dom called me back. I was ready for a grilling on my mountaineering and biking experience; to admit my weaknesses and push my strengths – the main plus point being the fact Phil is a fab mountaineer and I'd done a fair bit too. Dom had a very posh military-style accent which resonated with my army connections. He was friendly and polite and oozed confidence without sounding arrogant. He was obviously keen to find two more team members as a couple had just dropped out due to injury and work commitments. He already had four, plus two more in his support team. Getting six people to Everest Base Camp fit and well after going through some of the hardest areas of the Middle East and Asia was going to be a challenge, never mind the mountain. I bubbled with enthusiasm and that could have put anyone off. Warning: middle aged woman with an excitable disposition and a tendency to babble. How many people would be prepared to risk spending six months with that? Fortunately, he needed people with two arms and legs and the fact I had so much mountaineering experience meant I was in. Biking endurance would come as the trip developed.

Ok, now the hard bit. How could I sell this to Phil? He wouldn't enjoy long distance cycling or want to put his dream job at risk by asking for time off. Mt Everest wasn't on our 'must-climb' mountain list, although if a cheap or free opportunity came up we had agreed to consider it. That brings me to another big one - money. It was going to cost me about £7,000 to do the whole thing and him £6,000 to tackle Everest; we would lose nine months salary between us in one year and had no savings as we had just bought the flat. These may seem like obstacles, but the secret to success is to turn obstacles into a challenge and find a solution. Oh, I love the corny bits of this book, don't you? I needed solutions before I put the challenges to him, then I'd subtly drop the big question into the conversation during a particularly positive time. Maybe, a good meal and glass of wine might help too. Manipulative or pragmatic? I prefer to say pragmatic as I know Phil well enough to appreciate he sees obstacles; by thinking like him, I could avoid being shot down and left frustrated and angry at not getting past first base. The reality is our opposites compliment each other.

All went well as Phil was surprisingly open-minded. He sent me off to answer more detailed questions such as who, what, why and where. But, as the next week went by, he became adamant it was inappropriate for us financially and safety-wise due to the inexperience of the mountaineers in the team (he had read the profiles of team members on the Everestmax website). I struggled not to agree. Eventually even I conceded it was a big ask and tried to put it to bed.

Phil and I had endured a hard time over the last year or so. We had worked through an unsettled time of growing pains in our marriage and were moving into the next and better stage. I had been given a superb piece of advice once by Mrs Ratigan, who said that, if you have 70 per cent of the man of your dreams, you have the man of your dreams. I had more than that with Phil but this advice helped us both accept we needed to accept each others shortcomings as nobody is perfect. We realised that most of the time we were way over the 70 per cent and were lucky. I don't know why hard times are so good for people, but they were for us. We both became better people as we were made to reflect, accept and adjust. We did all this because we loved each other and the journey to the next stage was worth all the effort. I knew I would rock the boat by pushing for this trip, so I was in a dilemma.

I couldn't sleep at night without thinking about Everestmax. I tossed and turned, dreaming about cycling through Pakistan and the picture on Dom's flyer staring me in the face. Everest wasn't the big draw; it was the journey and a unique challenge that gave my stomach butterflies. Dreams aren't always sourced from childhood, they can come to you at any point; they may change your life if you follow them or frustrate the hell out of you if you don't. Each person is responsible for creating their own destiny and it is up to you how much you are prepared to do to make things happen, or prepared to accept so they don't. I was told once that the biggest block to dreams isn't money, time or career but the fact we are prepared to make do with what we have rather than risk losing it for what we can't guarantee. Is that contentment or merely make do? I know a lot of very content people who are living the dream by having a very happy regular life and I will never knock that. Contentment is success but if, like me, things keep cropping up to unsettle you and stimulate you, it gets tricky! Is it wrong to constantly see opportunities that will add to your life? Does that mean you will never be content? I don't think so.

Another great question I read once was: 'What would you do if you thought you couldn't fail?' I wasn't worried about the possible failure of the expedition, but I did mind my marriage failing. The other side of the coin was whether I'd blame Phil if I didn't go? I knew he wasn't being unreasonable: how many husbands would say: "Off you go darling; I won't worry about the debt, our careers or the fact you want to cycle through the most anti-western area in the world and then do a notoriously dangerous climb on the world's highest mountain with a team we don't know!" He had a point.

I had regularly cycled the 17 miles to work over the summer from Grantown, via the Ryvoan Pass to the Lodge which must be one of the best commutes in the world. Now I was cycling as much as possible, just in case I was able to go on the Everestmax expedition. I had become friends with Louise Ramsay, the marketing director at TISO, Scotland's largest outdoor retail supplier. I had got to know her well because she was responsible for Tiso's sponsorship of Glenmore Lodge. She was introduced to me as a VIP but it wasn't long before our banter took her down to my level and she became a good new mate in my new world. She was incredibly supportive of me wanting to do Everestmax as she could see how unique and special it would be. She didn't want to rock the boat for me with Phil, so promised Tiso would sponsor us with gear in return for a roadshow of talks afterwards. Phil's ears pricked up as Paul Casey, from Marmot and a sponsor of the Lodge, said the same thing. He could also see how Marmot would benefit as the kit would be used for such a diverse and extreme range of situations. Phil was being pushed into a corner as having the correct equipment was essential and expensive. Then another generous offer came form Eadaoin Hutchinson, a good friend from The Lakes, who offered us bomb-proof kit bags from the North Face. Faith and support was flooding in from every angle and we were on our way to a point of no return. I had gone through the finances with a fine toothcomb and worked out how we could afford to do it. The masterplan involved a bank loan, renting out the flat and Phil living in the van over the winter while he worked at the Lodge and I was cycling. He would then join us in Kathmandu for the mountain.

Scotland is great from any angle!

The only thing left was for me to get permission for a six-month break from work. Phil was convinced this wouldn't happen as I was new in the door and had started to do some good stuff. He said that, providing Tim agreed, we would seriously consider making it happen. I couldn't say fairer than that; so I went into Tim's office, sat him down and made sure he had a nice cup of tea. I started by confirming he liked the work I had done so far but force-fed compliments weren't as easy as I thought. I explained about this amazing six-month journey and that I desperately wanted to go. I'd even found someone to cover for me and they would be great so... please, please, please. There was a very long pause... I could hear my heart beating. If he said no, my journey would probably be over before it had begun. Tim sat up, looked at me in that fatherly way, and said: "The strap line for Glenmore Lodge is 'inspiring adventure'; if a journey like this doesn't inspire adventure, nothing will. Off you go." I had never fancied an older man before, but wanted to snog him senseless.

I jumped up, gave him a big hug as an appropriate alternative, and ran out the door.

Mixed emotions were flooding in. Phil didn't want any of this to happen and Tim had been his last hope. I had to tell Phil without being too excited, but a huge feeling of guilt made that easy. I was asking a lot of him to join in or just let me go. Phil's face showed he was gutted and we had some serious talking to do. Did Phil want to come and do Everest? We agreed to ask Dom to meet us so we could get a proper handle on where the Everestmax team stood. They could be a hoax gang getting money and then running away with it for all we knew. Dom very kindly flew up from Bristol to Inverness and Sarah Lyle, the other female cyclist, came up with him to meet us for a mutual 'sussing' out session. They came for dinner, stayed the night and flew back down south the next day. Phil was ready with a list of questions as long as your arm and I made them welcome before he began the Spanish inquisition.

Sarah was in her early twenties and full of all the enthusiasm you need to make these things happen. She wanted to know what the other 'girl' would be like: for 'girl', read 'mature lady'. I was now 41 which must have seemed ancient to her. I could instantly tell Sarah would always try hard to do the right thing; we didn't share a natural chemistry but it wouldn't take much for us to become friends. She was blonde and blue eyed and her physique, being a rower and rugby player, spoke of strength and endurance; perfect for this kind of trip. As for Dom, he looked like he sounded: fairly military, yet relaxed and confident. He was professional on the relevant issues, but very socially gifted at a banter level. He explained away being pretty chubby by insisting he needed to bulk up as he would lose so much weight cycling and being on the mountain.

Phil was charming and welcoming over dinner, and then got down to business. He asked all the right questions, the ones I wouldn't have thought of. Dom could see Phil knew his stuff and left really encouraging him to join us on the mountain as the team was very short of the appropriate level of experience. Dom had been on Everest when he was in the army but suffered a bad case of pulmonary oedema[11] at the North Col (7,200m) and that was the end of his trip. Dom had other people lined up to join us on the mountain with varied amounts of experience, but none more than Phil and me. This set alarm bells going for Phil, who was also concerned about as yet unresolved issues over weather information and oxygen supplies. Phil had to go or his wife would be on Everest with too many variables he would have no control over. After all, he wanted me back alive.

The major turning point for Phil was when our friend Carl Harbel came to the flat to talk through the pros and cons of him taking part. Carl could see both sides but turned to Phil as he was leaving and said: "When you are 50, you may have done some of the best climbs in the world...but Pauline will have done Everest!" That was the nail in the coffin of uncertainty: Phil was in as long as his boss gave him three months off to come and do the mountain. Phil had a whole speech lined up next day when he went to ask Nigel, but it wasn't necessary. Nigel cut him short and said: "I'm surprised it has taken you so long to ask... of course you can. No pressure, but we have never had an instructor summit Mt Everest, so over to you!"

We were off. In mid-October, I confirmed with Dom I was in for the whole thing and Phil for the mountain. He was delighted and I started to cycle in and out of work more than ever. I had about six weeks to arrange for the flat to be rented out, get the loan in place, collect our kit together and do enough marketing to ensure my life-saver and stand-in Lisa Fuchs didn't have a nightmare to handle. As I cycled in and out of work in the dark and the rain, I kept thinking of the promotional flyer and how much I wanted to do it. The weather in Scotland was hardly friendly, but I was even enjoying it there in the November conditions. In fact, I loved it. The odd deer jumped out to frighten the hell out of me on an otherwise quiet and remote commute through the forests, but I couldn't stop thinking of everything. My mind raced with things to do and people to see. Cycling gave me head space to get things in order, no easy thing when you are just busy being busy.

Once Phil had decided it was happening, he put his heart and soul into it. Each night, we went through a mixture of practical chat about preparations and sentiment about our potential separation and frustration with each other. It wasn't until the day before I was leaving that the gravity of how we felt really hit me. Phil and I spent the day cleaning out the flat for our new tenant who was moving in the next day. Every now and then, Phil just grabbed me, hugged me and loved me, then we shared a laugh and I had the odd blub. At night, we went out to dinner and had a mutual admiration society. We had gone through a hard time but loved each other more than ever and this adventure highlighted our complete devotion to each other. Sitting at a candlelit table in an Italian restaurant, Phil made me laugh lots as usual before pulling out a small box. I was overcome with emotion as he gently kissed my hand and gave me the box - if it had been a rats tail, I'd have loved it. As it was, he had bought me a beautiful necklace with two linking hearts in silver. Well... boo hoo and some! How dare I leave this man for so long?

We spent the rest of the evening at home trying not to go to bed because we would have to go our separate ways when we woke up. Eventually, we fell asleep holding hands tightly. I got a lift to the train with a friend and Phil drove to work. We had four attempts at saying goodbye: each time he stopped the van,

We spent a lot of time going west in Brian our van in 2005. Who needed more?

got out and kissed me again. It felt overwhelmingly emotional as four months suddenly seemed like a lifetime. We had been used to separation years ago but since had enjoyed our full time 'normal life' together. I had put an end to that, even to the extent of renting our home out. Was I mad?

The train journey gave me rather too much time to ponder what I was doing: Phil was now involved, so we would always share the experience. Our love for each other had been re-enforced and I needed to do this for me. I was over 40; we had agreed we weren't having children, and living and having adventures was my driver. Not going because it was expensive and meant a few months apart from Phil would be crazy. I would have followed the journey on the website and ended up begrudging Phil for not letting me go. Naturally there were as many arguments not to go; I just never gave them air time!

Next few days consisted of saying my goodbyes to family and friends. Subconsciously, I knew it was a potentially fatal expedition, so saying farewell to Mum and my brothers meant more than usual. I couldn't let go for minutes as Robert gave me a big hug at Guernsey airport. I never even told Mum I was climbing Everest: this was the only mountain she knew about and only that summer she had told me never to even think of climbing it. I told her about the cycle ride and that we would end up climbing a Mt Everliar! Penny and Martyn helped keep the secret throughout the Everestmax expedition by bringing her over-printed copies of the website updates, always deleting any mention of Everest. I will always be grateful for their kindness as she was over 70 and would have spent six months worrying rather than just enjoying the odd phone call from me on one of my adventures.

David and his family were extremely excited yet concerned about the whole thing. Big events bring out real emotions and David gave me the big brother cocktail hug of love, concern and pride. My niece Lydia couldn't stop crying as they dropped me off at the station. Bless her, she thought I was the living version of Lara Croft but without the D cup and long legs. She was only eight and knows better now! I had a London gang goodbye party, too, at the Hardy house, always willing hosts to my capital gatherings. Andy Cooke, another great friend, found time to come to London, take me for lunch, buy me a rose and wish me luck. People found it hard to get their head around the scale of the trip: lots of people do Everest, but nobody they knew had cycled there from the lowest place possible with a bunch of strangers. Carol Lovel turned to me and said: "What if after a couple of weeks the team drive you nuts and you want to get out?" I hadn't even thought of that. Anybody who signs up for a trip like this must have something in common with the others... surely?

I got news from Dom that our visas were delayed and we might not be able to fly until the Friday (five days late). Not a great start, but at least this gave me more time to catch up with godchildren and friends. I moved to my London base camp, namely Paul and Vics Ratigan's flat in Chiswick, where I'd once lived with him and Simon and Elaine. Such good memories. Paul and Vics have always let me use my old room since I left in 1994 and make me feel like it is still home. Even Phil is comfortable there despite it being in London.

I had a leisurely day to get the train over to Surbiton to meet the third member of the team, Nic Clarke. Greeting me in a really flash car, he looked offensively fit and clean cut, but was incredibly charming. I could tell straightaway he was a caring sort who was more than able of taking care of himself. He was more reserved than my average playmate and I tried to hold back the excitement as he showed me a new Marin bike he had been keeping for me. He had fine tuned it for me so we could cycle together to Richmond Park. He was incredibly comfortable cycling in London and, having been a fitness instructor and a marathon runner, as fit as a butcher's dog. I was suitably intimidated and paranoid; I had presumed they would all be fitter than me and, if Nic was anything to go by, I was right. Luckily, his goal wasn't to prove a point but to get me back to Chiswick in one piece.

I cycled home with a big smile on a gorgeous day. Paul and Simon Ratigan joined me for a great night out, celebrating our shared history and our future. All was good in the world. We got news on Friday that our visas were ready and we were going to fly on the Sunday. Paul and Vics were away for the weekend and that suited me just fine as I enjoyed my own space for the last time for ages. I had a suitably long chat with Phil and family as I knew phoning wouldn't be easy from now on. I felt guilty knowing Phil was now living in our van alone and he is not an 'alone' person. Oops!

Sunday came and I got a taxi to Heathrow airport. The first person I saw as I pushed my trolley into the departure lobby was Nic. Hooray, it wasn't a spoof. Then Dom and the rest of the team arrived in a Cheltenham College van and I really had to contain myself from grabbing and hugging complete strangers as if I'd known them all my life. I knew they had six months with me and first impressions counted. Fortunately, Sarah does do excited, so I vented some of my exuberance on her.

Jamie, the fifth cyclist, was 23 and looked fit and lean - thank God for bulked up Dom. Jamie had confidence beyond his years without being arrogant, was easy to chat to and possessed a ready smile that puts you at ease. Richard (Dickie) and Rowenna (Ro) were the support team: Dickie, in his early thirties and the only real heavyweight of the team, was a large fellow with a bib and tucker accent, yet endearingly scruffy and lovable. As an ex-naval officer, he had all the credentials to be organised and run the support team like a military operation. He was obviously rebelling against the clean cut look now he was a civilian. Ro, or should I say 'Hair', was a petite lady in her thirties with a disproportionate amount of thick hair. She had a distinctively posh, but not plummy voice, and an intelligent look (maybe it was the glasses). She seemed the most independent of the pack and wasn't girly either, ensuring the female pack was in sync. I gave her some space as we all blended in.

We boarded the flight without problem but were delayed for a couple of hours in Frankfurt. This was the first indication of how we were all going to handle 'stress': it was the middle of the night and we sat on the floor of an airport almost buried with hand luggage. What did we do? We laughed; a small sign of things to come.

CHAPTER **SEVEN**

Starting at the Dead Sea.
From the left, me, Sarah, Nic, Jamie and Dom

JORDAN
Population: 5,795,000
Capital: Amman; 1,237,000
Area: 89,342 square kilometers (34,495 square miles)
Language: Arabic, English
Religion: Sunni Muslim, Christian
Currency: Jordanian dinar
Life Expectancy: 61
GDP per Capita: U.S. $4,300
Literacy Percent: 91
Industry: Phosphate mining, pharmaceuticals, petroleum refining, cement, potash
Agriculture: Wheat, barley, citrus, tomatoes; sheep
Exports: Phosphates, fertilizers, potash, agricultural products, manufactures

Let the Journey Begin - Jordan

We arrived in Amman and got two mini vans to take us to our hotel where the host, Fayez, waited up and insisted on having tea and a chat before we went to bed. He was an entertainer and proved very helpful over the next couple of days. I spent the next few days observing the characters in the team. I knew I would irritate them in full excited mode, so tried to be a calm team player and demonstrate enthusiasm without excitability…bloody hard! I weighed up the other members of the team and how to approach them individually. I had done enough team development to know I could help myself by looking for their characteristics before establishing my own inimitable and potentially quite irritating persona.

Jamie and Nic shared a natural lads' rapport, always laughing between themselves, but without creating a clique. They were just building on a relationship that had started several months before. Nic was in charge of the route plan for the journey and the Marin bikes being set up for us. He took things seriously but was also up for a laugh when appropriate. He would need his own space and was more of a one-to-one than a group person; hence he and Jamie were good together. I could also tell he would be very generous with his time to help in areas he was strong in... like bikes! Right on both counts. Jamie would be easy to get on with despite our age gap, was a classic team player with no aspirations to lead, but never shy to give suggestions and make things happen. His role was to liaise with our charities and ensure they received the profile we had promised. Otherwise, he had no specific assigned role but lots of initiative, having worked with the team for long enough to know what needed doing.

Ro had known Dickie from when he was co-ordinating the media coverage of the centenary of Trafalgar for the Navy. Ro was a commissioned artist on his ship and he took personal care of her to make sure she got the best spot. I bet he did! They were only friends for a short time before he asked her if she would be interested in being part of the support team. They had a good rapport but were still getting to know each other. Dickie was in charge of border control, any bureaucracy and the general admin of the trip; Ro was chief of shopping and co-ordinating life. Together they were responsible for the cyclists' welfare by finding places for us to sleep and eat good food. It was even more essential they worked well together than the cyclists... fortunately they were the perfect partnership.

Dickie was easy going and fun as a person and made me laugh unwittingly. I think it was the mixture of the officer in 'civvy street' that did it. Ro seemed distant from me for a short while. I discovered later it stemmed from when we were sitting in our room on day three and I started unveiling more of the real me. I confessed to having been mellow thus far, but Ro found me somewhat full on and wondered how on earth she would be able to spend the next six months in such close proximity. Not the best start!

Next day we found our 'mutual experience' and bonded for the rest of the trip. Ro stood in the hall of the hotel where we had unpacked and built the bikes. Suddenly, she jumped into a large and lonesome cardboard box and started to rock. Asked why, she replied: "I have always wondered why children find boxes so fascinating, so I'm going to experiment." Before long, she had made it into a ship, house and a tank and I was with her all the way. We laughed hysterically for about half an hour and never looked back. From that moment, I just had to look at her and she made me laugh. Her wit was sharp, creative and different from the rest of the team and she was to prove a huge asset for me.

Sarah had obviously been Dom's right hand girl for anything to do with computers and was an important part of our day. We had promised sponsors and charities we'd keep our blog updated daily and Dom was still co-ordinating the trip to Everest. Confident, intelligent and very able, Sarah's youth and eagerness to please and contribute meant she could never relax until she felt her part had been completed successfully. She would be on the computer trying to make things work late into the night amid moments of pure exasperation, classic female tears and emotion. By the way, boys, that doesn't mean we are out of control; it just means we are frustrated and somehow this connects to our tear glands and we cry. Her persistence paid off and it was called on again and again throughout the trip. Especially when it came to teaching me how to do my IT bit.

Dom was a natural leader, never looked phased by anything and was happy to delegate to anyone if he could trust the job would be done. Not particularly emotional, but good at making you feel valued without the touchy, feely stuff, he had a very dry sense of humour which developed more and more. His posh manners were soaked in sarcasm, the very best form of British humour and the dominant one throughout the trip.

I still felt a bit of an outsider by day three because I didn't have a real role. I wrote in my diary how civil everyone was: they all knew each other, but not really well. The most time they had spent at one time together was doing Mt Blanc that summer and that was minus Dickie and Ro. Part of me puts the successful dynamic of this team down to that fact: we are far more patient with people we don't know well and got to know each other's habits, slowly and with more tolerance.

We all had jobs to do like shopping for cookers and camping kit as well as buying a van to be used as a support vehicle. Already a week behind schedule due to the visa problems in London, everything needed to happen yesterday. Getting the new van proved tricky as we were told we could get it duty-free as long as we got it out of the country within three days. Only problem was how and where to buy it; two whole days were spent chasing the right people to take us to the right office to get the right paperwork for another office in another area - get the idea? This was a bureaucratic nightmare solved by us all taking turns at being persistent. We ended up with a blue van which the girls called Martha and the boys called 'van'. Dickie and Ro sealed the deal along with adjustments such as having ladders welded on and a roof rack. This all meant a delay to our first cycling day.

That brings me to my big test: I had never cycled, climbed or done anything with this team. If they left me for dust on the first day, there'd be 7,900 km of playing catch up! Nervous in an excited but humble way, I was prepared to accept that I would pull out, if necessary, as we couldn't afford to wait for a slow coach. Dom insisted fitness would come with bike time, yet our original goal of 100km per day would need to increase as we had already lost a lot of time and had to allow for more delays... help! I tried to talk myself into sleeping the night before which made me even more awake. I saw every hour on the clock; just the start I didn't want!

I was obviously running on adrenalin next morning as I didn't feel tired despite my broken sleep. We all piled into two taxis to take us to the Dead Sea as our van wasn't ready yet. We reached our starting point on the shores, a lovely area where people come for their holidays although this was obviously out of season. There were beach umbrellas and shower taps; a very civilised start. We posed in a line with our back tyres dipping into the water at -420m, posing and posing for the camera and DVD. History was about to be made; it felt great and we hadn't even cycled a single km yet! After the shoot, we stripped off and went swimming in the sea. How much fun was that? Doing the breaststroke, I found it impossible to keep my bum down in the water due to the salt (nothing to do with the fact my backside had lots of floating fat agent). It looked funny and felt hilarious. Sarah was warned not to get any stinging water in her eyes but, being the scientific, inquisitive sort, felt compelled to try... big mistake, firstly because it really hurt and, secondly, she was ridiculed for the rest of the day. The precedent had been set... do something stupid and you will be the source of humour until the next victim comes along. This wouldn't work for everyone, but it worked for us and we all had our turn as the victim. Some more than others; why are you looking at me?

Nic, Jamie and Sarah enjoying a mud bath pamper session before jumping on the bikes for the first day

My palpitations really started when it was finally time to start. The drive there had shown we had an elevation of 1,200m to gain and we estimated that it would take 45km using the main road. So we made the good choice of the longer scenic route; albeit it took 75km. It wasn't long before I knew I was with the right team. We agreed to stop at regular intervals or at obvious directional changes – in this case, the top of each very long uphill. Egos and competition were out; it was just support and humour. Good job, as I was always last and that seemed no problem at all. I loved them!

The banter grew stronger at each stop. On my bike, I liked my own head space to take in the scenery and drink in my own thoughts, all very cathartic and energising. Then, at the stops, I couldn't shut up. Cycling through one small town on the outskirts of Amman, a policeman was the obvious choice to point us in the right direction. He even escorted us on his motorbike and took the mickey by imitating our cycling. This boded well in a country that still had its fair share of bad press as a destination for westerners. That was before we got pelted by stones by local boys. One hit my foot and one hit Sarah's helmet… good job she was wearing it. Funny enough, it felt remarkably unsettling to be on the receiving end of hostile behaviour regardless of the motives. I started to think of the more 'hostile' countries to come and whether we needed body armour. As usual, we discussed and dismissed negative thoughts within the same breath, knowing we would deal with the challenge of each day as they came. We were right not to look for trouble in countries we hadn't even been to. That night, the others were fine, but I definitely felt most tired after a long, hot day. I was pleased when Dickie and Ro said the van wouldn't be ready to go until the next day... meaning a compulsory rest day before we started our journey in earnest.

Dom getting evidence that we were at the Dead Sea

Did this bode well? Just another 7,925km to go with a provisionally planned day off every week to 10 days and I was stiff on day one. Let the challenge begin.

Day two in the saddle took us from Amman to the border and into Syria, the least troublesome of all the borders that only took a couple of hours. However it was the most disconcerting for me: handing in our passports, two different people asked if Jamie and then Sarah were my children... I know what you are thinking, how ridiculous! How could they look that young? I consoled myself with the thought teenagers often have children in Syria, so I could still look young. The others took no time in celebrating my humiliation with ageist humour for the rest of the day. I don't actually have an age hang-up, but that nearly helped me find one.

CHAPTER **EIGHT**

Welcome to Syria. Jamie enjoying the space

Flat is Fab - Syria

SYRIA

Population: 18,389,000
Capital: Damascus; 2,228,000
Area: 185,180 square kilometers (71,498 square miles)
Language: Arabic, Kurdish, Armenian, Aramaic, Circassian, French, English
Religion: Sunni, Alawite, Druze and other Muslim sects, Christian
Currency: Syrian pound
Life Expectancy: 70
GDP per Capita: U.S. $3,700
Literacy Percent: 77
Industry: Petroleum, textiles, food processing, beverages
Agriculture: Wheat, barley, cotton, lentils; beef
Exports: Crude oil, petroleum products, fruits and vegetables, cotton fiber, clothing

We cycled off with our first country under our belt; on a journey like this, every opportunity to tick a box is a good way to keep motivation going. Just as well, as the heavens opened and we were cycling in monsoon-like conditions. It was about 30km to the next town where we hoped to get somewhere to sleep. Dickie and Ro went ahead and, after a long search, found one hotel which by co-incidence had already been booked out by 40 German cyclists due to arrive that night. These were the only western cyclists we were going to see for the next several thousand miles. We insisted on hanging out in the lounge area for a hot drink and food just in case somebody had dropped out. Looking like drowned rats, we were also playing the sympathy card by appearing to need shelter at any cost. Luck was on our side and they were able to free up a room with a pull-out bed and three singles. Phew, the relief of not having to go back out into foul weather in the dark and hunt for somewhere to stay. The team showed a great sense of tolerance that day; nobody showed signs of irritability or discomfort, each obstacle was a challenge not a chore. Corny, but true - it would take something pretty mountainous to bring this group down.

Cycling in the outskirts of Damascas on Christmas Eve. It was a tad wet

Syria is a predominantly Muslim country and the capital city Damascus was our destination for Christmas Eve, the following day. Syria was also one of the countries on the 'be careful, you are western' check list. Instead, we found nothing except hospitality and generosity. We went back on the bikes in torrential rain and had been going for an hour or two before taking refuge under the awning of a shop that looked closed. The five of us were looking wet and uncomfortable when out came Mohammad, the shop owner. It took no time at all to recognise that this man was a good character. International communications strategy kicked in – body language to you and me - and, before we knew it, he invited us in to get warm and have some tea. We gestured we were too dirty and wet, but thanked him. He put his head in the door and shouted to someone inside. We continued our kung fu-style communication, then a young lad turned up with a tray of hot coffee and six cups. Some body language is more easily understood - for example it was very clear he didn't hold George Bush in high esteem when he did the cut throat gesture after saying his name. We decided it would be good for international relations generally to avoid the classic topics of sex, politics and religion... let trivia rule and stay alive was a good plan.

The kind gentleman who saw us looking cold and wet and brought us tea

Our cycle continued to Damascus where Ro and Dickie had done an exceptional job finding a cheap and bike friendly hotel in the city. The proprietors had been warned we were coming but still bore that slightly overwhelmed look when they saw how dirty and wet we were... too late, we had signed. Girls being girls, we had a sense of occasion and were desperate to find tinsel to decorate our table that night and the next day for Christmas. Boys being boys, they found it all unnecessary and trivial. So we went our separate ways; them mocking us and us pitying them for their lack of occasion. Both groups found fulfillment and all met up to go to the souk (market area) which proved colourful, busy, noisy and everything you would expect from a lively city. Yet I wasn't expecting some of the designs in the ladies dress shops: this was a Muslim country, but some of the dresses were positively sexy! One dress was stunning and fit for Cinderella with a hooped long pink skirt and an off-the-shoulder bodice. Stunning, but not what I anticipated your average Muslim woman to have in their local shop.

Fascinated by pretty dresses in Damascus

We had compulsory tinsel at dinner - which the boys begrudgingly found festive – but meant the girls went to bed happy. Sarah was as excited as a five-year-old as Christmas was a very big deal at her home. Ro was very good at recognising this. When we had gone to sleep, she stayed up decorated the room by sticking tinsel to the wall in the shape of a Christmas tree. Sarah woke up and was beside herself; a good job we three girls had our own room. As Sarah opened her presents from home, I wanted to be festive but felt I needed some 'me time', so I went to the loo and had a bit of a girly sob: Christmas is a family time, Phil was my husband and my family and we weren't together. No amount of logic can dismiss emotions that come from the heart. I wear my heart on my sleeve and, although not moody, wasn't my normal self.

The solution came in the form of a quiet chat with Ro and our team Christmas treat of an 'eat as much as you can' breakfast buffet at the four star Four Seasons Hotel. Dom's sister put us onto it by email and, although we looked the roughest guests there, we certainly had the biggest appetites. The food was exquisite and we felt very posh and decadent. We hadn't lasted long at roughing it, had we? We could justify the expense as in real terms it was seriously cheap and now we were fed, watered and recharged ready for our Christmas ride.

We set off and planned to meet Ro and Dickie en route as they normally went ahead, then waited and checked on us. Between times, they bought food. On the last stretch of the day, they would look for either a camp or a cheap hotel. They left us once we had managed to negotiate our way out of Damascus after breakfast and we didn't see them again until 6.30pm, by which time it was dark and cold. There was no sign of them, so we decided to pull off 200 meters to the side of the main road where we found a derelict building. It was already sunset, so where were Dickie and Ro? Nic and Dom waited at the roadside to stop them driving by while Sarah, Jamie and I performed aerobics and anything else we could think of to keep us warm. We waited for a couple of hours before they were spotted and flagged down by Dom and Nic. It wasn't a busy road, but it would have been easy to miss them and that would have been a disaster. As they drove into the site of our home for the night, they saw Jamie, Sarah and I in a circle hugging each other and jumping up and down. Ro confessed they had been shopping for wood to make an awning for the van and ended up having tea with the woodman. As soon as she had seen us in our frozen huddle, she felt racked with guilt "Good, that was our intention," I said, then laughed it off. Lesson learnt, they never put shopping before the cyclists again.

A satellite phone enabled me to call Phil and my family from the middle of the Syrian dessert to say Happy Christmas. Behold, the joys of modern technology. Phil had been waiting for my call and I cooked for the team with a renewed spring in my step. We popped a cheap bottle of bubbly, had vegetable mush and cleaned our bikes ready for the next day. It was then we picked up on the Nic 'McSlick' tendency to polish his bike; not just clean it but really love and cherish it at every pit stop. He was a role model for bike maintenance and our next easy target for ridicule. Jamie started to take subtle footage of him cleaning it, so we could use it as an on-going humour line throughout the movie we were hoping to make of the expedition. Dom, at the other extreme, only addressed bike hygiene if something was going to break. There must be a happy medium?

Next day saw us cycle 100km by 2.30pm to reach the historic town of Palmya where we met Dickie and Ro at a hotel they had found. The cyclists were starving and starting to have sense of humour failure when the faffing started, so they biked off to a café for food. I waited for Ro and Dickie to show us where we were going to stay; this was the first sign of tension en masse I had seen but, sitting around a table with a beer and a pancake, laughter resumed and ridicule replaced the uncomfortable silence. I had started to learn that these boys really did just deal with the moment and move on. If they got frustrated or annoyed about something, they didn't have to analyse it or discuss it. Women tend to try and understand too much for too long and for all the wrong reasons, so becoming more and more in touch with the male mindset as the trip went on made life easy. Yet when the three girls got together on our own, I fell back into my more natural hormonal state as we put the world to rights. I found that equally refreshing.

Leaving our fabulous shelter on Boxing day

Palmya was a tourist town with ancient ruins, camel rides and souvenirs. We fell straight into tourist role; I managed to avoid a camel ride but got a great blast on the camel owners' motorbike just for a giggle. We took the obligatory photos, read the appropriate history leaflet and got back to the appropriate bar for a good social. I wrote in my diary: 'today is the first day that I feel I am part of the team in my own right and no longer the new kid/granny.'

Having a nice chat in Palmya

Computers were a part of our nightly ritual to update our blog and download images. IT expert Sarah felt responsible and, if necessary, would stay up late as would Dom as he was still co-ordinating preparations for Everest. The rest would do admin like cleaning bikes, writing diaries or amusing ourselves with various things like Bop It, a very noisy, lively game where you have to beat a computerised toy by hitting and bopping and twisting things. Such a mindless but active game kept us entertained for ages and proved a great source of competition over the coming months. It was probably a tad ambitious to keep it going too long in a tent designed for four and sleeping seven without being hit yourself.

Camping in Syria was always spacious

The great thing about Syria was that it was flat. I was still at the back, but my fitness was growing all the time while I was still able to enjoy the view, heat and quirky sights of a foreign country. Syria, as I expected, was incredibly barren and it was great we weren't cycling in the heat of the summer as we were effectively cycling through a desert. It was flat and sand-coloured for as far as the eye could see. Occasionally, we'd see small herds of goats with children or men looking after them in the odd areas with green bush. I was enjoying doing long distances with my MP3 player. There was something wonderful about music, cycling and endless horizons. We stopped every 25 to 30km for refreshments and chat. I loved this form of travel as I could see, smell, hear and feel a country in a way you can't from a motor vehicle.

Stretching out on a typically flat road in Syria

We stopped in a small place that looked like a cross between a ghost town and a deserted building site. Ro and Dickie weren't with us when we saw a sign on a small building that implied they sold Coca Cola. Judging from the fact the windows were substituted with cage-like mesh, we started to wonder if this place was actually a good place to stop. Was it to keep the customers in because their produce was so bad or keep the street violence out? We brought our bikes into the café area and, although the streets were deserted, all felt an air of mistrust. Anyway, we managed to order a few drinks, the man was very friendly and jolly and we all chilled. Then slowly, slowly, children started to appear peering into our cage. Suddenly we were in a zoo - and we were the main attraction.

It's always tempting to deal with a bunch of inquisitive kids staring as if you were a bunch of aliens by running or roaring at them. However, we didn't know if they had parents ready to defend their precious children, so started by smiling and I ventured to do my disappearing hanky trick (very good, even if I say so myself). My very over-the-top party piece captured their total attention as they loved the magic and were totally intrigued. For the next Everestmax slot, Jamie got them to repeat his words of 'Big it Up!' while doing some youthful hand gesture associated with street culture - stuff I wouldn't get away with. They all looked like a bunch of street-wise rappers having a great time. Time for a sing-a-long and I started the ball rolling with 'I Iove you yes I do coz I know that you love me too'. They all got it really quickly; the Pied Piper effect kicked in and we had about 40 children running down the street after us as we peddled furiously to get away from our new fan club. The joys of celebrity status...

That day ended at a great campsite found by good old Dickie and Ro with a gin and tonic before dinner to loosen the vocals ready for Jamie and Nic to do their 'Big Brother' interviews for the video. Who said this adventure lark couldn't be civilised? Our days of alcohol were drawing to a close and you always want more of what you can't have, don't you? The interviews had Jamie and Nic in stitches for the rest of the night. We never watched each other's, but it was just as entertaining listening to them laughing uncontrollably.

More seriously, Dutchman Gerry Winkler was attempting the same challenge as us, so became our mock public enemy number one. It was the first time it had been attempted by anybody; yet, in the same year, two attempts were being made. How dare he? We knew he had started ahead of us but also that Everest would allow us to catch up. Nobody can race up Everest unless the weather is right and the weather wouldn't be right before May. He could race all he liked, as long as we were there and ready for Everest, we would be ready for him.

Camping was a team favourite. Our tent was big enough for all of us to sleep in at the same time – just. It was a hive of activity with cooking on one corner, computer updating in another and a game of 'Bopit' in another. Life was never dull and somehow we never felt we were on top of each other to the point we were getting frustrated. When not raining or snowing, it was a great time to spread everything out, get bikes cleaned and sorted, play hacky sack and generally enjoy our surroundings. Camping was great.

The 7 of us loved camping despite the lack of personal space

"Don't move: relax and stay where you are." We weren't being held up by bandits, but trying to get everybody to relax after a good night's sleep to fill in our weekly stats report. We updated our blog with weekly reports on our weight and heart rate. It made good reading as, after good food and good sleep, how could we have anything less than a low and healthy heartbeat? Unless you are Sarah, who had an 'action' dream and needed to go to the loo so much her heart was racing. Our star support team, Ro and Dickie, kept presenting pleasant surprises at meal times such as chocolate spread to try and make flat bread more interesting. They also kept us away from dismantling our gorgeous tent as our 'that will do' attitude could have meant it not lasting the trip.

Nic, our illustrious navigational leader and 'clean bike champion', led the way with a tail wind, meaning he was even faster than normal. One of our stops was near a small group of tents where a woman beckoned us with an enthusiastic wave to come near as a smart car pulled out. Curiosity prevailed and we cycled up to introduce ourselves: all the other roadside women we had seen were shepherdesses, but this lady had lots of makeup and a revealing, rather tight fitting, dress. The penny dropped and we realised we had met our first 'lady of the road'. Our normally cool and collected men decided we needed to go but not before Jamie asked for a photo for his cultural collection. Funnily enough, he was refused. Ah well, don't ask, don't get.

We cycled to Deir Ezzor city where Ro and Dickie led us into town via chaotic roads and alleys. Ro was on the roof getting film footage of how much fun it can be dodging cars children, bikes and carts. Dom's previous bike courier days meant we had a natural leader and the fact we were here at all created a Mexican-wave reaction in the market streets with men and children crying out greetings of welcome. Syria exceeded our expectations of hospitality.

New Year's Eve was a day of firsts: our first 100mile day, completing our first 1000km and, as if that wasn't enough, Nic led our first 'ogi, ogi, ogi' to celebrate. We had been forced into our first 100 miles by circumstance as we had got to a potential camp site by 5pm, but the police said 'no'. We couldn't really argue, so there was a team chat and we decided to push on another 55km to the border town – hence the first 100 mile (160km) day. The decision-making process was in full swing

A team lunch stop with Martha our trusted van

by the time I had pulled in. When told we had a few more miles to go, my face said it all - nothing a few expletives couldn't have done equally as well, but apparently much more amusing. Of the others, Nic did the British stiff upper lip and onward and upward; nothing stops Sarah; and Dom and Jamie get off on things being ridiculously arduous.

Ro rose to the challenge by getting the cooker on and getting some great food down us before the late night push. One of the problems I stupidly hadn't anticipated was riding at night so I had my head torch but no bike light. The next 75km on the equivalent of the English M6 motorway was done by cycling between the team and scabbing some of the benefit of their lights. Sarah had her glow-in-the-dark jacket which, although sad in the world of cool, became a big asset. Once the mickey taking stopped, we all secretly wanted one. Despite it being cold, dark and late, we had such a laugh. This group was meant to be together doing this sort of thing and banter fuelled our energy.

Ro and Dickie made a timely tea break stop while we did the ritual cold dance; then took off ahead again before returning with the best news: a hotel that took smelly, wet cyclists, had hot showers and clean sheets, plus was willing to give us food late on New Year's Eve. Never had two people looked more attractive and kissable – well, apart from Phil. We probably looked like we were on drugs we were in such high spirits. I bounced on a posh bed and hugged the crisp blue sheets before diving into a gorgeous shower and meeting the team for dinner.

As a New Year treat, I decided to bring out my harmonica and play them the two tunes I knew. Dom hated anything like that and that made it all the more necessary for me to do it; fully supported by the team, of course. This musical bonanza was followed by a dose of pub quiz - hosted by yours truly - before bringing in the New Year bouncing on each other's beds and singing Old Lang Syne.

CHAPTER **NINE**

A coffee stop near the Iraq border

TURKEY

Population: 72,907,000

Capital: Ankara; 3,428,000

Area: 779,452 square kilometers (300,948 square miles)

Language: Turkish, Kurdish, Arabic, Armenian, Greek

Religion: Muslim (mostly Sunni)

Currency: Turkish lira

Life Expectancy: 69

GDP per Capita: U.S. $7,300

Literacy per cent: 87

Industry: Textiles, food processing, autos, mining, steel, petroleum

Agriculture: Tobacco, cotton, grain, olives; livestock

Exports: Apparel, foodstuffs, textiles, metal manufactures, transport equipment

Hills Are Hilarious! - Turkey

Dickie and Ro went ahead to the next border and we followed an hour later, managing to get through in an hour without a problem. They meanwhile hadn't even got past the start line because of Martha. Officials insisted this border couldn't accept the carne we had (this is like a passport for vehicles) so Dickie and Ro needed to travel a couple of hundred km to an alternative border crossing. There was no choice but to separate and see them on the other side in a couple of days. They knew our route and would be able to catch us up, yet it felt really odd saying goodbye. We packed what we needed to be self-sufficient knowing we would sleep in hotels and eat in cafes. This wasn't a problem as our itinerary could take us between towns with no need for camping. The rest of the day was spent on the other side of the border in our first Turkish town, eating, drinking and doing emails. We were recharged and ready for the next day.

We knew we were in for our first day on hills for a long time after flat Syria. A hearty breakfast in the local bakery gave us an opportunity to see local teenagers in their element. Wearing shirts and ties from their uniform worn in a way to look defiant and 'cool', the boys hunted in gangs and the girls looked nonchalant and disinterested while flashing the odd glance, then bursting into hysterical laughter. It's the same all the world round. You can change the religion, but not the hormones!

We set off and, as usual, I was last at every stop - but big deal. The terrain had changed dramatically. Winding our way up a gorge with a river cutting through it, I couldn't believe I was saying it, but it was good to be doing hills. We got to the top, had a banter and all set off down. The huge downhill felt fast and it was novel to be freewheeling. Yee ha! We ended in a small village with a big high school and waited for Dom, who had taken my last place. Before long, Jamie was playing football with the local boys' team; Nic and I were in with the headmaster explaining our journey and interest in Turkey; and Sarah was guarding the bikes from the now growing crowds... but still no Dom. We had been waiting for about an hour and, even if he'd had a puncture, he should have been here. Then we saw him and discovered the reason - just after we all left him, he got a puncture, having just given the pump to Sarah to fix hers. So he had to walk five km to get to a place that had a version of a pump. We were sympathetic but only after howling with laughter. As nobody was hurt or dead, it was funny, especially as he had missed the best downhill of the trip so far.

After about 80km, we caught sight of a gorgeous blue van that looked just like Martha... yes! Dickie and Ro had made it and the reunion was as though we hadn't seen each other in weeks rather than a couple of days. Then Dickie broke news he'd had to give them $1,500 as a bond for the vehicle which we could claim back at the border when we left. He had done well to negotiate it

Nic loving the hills

down as the original demand was much higher. Our hearts sank a little as even I, with my irritating optimistic condition, felt we had just seen the last of that money. I was equally sure Dickie had done a great job getting the best deal he could from a bunch of corrupt officials.

We stayed the night in a great hotel in the city of Batman, complete with Turkish bath and masseur for the amazing price of $5. We all got 'detogged' and sat in the Turkish bath together, with us girls being very aware of our hairy legs and bikini lines – well, we weren't expecting to undress! All this was chivalrously overlooked by the boys once they'd had five minutes to get it out of their system. Then came the masseur. It was amazing, albeit a tad unnerving, that a man from Turkey was happy to be so intimate with a woman. He pretty well massaged everything, apart from my nether region. What started out making me relax into a jellyfish, changed into me becoming a slightly overcooked joint of beef. The girls compared notes and felt the same, but somehow didn't really care as we knew we could have shouted the boys for help if he had gone beyond the line.

Next day, Ro and Dickie were held up and very late getting to us for our lunch break. Hungry after cycling at least 80km, we all pulled up together on the side of the road. There hadn't been a shop or village for miles and there was no prospect of one coming up soon either. Sarah and I went for a walkabout to some small houses we saw on a nearby hill. We weren't expecting a local Spar shop but a small stall with biscuits and sweets looking like they'd been there for years would have been nice. As it was, we ended up having a laugh with a couple of kids, creating the Pied Piper effect again. A smiley young man joined us and, after we tried to explain we had money for food, led us to his home and introduced us to his pregnant wife, mother and five children. He must have started very young! He took us into the equivalent of his lounge, a concrete floor with rugs on the floor and three photos on the wall. Body language kicked in with the grandmother, our smiley man and two of his children before, much to our surprise, his wife walked in with a tray of tea, fried eggs, bread and cheese. Wow! It was delicious and both Sarah and I soon overcame a moment of guilt about the boys being left hungry on the road. This was a hard working, welcoming family we would never have met save for our bikes. We took out the money to ask how much and he refused to take any. This was too generous as he had five children and a mother, never mind a pregnant wife, and we left humbled and uplifted by another example of human kindness not enough people witness in our busy consumer life. Back at the roadside, Ro and Dickie created a feast. Village children followed us, cue my magic hanky trick and Dickie got into the mood with his clown act, making them laugh and run after him for ages. He was a natural.

Turkey surprised me as I'd imagined the whole country to be a lot more westernised in its infrastructure. Elements in the city were such as their famous seaside resorts, yet pockets were more like a Third World level of living in a country about to enter the EU. Political problems with the Kurds were also very obvious even to folk with limited exposure to people's comments. This was highlighted by the fact we were cycling so close to Iraq (50 miles from the border) where most of the Kurdish people live. We stopped in the early evening and camped that night in a green field by a river, overlooked by a military post. They came to visit but were fine and we probably felt safer knowing they were keeping an eye on us. We just had to choose our toilet areas carefully when we went off with our trowel.

I was chief cook that night and Dickie was my helper. Well, talk about opposites: I am a chop and cook kind of girl; Dickie is a process, systems, detail kind of boy. All he had to do was peel and cook the potatoes but, by the time I had done the veg, prepared the water and generally aged another year, Dickie was still working out how and where he would achieve his task. Far from being annoying, I found this incredibly funny, laughing and taking the mickey out of the fact officers in the forces can't even go to the loo without proper procedures and systems in place. We went to bed that night and I couldn't find my eye covers, a big set of red lips made of felt (yes, lips). I wake up at the first sign of light and, without them, I knew I would lose badly-needed sleep. The girls were particularly good at helping me search but I didn't find them and went to bed ready for a short night.

Next morning, before we had even got out of the tent, Sarah and Ro said it was the first time they had seen me looking close to 'distressed' and had thought of a way to make me some more red lips very easily. I was taken aback by their thoughtfulness, a good example of how we had all come to care about each other in a very short time.

Next surprise was the weather: we went to sleep in a green field and woke up in a white one! It had snowed and was freezing. Nobody in the team was fazed by this and it became a 'bring it on' moment. I was a little less that way as I had just experienced a bout of diarrhea; not a good start to a very challenging day. I decided to take some loo roll in a water-proof bag and hope we had lots of bushes along the way. I didn't feel ill but was aware of the potential drainage on my resources as diarrhea causes dehydration. Often it's best not to eat to get rid of the bug but you need energy... oh the dilemmas! You just need to get on with it and react if you feel bad, rather than wasting time anticipating feeling bad. I focused on good things like Phil,

Camping the night before the snow

Warming up with the army

family, parties and the journey ahead to Iran. Off we went into the snow, wind and rain with Ro and Dickie sticking to us like glue. We had regular snack and hot drink stops with hot chocolate, pasta, sweets and bread coming at us fast and furious... my appetite returned during the day and I blessed Mum for my very robust disposition.

We had a lot of hills to tackle. One, in particular, was long with lots of false horizons so it was even longer than we thought and a bit of a psychological battle. You expect the best at each bend only to come face-to-face with yet another huge hairpin. This became our longest day to date and at 4pm we decided to do a final big push into the city of Van, another 60km away. Of course we were up for it! We cycled over 155km in hard conditions that day but with amazing views, especially over the lake. Good banter stops ensured distance was no object. At our last tea stop, Ro and I found singing Frank Sinatra songs very uplifting and amusing while, for some reason, the boys found it a great incentive to get back on their bikes. The last 30km were incredibly hard; the team could tell I was exhausted and almost did a bike escort for me as we pulled into the town. I was the slowest of the pack but never once did they make me feel it was an issue. We got in at about 7.30pm and found a hotel where the girls discovered heaven; our own room with a hot shower. Out came Sarah's copy of Pride and Prejudice and we proceeded to eat and watch movies on the computer in our room until noon the next day... perfect!

The following day had been deemed a rest day anyway. The boys needed their fix of tweaking bikes and kit and tried to entice us out of our rooms but to no avail. I really needed the day off, being a bit older and not knowing when the next one would be. I needn't have worried as the snow was a couple of foot deep in places next morning and we weren't going anywhere. This was the coldest winter Turkey had experienced in more than 30 years and the streets were hard to walk in, never mind bike on. Nic and Dickie went off in Martha to assess the road ahead and came back with reports the road clearing was actually very good - as soon as it stopped, we could go. Meanwhile, the hotel proprietor spoke good English and made the most of our delay by organising for the Turkish TV and papers to come and tell our story. I love this kind of thing and was happy to jump in front of the cameras and chat away in the snow, next to the bikes for dramatic effect. If I'd been watching the news, I'd have thought we were mad too. However, when you are doing the mad thing it doesn't feel mad at all. It was as normal to us as getting up for an office job.

Having time to organise somewhere to stay in advance, our friend the proprietor booked us into a school house about 80km away. Another older man asked about our story and our route and his

Bird Flu and bad weather in Van stopped us for a couple of days

face said it all when we explained our plan to cross the border to Iran. He warned that our route involved crossing a 3,000m pass, a current impossibility on our bikes, and we knew two people had died of bird flu in this region as it was all over the news in the UK and Turkey. We were in danger of having our plans curtailed if they wouldn't let us through our chosen route. Our only answer was to wait, write emails, watch DVDs and hatch a contingency plan... there wasn't one! Our route choice was non-negotiable if we were to get to Everest Base Camp in time to climb.

Every extra day chipped away at any floating days we had given ourselves for illness, weather or unpredicted delays. Also we liked being on the bikes and moving on. As much as we enjoyed seeing local attractions and spending time relaxing, this journey was about something different. We wanted to be on our bikes and enjoying the scenery, exercise and opportunities it gave us.
We set off knowing the roads would be icy, from the previous two days of snow and having changed to our knobbly tyres for more traction. The roads had been cleared really well to reveal long patches of snow but no real sludge. Bird flu officials stopped us but didn't spray our bikes - at least we knew we could carry on our route, removing another question mark. Two food stops at cafes broke the journey well and Ro got on the spare bike for the first time. Girls being girls, we rode together for the next 20km chatting away. Sarah and I took the mickey out of Ro as she and Dickie were showing signs of natural compatibility despite her protestations they were 'just friends'. Most couples don't get on as well as they did. Ro and Dickie were our TV soap: would they or wouldn't they?

After digesting some dodgy looking stew at the second café, we cycled into the night and over the last 10km I could feel myself get progressively weak. Ro and Dom spotted I wasn't on form and stayed with me until we got to the school which the others had found. I told Dom I may not be feeling great the next day and knew if I couldn't cycle the whole team would have to wait for me. We had never had a team discussion over what we do if somebody got really ill and needed a week to get better. Our schedule was already tight but Dom talked it over with the team and it was agreed we would give anyone three days; after that, they would have to get into the van and the journey would continue -devastating for the individual, necessary for the success of the expedition. We only had one chance at Everest and needed to be there in time. The weather window always comes in May to early June and, if we didn't arrive by early April to fully acclimatise, we wouldn't be able to climb. Being a week or two late wasn't an option.

I went straight to bed without eating and feeling exhausted and anxious. The girls kept checking on me and feeding me water and, luckily after 12 hours sleep, I felt much better and even managed to eat some cornflakes. My eyes looked like I'd done 10 rounds with Mike Tyson, but I was ready to get on the bike. That morning was so cold that, as Dickie poured boiled water into our water bottles, it froze. But the sky was blue and there was very little wind, just as well as we had a target of 100km and a 2,700m climb over the pass. Bring it on!

Ironically, this proved to be one of my favourite days of the journey to date. Ro and Dickie were there with as much food and drink as we could manage at regular intervals and Ro created fun challenges at our different stops. One of these was a superb toboggan run up a steep bank: we all had a go at racing each other to the top and sliding down, dressed in our waterproofs. At another stop, she built a snowman which ended up being

Ro and Dickie test the sledging course

Nic and Dom snow cycling

destroyed by Ro and me in a snow fight. Jamie and I shadow boxed to stay warm – I'm sure I got him in the first round. Dom looked on like a proud dad who didn't need to join in to get the fun.

The pass was a long and challenging uphill. As I pulled into the summit, I saw the van with the team jogging on the spot to stay warm. The blue sky had gone, the snow was pouring down and I was about 20 minutes behind the first riders - a long time to wait, but nobody rushed me. They were freezing as they watched me drink my hot chocolate and it was incredible nobody was irritable or impatient in these conditions. They knew I was doing my best and encouraged me to get ready for the next stretch without hassling me. I was ready to go really quickly as it was so cold. I could see their smiles as I said this.

I loved the next downhill stretch which was more like mountain biking with the road covered in a mix of ice, slush and snow -

We started the day in wet kit and finished it in frozen wet kit

quite treacherous conditions, but I didn't look on them like that. I had never really biked on snow before, so it just seemed like a fun downhill. I was ahead of the gang for the first time and loved the speed and fun of it all; the others were more cautious as they were a lot more clued up over the consequences of coming off. My age didn't always reflect my level of wisdom! Along our journey, we stopped at an army post under a big shelter with a stove going and they wanted to see our passports. They laughed at us for being on bikes but offered tea and stood back while we warmed ourselves by the stove.

We made it to the border town by dark and found a hotel to stay in. Ro and Dickie went straight to the border as we had a deadline to get the van to the border and would be fined if even a day late. They also needed as much time as possible to try to get our $1,500 bond back. They reported back we would need to wait another three days as there was a holiday and the bank was closed, biting into the time we needed in Iran. We had limited time on our visa for Turkey so would have to cross the border. Each day we waited for Dickie and the van would detract from our 30-day visa for Iran and we had over 2,800 miles to cycle. We needed all 30 days and there was no guarantee we would get the bond back anyway as the border control officials weren't being helpful. We took a team decision to move on as we had very little faith we would see our money again. Tough call, but the right one.

Our last night in Turkey proved to be one of the most entertaining as Jamie, Sarah and I went with Nic to get a haircut. That was great but it was the extras that added such good value as Nic proceeded to have his neck, arms and back manipulated in an almost brutal fashion. With each pull and jerk, I was more and more alarmed but Nic was still smiling and, in a funny masochistic way, actually enjoying it. Then came the threading: the man took two strands of thread, twisted them and proceeded to roll them down Nic's cheek which was like waxing his face! I'd had it done for my eyebrows in Nepal but never seen it on a man. We didn't want Dom to miss out on such a good body workout, so I went to fetch him and sold the luxury experience as a 'must do'. As he got into the chair, he started to suspect something - something to do with the way we were all smiling like naughty school children setting up their teacher. The haircut, as before, was fine, but our main artist clearly didn't want to disappoint us. What seemed shocking watching Nic was now hilarious on Dom. We laughed so hard with each tug and grunt, I was actually crying. Dom was a superb volunteer, groaning and screeching as I crumbled into a heap of laughter on the floor. Why do Brits love laughing at each other? It was a great show and I'm sure Nic and Dom both felt better for it even if their arms seemed longer than when they went in!

Ro was always there with food hot drinks and a smile regardless of how long she had to wait

CHAPTER **TEN**

Sarah and I fixing a puncture

IRAN
Population: 69,515,000
Capital: Tehran; 7,352,000
Area: 1,648,000 square kilometers (636,296 square miles)
Language: Persian, Turkic, Kurdish, various local dialects
Religion: Shiite and Sunni Muslim
Currency: Iranian rial
Life Expectancy: 69
GDP per Capita: U.S. $6,800
Literacy Percent: 79
Industry: Petroleum, petrochemicals, textiles, cement and other construction materials
Agriculture: Wheat, rice, other grains, sugar beets; dairy products; caviar
Exports: Petroleum, carpets, fruits and nuts, iron and steel, chemicals

Desert and Snow Cocktail - Iran

WESTERNERS have their own ideas about what it is like to visit Iran; most I talked to expressed huge reservations about going to a 'hostile' country which treated women as second class citizens, and all westerners as a threat. The border was our first Iranian experience, starting with cycling in frozen conditions of snow and ice on the roads and surrounding land. It felt very remote and kind of exciting that we had been cycling in these harsh conditions for the last week. It made me celebrate how lucky we were to have such a great bunch of people in this team. Attitude is very contagious and one person being a doom and gloom merchant would probably have had a big impact on the group. As it was, we were all feeding off each other's enthusiasm.

The cyclists separated from Ro, Dickie and Martha at the border. We had a relatively straightforward process and were through in an hour or so. It took them 44 hours so it was just as well they went ahead. We all left the border control together and went about 500m to what looked like a popular café in a street that, befitting border towns throughout the world, appeared bleak and tired. We didn't know the protocol about women; looking like aliens in cycling gear covered in dirt and snow, we took a table feeling very aware we didn't blend in. However, we were all very excited about being in Iran and had talked about how Sarah and I should dress on the bikes. We had bought head scarves in Jordan in anticipation and wore them under our cycle helmets straightaway to avoid offence. They also kept our ears warm and I liked the nice shade of blue covering up my constantly greasy hair.

Once the locals had taken time to stare, we got the attention of the waiter. None of us could speak the language and our short phrase book was getting us nowhere, so I decided to lead the waiter to the kitchen and point to the things we wanted to eat. The team found this amusing but never knew whether I would get them into more trouble. As time went by, they began to trust that somehow people found me completely unthreatening. I had a gift for body language that made people smile and humour my pathetic attempts to communicate. Here was no exception and, despite me being a woman, these men weren't fazed and found it all rather entertaining. The other cafe guests probably hadn't had such good lunchtime entertainment in ages.

There is very little choice in Iran in small town cafes, so kebabs and rice became our standard diet. We had no idea we were about to taste the best Iranian stew we found anywhere in the country. Despite it being a traditional meal and our great efforts, we only got to try it once more. The main character of the place was a mature man in his fifties with a big head of grey hair and beard to match. In front of him was a 'hubble bubble', an ornate glass jug with a tube you inhale the smoke from. He was blowing such exceptional smoke clouds we started to applaud him. Another table of men (did I mention there were no women in there?) enjoyed the hubble bubble and, sensing our fascination, invited us to have a go. Sarah and I couldn't resist and did our best to take it seriously. Not being a smoker or drug taker, here I was in Iran, with a table of men, breathing in smoke from a bottle of bubbling funny-coloured water with no idea of the potential consequences. As it was, it was all harmless stuff and we got the feeling this was a good preview of the way women would be received in Iran. Having a bunch of strapping men with us was a big incentive not to worry about anything. Iranian men were encouraging the girls to take part and our western men were supporting. We were already loving the place and the people with western misconceptions crushed within a couple of hours at a local transport café. Excellent. The other great thing about Iran was the cost. Everything was cheaper than in previous countries and more in line with our budget. We could now start to make up for the lost $1,500 without short changing ourselves of the odd luxury.

The weather continued to throw what it could at us, but now it was mostly sludge so we and our bikes were caked in mud. After 110km, Ro and Dickie had still not found a hotel and were doing their best to find alternative accommodation as camping wasn't an option. This part of Iran consisted of big roads and there was no suitable place to pull up and camp. Then came the good news they had stopped at a Red Cross organisation complete with makeshift hospital happy to let us use an empty ward. They had obviously done a good job of translating our story with help from one of the English-speaking residents. They drove back to tell us we didn't have far to go and pulled over at a lorry wash area. One lorry driver saw the state that we and our bikes were in and offered to use the power hose on us.

Bike maintenance was challenging in consistant snow conditions

Before we knew it, the five of us were proudly inspecting the cleanest bikes we had seen in ages, typical of the constant acts of kindness we witnessed on our journey through Iran

Ro and I used the kitchen at our Red Cross camp to make dinner while Sarah, dedicated as ever, fought her nightly battle with the computer. I had developed an 'allergy' to the computer as I felt it dominated our routine and had become an obligation and a real chore. Sarah was taking far too much personal responsibility for it and we were all taking the blog too seriously. I made a point of only taking 20 minutes to write my blog rather than what had become a nightly epic, losing us a team member each night. I chatted with Dom, who was always great at listening to our points of view.

Back in the real world, Jamie and Ro practised their juggling; Dickie and I did a fantastic rendition of Patricia the stripper; and Nic managed to pretend to sleep all the way through without moaning once despite it all going on far too late. This was also the night we discovered the heavenly nature of massage. I gave Dom, Jamie and Ro a massage - all barriers are down when happy to have your body manhandled in a public area and grunt with pain or pleasure. We really had become a close and effective team. Next morning, we cleaned up to ensure we were leaving the place better than we had found it and tried to make a payment. They refused and only wanted a photo with us for their album. This we arranged with pleasure, humbled by yet another act of generosity.

It was a long, tedious day of cycling in the cold minus Ro and Dickie, who had to go and source Iranian number plates as a condition of their visa. We caught up with them just outside the city of Tranzin about 140km down the road where they had picked up a local guide to help them with the plate and help us find a hotel in our first Iranian city. It was dark and busy and the traffic relentless. We were riding as close to Martha as we could without being hit. I cycled past a parked set of cars with a lorry pretty tight on my left side when a door opened in front of me without warning. I managed to pull out and do a recovery move that may have looked incredibly cool, even gymnastic. I, of course, was only able to do this due to a rush of adrenalin which soon deteriorated into a version of tourettes. I wasn't sure how a woman swearing in Iran was likely to be received - never mind, I had just missed being squashed under a lorry before even getting to Mt Everest!

City life in Iran is as decadent as any western city with pizza and burger bars, restaurants and cinemas. We went out for a great meal with all the trimmings. Sarah inhaled a burger and chips and, after due feedback from the group, slowed down the whole eating process. We were only trying to help, honest: who would want to lose a man over a romantic meal by doing a really bad impression of a Dyson? She took it well.

We had a lie-in until 8am the next morning. Jamie had started to feel ill the previous night and was still not feeling great. Our fun fights and banter meant I suddenly became a protective big sister and felt the need to ensure he had water and rest. Sarah came in from another frustrating experience with the computer. I was in the 'I hate computers mode', stuck my fingers in my ears and made loud noises to indicate I couldn't listen to anything else about the thing. It was our first tense moment. I knew she was taking on a big job and how important it was to the journey but was the wrong person to share her concern. Selfish maybe, but true. To me, the journey was the important thing and it was starting to suffer from 'techno stress', the very thing these trips normally take you away from. With retrospective vision, I recognise the benefits of the blog and technology were huge but, as a middle-aged traditional adventure lover, forgive me for struggling with the modern approach.

Although weak, Jamie said he could continue to cycle so we made a late start and cycled 50km to the next town. He struggled up the hills in freezing weather against the wind and, we eventually got to Bostanabad, where there was no sign of Ro and Dickie. We found a café off the main road and took turns to look for Martha. Meanwhile the café gave us tea and cakes and Jamie tried to warm up and eat something. Dickie turned up about an hour or so later, saying they'd found a hotel nearby. Jamie got up to leave and fainted as we opened the door. We got him back to the hotel in Martha. The hotel was a café downstairs, with a couple of showers and basic rooms upstairs. We all had the same room; seven dwarfs-esque but cheap and dry with space to store our bikes and Martha. Absolutely perfect.

Jamie was feeling better next morning but Sarah was in a bad way and couldn't get out of bed. It was freezing outside and we all decided to give her a day to be ill as we cleaned our bikes and did admin. We heard about the hot spring pools and all of us (except Sarah) got our togs and jumped in a taxi. It was an impressive building and the boys went to their half and Ro and I went to ours; a great opportunity to mix with women and girls from Iran with no men around. We were greeted with open arms and, for the vast sum of about £1, were treated to a very funky mop cap that was compulsory garb. The changing rooms looked quite grand with ornate shower areas but otherwise provided open plan changing. Walking into the pool area, there were about 10 ladies between the ages of four and 70 having a great time, with the best swimmers just about managing a version of the doggy paddle. They wore the western equivalent of 1920's male-style swim suits, all too big or too see-through and none likely bestsellers for Gucci. It was like watching a ladies' scene from the Jane Austin era with everyone having lots of fun together away from polite society and men... are the two interchangeable? They were very tactile, hugging and holding hands as they giggled around the pool. Ro earned the equivalent of a standing ovation when she accidentally stepped back into the pool. We obviously wanted to interact and they led the way by demonstrating how to have water fights with a convenient hosepipe. I found my genetic strain of the Terminator and took my turn at the hose until the staff decided enough really was enough.

There was a big pool full of warmish brownish spa water and plunge pools of freezing water to stimulate the parts others couldn't reach. Ro was particularly brave. I did one plunge, enough for any average masochist. The Iranian swimming style seemed to be a five meter stretch complete with nose clip. Being compulsory control freaks in the west, Ro and I gave swimming lessons that were received with more laughter. How lovely were these people? Ro and I left having had a great time and met the boys claiming they had spent most of their time jumping in and out of the freezing plunge pool... yeah right!

Ro and I went headdress shopping and a little old man in a little old shop had lots of fun with us. No idea what he was saying but by the end we may have given him a licence to be over familiar. Remember these people see a lot of illegal western films and MTV where women can easily be perceived as 'sexually free' so we were always super careful to have rapport but not flirt. Being not exactly the most feminine girly girls, Ro and I had very few problems.

Our next stop was watching men make bread in an oven. It smelt gorgeous and, knowing we needed to 'bulk up' for the mountain (good excuse and I'm sticking to it!), took time to eat a whole plate of cakes before dinner…delicious! The food in rural Iran is incredibly repetitive: usually either rice and kebabs, or kebabs and rice (with the exception of that unforgettable stew). However, their cake shops are fantastic and neglecting such a cultural insight would have been positively rude!

The rest of the day was spent with Ro trying to audit some of the film we had taken and Dom and Dickie attempting to make the accounts balance; Nic wrestled with his satellite connection, a feat requiring the patience of a saint whilst Jamie and I braved the freeze and made a respectable stab at cleaning the bikes. The kitchen cooks kindly let me in to try and make some Sarah-friendly food – anything other than rice and kebabs or kebabs and rice – and I returned the favour by washing up. All this was negotiated in our very best body language, both Persian and English. We had a giggle cleaning up whilst being stuck in the coldest town in Iran. Final food warning: I may not be famous for my culinary delights but, with the considerable help of a slow cooker, created a masterpiece of a bread and butter pudding and won bags of brownie points for it. Taste buds, bored by kebabs and rice, scored my offering positively exotic.

That night the temperature plummeted even further to -29 degrees. The depth of the freeze was demonstrated really well by Ro producing a classic comic moment by going to our food store in Martha and dropping a tomato into a plastic bowl. The resultant sound was more like rock on plastic rather than a plump red tomato. Even poor Martha was frozen. I managed to talk/smile a local lorry driver into towing her onto the main road where he got out his gas cooker and placed it under the engine... health and safety is so yesterday in Iran! Nearly every truck parked up on the main road did likewise. Fires under engines were the ideal, if hazardous, solution to thawing out the fuel pipes. We stayed close enough to express thanks and interest, yet far enough away to show healthy respect for fire and explosions!

The alternative approach to warming up the engine was to light a fire under it

Maintaining dear old Martha was the order of the rest of the day. Once she was ticking over, the boys took her for a drive and felt so confident after 50km they even stopped for lunch...note the fatal word there, STOPPED! Top tip they came back with was never travel to a country with freezing temperatures without knowing the words for 'jump leads' and 'help, please'. True to form, the local Iranian people pushed, towed and jump started Martha back to base to fight another day. Jamie and Dom got the bonus of a testosterone fix as one of the mechanics at a garage said they just needed to change a part (don't ask me which). They got right in there and came back to the dining room with man-tales of grease and elbows.

Another rest day to help Sarah and Martha fully recover provided another opportunity to see more of a different side of Iran as we took a taxi back to the nearest big city of Tabriz. Our relations with Iranians had been so good so far and we lost a few more inhibitions bantering at a market stall. Somehow I became involved in a singing competition with other stalls - just like being back home at Leicester Market. The stallholders almost sing about their goods to entice customers to stop and sample them. I had no stall but became a cling-on to the friendliest and started to shout out in a singing tone: "Roll up roll up, buy your fresh vegetables here. Cheap fresh and oozing quality" (or words to that effect). I found myself becoming a tad operatic; well, I do have a tendency to go the extra note. The all-male stallholders humoured me and let me carry on despite the fact I probably frightened off a good many more customers than I attracted.

Let me tell you about another lovely stallholder. He looked like Pinocchio's dad, a kind old man with a smiling face and dedicated to his work station. All day every day he hammered and chiselled large blocks of sugar into small cubes ready for sale. What a gloriously simple life. Don't we over complicate our lives with materialism and excitement? Then there was a really kind and chatty lady in a ladies shop who spoke great English and explained that, as city guests, we didn't have to cover our whole heads up. She giggled affectionately at our attempts to show respect and fit in but warned we would have to be more conservative in the more rural areas depending on who was in charge. The moral police (holy men) have equal authority as the state police and tend to be stricter in rural areas than in the cities.

My sugar daddy. Happy with his life

We had come to the natural end of our rest days. All of us, apart from Sarah, who could have done with more time to recover fully, were gagging to get back on the road. It was another cold, beautiful day and we had left Martha's engine running all night – just in case. This sounds decadent but, with petrol the equivalent of 70p per gallon, it seemed a safe strategy. We cycled 107km with a 600m descent and blue skies totally compensating for the freezing conditions. Sarah did really well for somebody who hadn't eaten in three days... she's a hard gal, that one. We started to see almost Himalayan-like scenery with Mt Sahand (3,710m) standing immense in the background. We all dealt differently with our cold appendages: I favoured mittens rather than finger gloves to keep me toasty warm; I gave my spare pair to Sarah whilst the boys struggled with cold fingers; as for feet, Dom and Nic sported SPDs which are leather clip-on shoes. Despite having those over boots and becoming positively smurf-like, their feet were still often incredibly uncomfortable from the cold. I had new balance fell running shoes and never suffered from the freezing cold feet when cycling. Jamie found an ingenious way of keeping his wedding tackle safe for the future with yet another way of using Buff headgear. That annoying guy on the Buff promotional video would love doing a demo of that one!

No day was complete without some form of verbal or physical battle to keep the team rapport going. Nic and Jamie proved to be my constant playmates throughout the trip and we all had our moments of glory. This often resulted in the three of us being on a bed and the last one left being declared the winner. This could get very violent. Today was another physical battle royale, complete with snowball fight extraordinaire. My diary clearly states I had both of them on top of me at once... I'm not sure whether that makes me a winner of loser?

Competitive banter made the whole trip uncompetitive, if you see what I mean. Everyday we would talk about who was the fastest or the most stylish. The blog highlighted the hero of the day and, by pure co-incidence, it would often be the author. Nobody took themselves too seriously but all tried hard to keep up with the schedule. Nic could have gone a lot faster from the beginning but was almost pacemaking for us so that tail end Charlie (that's me!) wouldn't feel I was letting the side down. A regular topic of discussion was what we would leave at the top of Everest for the others as they dragged themselves up later. I pledged a hot flask of tea loaded with sugar as they would need all the energy they could get. Oh the hilarity!

That night Dickie and Ro found a great little hotel in a town called Miyaneh that was about £10 for all seven of us. They made such a great team as support. They really enjoyed each other's company – so much so that Sarah and I decided we were going to buy a nice hat in Kathmandu at the end of the trip;

know what I mean, Cilla? But Ro still insisted they were just good friends and the trip worked because they were platonic. So wise! Imagine having a bad day with your lover - you'd never be able to get away and, more importantly, neither could the rest of the team.

Next day was a complete contrast in both scenery and temperature. Within a stretch of less than 20km, the geography changed from snow-flanked roads over undulating hills and steep sided mountains into flat stretches with stunning sandstone ranges in the north with multiple stripes of different coloured sand. What a mouthful! They just rose up out of nowhere. To the south east were the snow capped mountain ranges we were heading for. Absolutely stunning.

Ro and Dickie took turns riding with us while the other drove. Dickie joined us and wore the 'numpty hat' (multi-coloured felt hat for a clown, if you're interested). It was good to see an ex-naval officer could still be down-to-earth enough to look a complete plonker. Needless to say, we gave him his space so he could go at his own pace and not because we wanted nothing to do with him …honest. Sarah struggled on and I stuck with her so she could draft me (don't worry, I'll explain later). We cycled 100km and there was an option of getting to the next town if we could handle another 40km - but a tea break revealed poor Sarah was at the end of her super human endurance. She was still not 100 per cent and had already done far more than any normal person so we took the opportunity to get back into the camping world. Camp was in a great spot and no longer in the sub zero temperatures. Infact, it was positively pleasant as the cold days of Iran were left behind for a while.

There were perfect views and terrain for a mini game of volleyball. The rest of us were feeling well and 100km wasn't a

Much needed respite from the snow came in the form of this glorious scenery

big day so we still had loads of energy. Dom and I challenged Jamie and Nic to a game of hacky sack. Sarah officiated while Ro and Dickie went to town to get food and spoil us. My team obviously had maturity, experience and athleticism on our side which was enough to put youth in its rightful place. I confess to a competitive spirit but that was just to beef up the game. Nothing is as boring as opposing teams being pleasant... how dull. I really don't mind losing as long as the opposition haven't sussed my attitude. Work that one out! In this case, I was able to ridicule youth for days to come. Dickie and Ro did us proud on the food stakes and I can't underestimate how important food is when cycling long distances especially in adverse weather. The boys, in particular, lost weight easily and needed regular fuel en route. So three cheers for Ro and Dickie, Iranian cafes and, last but not least, cake shops.

Farewell moderate temperatures, the snow and wind were back in force next day. Biting wind-chill and sludge on the roads made cycling treacherous. The hard shoulder, aka our bike lane, became increasingly reduced. Iranian roads are superbly made but all the good tarmac in the world couldn't make them easy to ride in these conditions. Road etiquette was a compounding factor with truck drivers enjoying playing 'chicken' by overtaking into oncoming traffic, leaving the hard shoulder (ie our lane) as the only place for them to go. They had the precarious belief that a two-way highway was sufficient for several vehicles to travel side by side. Unaccustomed as they were to seeing cyclists on their roads, especially in freezing conditions, they hooted their horns – either as a sign of support or a less generous gesture. When cycling on a road you can be almost oblivious to how scary it is when lorries skim past you rather than leave room for error. Dom was the only one to come unstuck and take a fall. Leader Nic pulled over for a natural break and some shelter and got his camera out to film us. The snow was covering a deep channel eating his front tyre and, before you knew it, we had priceless footage of Dom, the boss man, on his butt and the new victim for the day. Despite looking like drowned rats dipped in frozen compost, we found a café to let us in and eat. Even the kebabs and rice tasted wonderful.

We were only able to do another 20km in these conditions before taking refuge in a cake shop where a very sympathetic gentleman offered to let us come to his home. How kind! We gratefully declined in our body language and got back on our bikes before inadvertently making someone else feel sorry for us in our pathetic state just five km down the road. Unbelievably, the same man pulled his car over in front of our lead rider, waited for us and brought out another box of cakes. Incredible thoughtfulness. I just hope he wasn't hoping to take any home for his family as we gobbled the whole lot! Yet another example of Iranian hospitality over and above anything we expected.

Ro and Dickie saved the day yet again by finding us somewhere to sleep in a town with no hotels and where camping wasn't an option because of the terrain. They asked a local shopkeeper for help and he gave them an empty shop. We used the shop like a big tent, making ourselves at home while our hosts came in with hot potatoes for us. The shop window was just that as friends and family came to see what the living manikins were doing. Dom and I cooked and the photos and footage showed we were all looking a tad rough around the edges. 'If it was easy, it would have been done before!' was our mantra.

Next morning, it took us over half an hour to try and thaw out the bikes. We knew hot water would refreeze but, at least, it was clean ice. We chipped away until the wheels managed to turn. Even Nic McSlick was challenged to keep standards high in those conditions although he developed an ingenious way to de-ice the chain area – using his body to hose it down. Yes, that's peeing, to you and me and provided just the right temperature.

The day was freezing but with an absolutely blue sky and a perfect tail wind we did 136km to a town called Shai with no problems apart from the usual speeding horny trucks, a broken spoke (Nic), a puncture (Pauline) and a couple of stylish bike departures (Nic and Jamie). Ro and Dickie tackled the biggest challenge as there was nowhere to camp due to the heavily ploughed fields, no hotels and sunset was imminent. They told us to go and eat cake in a shop while they did some research. They returned with pride, having found a large building that looked like a bank but was empty apart from a couple of guards. They explained the problem and the guards were more concerned we would be cold on the floor as they showed us to a room to sleep in, a place for the bikes, a kitchen with no gas or water and a loo with no water. Perfect, well almost!

We were on our travels next day to Saveh (136km) and the cycling and weather was great with some downhill too. Dickie drove past Sarah and I and reported we were doing 50km/hr – what a change from the previous few days. Again the challenge of the day was finding suitable accommodation. We were sent to a cake shop but then joined in with the search as it was getting later and later. They had found one truly grotty guest house but, for the first time in Iran, we were rejected! However, a taxi driver picked up on our dilemma and heard the word 'camping'. We followed him to a set of gates where we were told to wait while Dickie was taken off to the police commissioner to sign us all in. This took forever and, despite hacky sack competitions, balancing on the wall challenges and Bop It competitions, there is only so much time you can kill outside a high walled campsite by a road.

A huge cheer greeted Dickie on his return but, before we were let in, we had to go to dinner with the chief of police and his friend Tamirah, an English teacher. We were taken to a restaurant where, despite being tired, we all tried to be really grateful and sociable. I didn't find it hard as I gave Tamirah the Spanish inquisition on being a woman in Iran. She was more of a traditionalist with no radical opinions and very happy in her world. We appreciated each other's values and lifestyles with mutual respect to the point we were both happy to be in our own worlds. They came back with us to the compound, enjoyed some photos and a giggle and didn't want to leave. Neither did we as it wasn't a campsite at all but a set of dorms that were clean and with beds and showers. Typical of the generosity of Iran, we were told it was for free.

Nobody was ready to get up early, despite the morning sunshine. It was also the first day in ages we were able to go biking without gloves and all the extras and the first 20km of the day whizzed by. I was cycling at the back (as usual) when a car slowed down and drove beside me. The lady wound down her window and offered me some dates (the fruit variety, silly). I was a bit thrown by this. They must have been going in the other direction, turned around and thought I needed the extra energy. How many people would do that for a complete stranger? I took the dates with a big smile and thanks and they drove off waving from the window. I love this country!

Unbeknown to us, Martha had blown a gasket and was limping by the time she caught up with us on the bikes after around 100km. Ro and Dickie struggled on to Delijan for another 26km and we cycled into town in the dark to be guided towards a posh hotel with pizza and strawberry non-alcoholic beer. Fab! The girls had one room and the boys the other and both had showers which were great not only for us but for catching up on washing from the last week. The only negative was the rooms were so hot we couldn't sleep despite telling them three times - and being assured three times - the heating was turned down. At least, the washing got properly dried.

We waved goodbye to Martha next day as she was put onto the back of a truck to be transported to Esfahan (our destination in two days' time). Ro and Dickie obviously went as well leaving us to fend for ourselves. We had been lulled into a false sense of security as the weather had been so good the previous day. We had wrongly convinced ourselves we were going south and the extreme adverse conditions were behind us. Almost as soon as we were on our bikes, the heavens opened and the head wind kicked in. Not long afterwards, the rain turned to snow as the lorries sped past fast and close enough to give us a regular adrenalin rush; the hard shoulder having now disappeared completely. Dom had a near miss (although he claimed he was just practising one of his fancy manoeuvres) when he did a 180 degree spin into the main road and slid off. He grabbed his bike and dragged himself to the side just before a lorry skidded to avoid him. Later that day, Jamie, our youngest and most in need of adversity for adventurous fulfilment, came to a shattering conclusion: "OK, this is not fun!"

We were all freezing and wet to the bone. Nic got a puncture but didn't have the dexterity in his hands due to the cold to change a tyre. Fortunately, some kind lorry drivers pointed us to a café three km ahead where we thawed out before mending the puncture. At the typical lorry driver stop off, there was a hot log burning stove and they served our favourite Iranian stew dish we hadn't been able to order since the border. Using a pestle and mortar to mash the meat ensured it was fun to eat as well as being delicious. We were all so cold the proprietor took pity and mashed them all for us. Sarah took off her socks and wrung them out. When he saw the dirty water, he took her to the kitchen and made her wash them so at least they were clean and wet. After this, the rest of us ensured we hung onto our socks for dear life.

It felt like a feast and a real paradise compared to the outside world but we knew we had to get back out there and make the next town before dark. We were now at 2,000m and stopped regularly to make sure we were all ok. Darkness had closed in by the time we made it to town and Dom managed to cycle past three very warm looking kebab shops - much to my disgust. I convinced him, as only a tired, hungry and wet woman can do, that we needed to go back to the last one and befriend a very big boiler. When we went in, I couldn't talk properly as my top lip had frozen. I felt like it had been injected with medication to freeze it and must have sounded very drunk. After 30 minutes of thawing and kebabs, we found a hotel of sorts consisting of four army barrack-style beds for the five of us in a 12ft by 10ft grey walled room. It also had a superb heater… now that was really paradise. We got into our dry clothes and spent the rest of the evening playing a pub quiz and generally having a good laugh. Another good day!

Ro and Dickie were overwhelmed by all that had happened to them. They got the van going and started on their way back to meet us only for sickly Martha to break down again outside a shelving shop. Ro asked for water and, before she knew it, the gentleman was on the phone organising for his friends at the local garage to come and help, but not before giving them lunch. The garage team was completely different from the average Brit who takes a well-rehearsed intake of breath at how much it will cost and can never do it before next week. In contrast, eight men on a mission worked into the night while Ro and Dickie enjoyed the hospitality of their shelving man who took them home and fed, watered and entertained them with his family and friends. Already humbled by their hosts' generous hospitality, they were then invited to the garage office to be told they had done all this work for free as guests of their country. Ro was still overwhelmed when telling us before we had reached Esferhan. Yet no sooner had they met us than the van was on the blink again (have you noticed I call the van 'van' and not Martha when she is acting up?) How could they go back and ask for more help? But they simply had to.

We cycled on and made our own way to a great hotel in the heart of the city of Esferhan. This was like no other city we had been to in Iran although, in fairness, we had only really been to Tabriz. Esfahan was famous for its cosmopolitan-style which became apparent very quickly. There were wide streets with beautiful trees, dustbins and even cycle lanes. The cafes and restaurants didn't just sell stew and kebabs but were marketing ice cream and all the food we had been dreaming of because we couldn't have it. It didn't take us long to start touring the city and indulge in all sorts of long forgotten pleasures. After a big meal supplemented by Mr Whippy ice-creams, we were charged up enough for Ro and I to have an obstacle course race down the street between trees and over flower pots – don't worry, nothing was harmed during the making of this!

A full-on tourist experience followed which so many people would repeat if only they knew our secret of how welcoming Iran is. It should be top of the 'must do' destination list. We kind of stuck out a lot and Ro managed to explain why. We noticed there was a tendency to stare, especially among men in the smaller towns with nothing else to do. At first, one or two stare, then more join and start a discussion. Didn't they have jobs to do? Ro suggested that, if a camel walked down the middle of an English village, people would stare, then be joined by others, who would chat about it for ages. No work would ever get done. I then started to think of us as camels. Every team needs an artist to think a bit left wall.

It came as no surprise when the local Iranian TV booked us for an interview; we let our intrepid leader take the lead but were there in the background giving him support all the way. We took it very seriously as you can imagine… if the locals thought we were a bit mad doing what we were doing, the interview probably didn't do much to change that view.

Esferhan is home to the amazing Emam Khomeni Square, the equivalent of St Marks Square in Venice. We were all soon in awe of the ornate artwork and blue tile roof of the Shah mosque. The fountains in the centre of the square were filled with clean water, adding another impressive element of beauty to this already magnificent area dating from the 17th century. Jamie and I had a balancing competition trying to push each other off one of the grass border edgings (all of two inches high). Unusually, I fell to the floor inadvertently showing quite a bit of leg as I was wearing a long skirt. An official came up to us and explained very nicely in broken English that Jamie shouldn't let me show my legs etc. However, he almost apologised for having to say anything. It was as if he understood our culture would have seen this as innocent but needed to educate us to keep us out of trouble with his culture. I appreciated it and we said thanks for the help.

We were then stopped by three young women who wanted to talk with us and the boys. I have a great picture of three giggling ladies in their headdresses staring with loving eyes at Dickie, Jamie and Nic. They moved onto us and had a girly giggle:

Iranian women enjoying the opportunity to talk to our men

one wanted to marry an Englishman and we had to explain the boys weren't available. These ladies seemed very liberal with their approach to life while being happy within the limitations of their culture. I arrived feeling the scarves and headgear would drive me mad but, infact, they are no great hardship. When you meet the people and see how happy and unsuppressed they are it feels more and more that different people are happy to live in different ways rather than our females have got it all right and they are the poor underdogs of life.

Later the girls went on tour and found some giant swan pedlows on the river running through the heart of the city. Fantastic! In we jumped and peddled to our hearts content as if we were on holiday. I inadvertently managed to entertain the crowds by missing the pontoon and falling into the water up to my thighs. Oops, I got the 'bish, bash, bosh' award for the day. Then we took refuge in what we called a 'hubble bubble' café. There were no women in there but we were welcomed anyway. It was located under the beautiful bridge, the centrepiece of the city spanning the river. The café looked like a wine cellar with tables in the alcoves. A myriad of articles hung on the wall and there was an almost medieval smell and feel to it. Lots of men chatted away over their 'hubble bubble' bottles with the smoking tubes. We bought one between us and attracted the attention of a couple of nice gentlemen who helped us to use it properly. It wasn't as if it was full of drugs and women didn't use them. It really was harmless and women do use them in the home but not out in public.

Being a city, it was less strict in its approach to western women. We may as well have got high we were giggling so much but decided we really wanted another ice cream – bulk up and all that. We had ice cream again and again, then went to the cinema and watched a fantastic film. It was surprising as the good guys were a couple of very 'city chick' Iranian women being bullied by a very traditional policewoman. They both got their just desserts in the end for being too liberal and too strict as the moral was to keep moderate. This was all in Iranian but it didn't take much imagination to follow the plot. It was as if they knew the girls were coming and put it on for our education. We bounced back into the hotel high on girl power to a less-than-chuffed bunch of boys who felt we hadn't used our time constructively for the team. We didn't lose any sleep over it and got all our chores done next day which ended with Dickie coming back with the unbelievable news that the van was fixed and yet again they hadn't charged a penny. We were ready to hit the road again.

Great cycling for 151km brought us to a town called Naein. Our accommodation, in a pilgrims' shelter next to a mosque, was stunning, consisting of three floors, each with a balcony facing into the centre of the building overlooking an open air garden with a magnificent tree growing past the roof. There were lots of options to discuss over dinner as Martha was still not right. We all gave 'airspace' to each other, dealing with all our frustrations. We agreed on a plan of Dickie taking the van back to Esferhan and Ro going with us in a taxi so we could have extra kit and food as the weather was closing in again. By the time we walked back to our rooms, the snow was falling heavily. The scene was almost magical as it was snowing into the middle of our home and light caught the flakes. Stunning.

So we said goodbye again to Dickie and Martha while poor old Ro sat in a car with a man who spoke no English and was distinctly musically-challenged. She did great and fed us really well en route as the weather stayed kind. Blue skies! Next day, she tackled a really chatty eccentric man and his wife. The trio managed to talk about religion, politics and social things despite only sharing about 10 words of Iranian or English between them. She remained sane but definitely started to have the look of a woman possessed by the end of the day.

Cycling was straightforward and Jamie and Nic were the leaders in the art of truck surfing. They had done this a few times and I had tried it once or twice. My balls were growing to coin a phrase. It involves cycling fast enough to be really close behind the truck so that you catch the draft created as it goes along. The trick is to maintain speed and then the draft speeds you up to much faster than you could peddle on your own. The danger is, if the truck stops or slows down suddenly, you will inevitably go straight into the back as you are too close to react. Dangerous, exciting and a great way to cover miles fast. Sarah and I caught the surf on the same truck and clocked up a steady speed of 50km. We even overtook other trucks... come on boys!

Another 100-plus km day took us to a small town called Mehiz. As we pulled into the main street, we were fascinated to see hundreds of men huddled around three huge cauldrons. It looked like a soup festival and, guess what, it was a soup festival. We dismounted and were welcomed to the party, given plastic bowls and had them filled with delicious soup. Amid all the noise and frivolity, I heard the occasional phrase that followed us everywhere 'welcome to Iran!'

Ro was up to her usual endeavors of finding us somewhere to sleep. Her taxi driver introduced her to his friend and we were escorted to the ultimate home for a bunch of people who seem to live off kebabs and rice – a kebab house! The owner had a balcony floor above the main restaurant and said we were welcome to sleep up there. It was perfect. The mood was good and we were all upstairs having a laugh when a very austere man came into the place. The owner asked Dom to come and talk to him. Ro and I hadn't gauged the seriousness of this man and ended up coming down to join them and having a girly fun scuffle until the austere man stopped us. We learned he was the moral police, part of the authority of religious men who carry the same level of authority as the police. We immediately stopped 'misbehaving' as he was speaking English and told us off through Dom – he wouldn't lower himself to talk to the women directly. We felt like naughty schoolgirls but without the fun. After the nasty man had gone, the shop owner explained he had come to check nothing immoral was happening as he had heard we were a mixed group sleeping in the same area. He had the power to put us in prison – and our hosts with us – if he wanted to. This is what the lady in Tabriz had hinted at; the rural towns were often more strict in traditions and etiquette depending on the leaders of the religious sect. So, not wanting to cause any trouble for our hosts, we stayed off the

We were made to feel very welcome at a giant cauldron soup celebration

streets for the rest of the night, ate kebabs and amused ourselves in our bedroom, ending in a pillow fight between me and Jamie with the others voting on the winner – selective memory doesn't allow me to remember who won.

The only negative about sleeping in the same place as the cooks and friends of the kebab house was that they seemed to be nocturnal. We tried to go to sleep from 11pm but they were downstairs singing, shouting and having what could only be described as farting competitions until past 1am. Sarah was about to go down and read the riot act until Dom calmed her down. Their antics didn't mean a later morning for them - they were up and bashing pans etc by 6am, so we left them with lots of thanks but great relief.

This was a great truck surfing day for Dom and he caught a long ride. It was dry and sunny and at lunch break the hacky sack was out with Jamie giving a great demonstration, followed by most of us looking like dysfunctional useless blobs with arms and legs. There was certainly scope for improvement. As the weather became more agreeable, hacky sack became a regular part of the break times. In town that night, Nic and Jamie went off to change some dollars and managed to get invited to a local school to help with the English lessons for a class of 14-year-old girls. They really enjoyed it and I am sure the girls loved having two young western dudes doing their best to impress.

The weather was getting warmer and warmer. Four days previously we'd left Dickie worrying about how much snow we would have to deal with, now we were basking in sun in an area claiming to be the biggest exporter of pistachio nuts in the world. We knew our goal was 100km to a town called Anar and that was now starting to feel like a half-day cycle especially in good conditions. There was no rush; so we optimised on creative filming on a new unused stretch of road. We all cycled in a straight line towards Ro, who was bravely lying with the camera in the middle of the road to get the effect of the heat on the tarmac. We all just peeled off alternately to the left and right as close to the camera as possible. Numpty here obviously got a bit too excited by the whole filming thing and got my left and right wrong, causing huge amounts of hilarity and leaving me as the ridicule victim for much longer than normal. All in a good cause, I suppose. We had the time and energy left for races. Although I could never beat the boys, I was good at sneaking up on them as they were riding calmly along and shouting: "1km, go!" They would oblige by catching me up and then breezing past with an encouraging 'call yourself a challenge' kind of comment. Jamie and Nic were always better than me, but still had to try. I had Dom a couple of times, although he refused to say he even bit. Sarah and I were too close to avoid it becoming real competition so never really challenged each other. These are the kind of things that broke up the cycling routine for me. I loved my personal time on the bike with no need to chat but I did enjoy a bit of a laugh, too, just to add a bit of variety.

Dickie turned up just as dinner was ready, sporting a newly grown beard and very tired as he had driven non-stop to catch us up after being away for five days. It was great to have him back and Martha in full working order as now we could really get some miles under our belt. We still had 700km to do and just a few days before our visas ran out. The next couple of days saw us cycle 157km and then 168km in great conditions. We were fit and the scenery was spectacular and in complete contrast to the rest of Iran. The scrub and 'green gold', the local name for pistachios, filled the landscape punctuated by desert plains with the backdrop of snow capped mountains.

The weather also meant the boys could change into shorts and T-shirts while the ladies had to keep covered up as we were going into the more traditional areas of Iran. I had bought a cheap man's shirt, cut the sleeves off and sewed them to my lightweight short sleeved cycling shirt. This kept me cool and my arms covered. We were all a tad jealous of the boys comparing their tan lines in the evenings... yes, they are just as vain as women! I also acquired a pair of what looked like MC Hammer trousers to keep me stylish (for some strange reason, my sense of fashion always goes a bit too native).They had the baggy legs with tight ankles and low slung crutch I had seen lots of men look remarkably cool and comfortable in. Whether a 5ft 2" middle

Jamie seemed to enjoy how fast the lorries passed us

aged woman on a bike could pull off such a double coup was another matter but it certainly felt like it. I inevitably became the team victim of ridicule for a while.

Truck surfing was becoming competitive as we were all into it whenever possible. One driver had seen Dom and I surfing his truck. We lost him as he sped up a hill so he waited for us and invited us back on. As we overtook Jamie, he was shouting out 'purist surfers don't book drivers!' He was turning green as he was speaking –hope he wasn't ill. Jamie and I were cycling together when we saw this most amazing tree on its own close to the road. It may as well have sported a neon sign saying: 'climb me, right now!' We jumped off our bikes and scrambled our way to the top. Moments like this, surfing, races and hacky sack made this journey such a success. We knew we would get the miles done much more easily if we gave ourselves time to enjoy where we were and the folk we were with.

Our next big destination was Bam, a place where 30,000 people had died only a few years before in a huge earthquake. I was listening to a mellow song on my ipod when I saw the sign for Bam and it hit home that whole families were wiped out here. My eyes welled up as I contemplated being in a similar situation. One of the charities the Everestmax expedition was raising money for was Merlin, which was fundamental to the rescue operation. We intended to visit their offices and get an update on how life was now.

When we arrived in Bam, we went to Abdul's guest house. He was charm personified and welcomed us like long-lost friends. Bam's post-earthquake international support really impressed local people. He talked us through his experiences of the quake; he had had guests in and the building had collapsed on them killing many friends and family. The official estimate was 30,000 dead – a figure locals believed was nearer 80,000.

Sarah, Ro and I walked around Bam next day while the boys went to find the Merlin offices and hear their stories of tragedy and hope. We chatted to some local people still living in makeshift tarpaulin homes. Two years on the town was buzzing with development and Akbar said foundations had already been laid for 80 per cent of the housing. Within another two years Bam would be rebuilt. Youths were full of optimism and we had a great time chatting with three young men. They refused to dwell on the past and voiced their thanks to the international community for responding so fast. They had lost their mother and sister but had a bright future ahead of them; so why ask them to ponder on the tragedy?

Ro, Sarah and I trying to fit in

Iran has very sophisticated and cosmopolitan areas contrasting vividly with very rudimentary basic areas where health and safety have no place. A small example was spotting a pick up truck full of long thin strands of metal tubes. Too long for the truck,

Jamie and I taking time to enjoy our surroundings

they were dragging on the floor behind. It was like watching a van driving along with sparklers attached to the back. This wouldn't have surprised me in other countries like India or Pakistan, but Iran isn't Third World. Road systems are superb and they even have a ski resort to match, yet there is a huge diversity of lifestyles and standards throughout the country. The boys returned more inspired than ever about raising money for the Merlin team. They didn't just pack up and go after the initial quake; they left a legacy of medical and health centres.

We took time next day to visit a very famous Iranian landmark nearly destroyed in the earthquake. It was a citadel more than 2,000 years old and had been a major tourist attraction in its previous good condition. Now it had scaffolding and lots of collapsed walls. We all left Bam inspired by the people and knowing they were on their way back to a good future.

That day saw us reach our halfway mark to Kathmandu. Only 4,000km to go! We were on a roll and knew, providing the team kept up this performance and had no dramas beyond our control, we could do it. Jamie kept us entertained by falling off his bike when we were all watching by slipping into a tiny gravel stream as he was slowing down. Such a pathetic fall had us all in fits and kept the boy hero in his place for a while. The boys were definitely on the leader board for falls. Meanwhile Martha (aka bag of bolts) was constantly teasing us with unhealthy sounds. We doubted her ability to do the whole journey but somehow she kept going. It's like she craved attention and, when she got her quota, would work again. Women!

Another great day in the heat saw stunning sand dunes rising out of nowhere. Jamie and I took no time at all to see the potential and were up on top. Wow, it's exhausting running up sand dunes trying to beat a 23-year-old! Sarah and Ro joined

Enjoying the dunes in my alternative bike trousers

us and we all had fun fights knowing the landing was going to be soft. These are the kind of places where thousands of pounds are spent doing photo shoots and we just spent half an hour having a laugh as part of another fab day.

One of our last stops in Iran was in the middle of desert-like terrain in an army fortress. When we pulled over, soldiers welcomed the company and let us use their backyard area which was great. We all love local facilities but camping was by far our number one choice. I took myself off to a private spot behind a huge rock to have a moment to myself with my MP3 and dance my socks off. Little did I know that Dom had seen me sneak off and took video footage of me, looking like a nutter doing my favourite Michael Jackson moves and singing badly out of tune - as you do when you think nobody is listening!

We had brought some videos with us and there was plenty of time as we had stopped at about 3pm. Dom hates the film Vertical Limits but was voted down. We had a great laugh as it started us talking about Everest and who would be the biggest hero. The tone of the Everest banter had already been set but this film just re-enforced it. We weren't going to take ourselves too seriously until we had to. The focus for now was on the cycling and there would be plenty for time for Everest. I think deep, deep down, seriously deep, Dom enjoyed it.

Woke up to a pillow fight with Nic and Jamie – always good to get the day started by putting the lads in their place. We had to give Martha her morning dose of attention and got the army boys to join in while we push started her down the sandy highway. That night we stayed at a police compound which was pretty grim from the point of view of being a dirty camping area but was at least safe. The police were also great. This south-east area of Iran isn't considered entirely safe for western travellers so they decided to escort us for our last two days to the border. We reached our destination town of Zaheden by lunchtime having done 100km with Ro patiently driving at our speed so our escort could keep us all together. We had a variety of police and army personnel with us all the way and I surfed the back of a police vehicle for the last 5km - why not?

The reason for the concern was that this town is only 90km from the border with Pakistan and Afghanistan is 30km to the north. There is a steady influx of Afghan refugees and Pakistan immigrants passing illegally through the area seeking the greater wealth and stability Iran has to offer. We found a nice hotel that seemed really posh as this town looked and felt a lot poorer. We attracted our biggest crowd ever with at least 200 gathering to stare at us while we were asking around about hotels.

We were coming to the end of our time in Iran and felt enlightened and privileged to have met so many wonderful people and been on the receiving end of countless demonstrations of kindness and generosity. The geography is so varied and stunning and the weather just added to the whole extreme experience of cycling through a country three times the size of France in 30 days. We were proud and humbled in the same breath.

Our early start to peddle the last 75km to the border meant we could get there in good time to get the paperwork done and minimise any delays. Unfortunately, we had again arrived at a border just before a major festival, hence our desire to crack on. Our escort had other plans and, just a few kms into the ride, we had to stop for an untold amount of time for them to change escorts. Out came the hacky sack for Jamie to demonstrate tricks from his misspent gap year. Sarah's grace, Dom's agility, Ro's style, Nic's determined face and Dickie's panache all added to the entertainment.

When we were off again, we cycled into the strongest headwind we had dealt with on the trip so far. I reassured myself that headwind and chasing the boys was good for Everest training (by now only seven weeks away) but, at this point, it just hurt. We decided to cycle as a pack using the leaders' draft to pull us along. Sarah and I took our turn but it was important to let the boys feel they were the Alpha males and have longer stretches. Ro cycled with us and, although fit in her own right, had to fall back from the pack – a sign we must be getting fitter as a pack.

At the exit border, Dickie puffed up his chest and went in to do his stuff. Nic was kind enough to go with him as he didn't like seeing his friend go into the lion's den alone. It wasn't long before we knew we were on the road to another long border crossing. When your head is programmed to get ready for delay it is much easier to chill out. We now had this down to a fine art: chat, cups of tea, rice pudding and hacky sack were the order of the day. Nic and Dickie returned with the news we were here for the night and potentially a couple more days due to the festival, plus a mistake on the forms made by the transport police. We were in 'no man's land' between Pakistan and Iran in a very basic hotel; either we were going to get really good at hacky sack or get moving soon.

The next day saw Nic and Dickie take seven hours to go back with various escorts to the transport police in Zahedan (only 75km away) just to get a stamp in the book the police said they didn't need the day before. Oh joy. However it only took them a couple of hours to get back with just two changes of escort so they were in good spirits and mostly relieved to get the stamp before the big holiday. We did our team hacky sack and got a record seven passes between us without dropping it. Sounds pathetic but, yes, that really was an improvement.

CHAPTER **ELEVEN**

Sporting Colours – Pakistan

One of the many great downhill hairpin bends we enjoyed

PAKISTAN

Population: 162,420,000
Capital: Islamabad 698,000
Area: 796,095 square kilometers (307,374 square miles)
Language: Punjabi, Sindhi, Siraiki, Pashtu, Urdu, English
Religion: Sunni and Shiite Muslim, Christian, Hindu
Currency: Pakistani rupee
Life Expectancy: 60
GDP per Capita: U.S. $2,000
Literacy Percent: 46
Industry: Textiles and apparel, food processing, beverages, construction materials
Agriculture: Cotton, wheat, rice, sugarcane; milk
Exports: Textiles, rice, leather, sports goods, carpets and rugs

ALL SORTS of things changed when we entered Pakistan; the biggest plus being everybody official talked English, making life much easier. Another thing was the tea (chai): Iran offered black tea with various styles of sugar (lumps, crystals, wafers) and always served in small glasses; here we had milky sweet tea and I was in heaven. I had always loved Nepalese chai, one stage closer to English tea!

The other major thing to change was the colours: Iran isn't a colourful country with lots of black, at least on the streets; Pakistan verged on the ridiculous as everything was bright. The trucks were works of art with every inch covered in patterns and paintings with religious beads and pictures hanging from every angle. This being the border, there was a whole lorry park filled with spectacular designs and proud owners.

We went into the main official area - a high ceiling, bland hall-like place with lots of men hanging around waiting for something to happen. We were about to join them; I went with Dom and Dickie as there was no limited area, just a long desk at the front of the hall for the officials with lots of seats in front of the desk for applicants. I sat on the bench at the side listening as they tried to explain our needs. They were terribly nice and very concerned for our safety as the next 500km to Quetta was notorious bandit country and they weren't happy to let us cycle there, instead urging us to put our bikes in the van. We tried to explain that our attempt at a world record and our fund raising would be a failure if we did this as we had to cycle every meter of the way. They kind of understood but threw into the mix the problem of the Dutch cartoonist, who had just published his mocking image of Mohammed with a bomb-shaped turban on his head and sent the Muslim extremist world into a frenzy. They explained all westerners should now feel worried about their safety. Due to bandits and religious reprisals, they were none too happy to let us go at all, never mind on bikes. Also Martha was in a quagmire of bureaucracy: we could take her to Quetta, the next city with officials that could make decisions, but would have to see from there whether we could go further. Where's a crystal ball when you need one? As it happened, they couldn't have been more helpful as copious amounts of tea and chat on both sides, starring the ever-patient Dickie, led to the offer of a solution. I wasn't sure whether they'd do this for everybody or just liked us but they decided to let us go and gave us an armed escort to take us to Quetta and then, hopefully, across the whole of Pakistan. How cool is that: three weeks of armed escort!

Dickie, the ever British officer, suggested the brilliant idea of a game of cricket to his new best friends when they knocked off. So we arrived at 5pm as best dressed as we could to prove the British Empire can still hold its own on the pitch. They obviously play cricket a lot in their down time and the stumps were set up in no time with an intimidating umpire sat in the shade. The cricket pitch was contained in the area behind the customs building, near a small mosque and flanked by the lorry park. They knew we would be rubbish so chivalrously suggested we split into two teams of 50/50 Pakistan and British. Dickie was the only Brit we could be really proud of; the rest of us being your average novices. They bowled with the speed and aggression you see on TV. We were lambs to the slaughter. I pre-empted one bowler by saying how good looking he was – and got 15 runs teaming up with Dickie! There was lots of laughter and mickey-taking between the two teams, especially when it all got too much for Sarah. She was in line for the perfect catch only for the ball to spill from her hands and onto the floor. Local transients and truck drivers took up their seats and squatting positions to watch the whole match. They probably hadn't seen this kind of thing very much but, let's face it, there really wasn't a lot else to do at a border town.

Sarah is ready to run with her team mate at one of the many cricket games we had

After a great match, they invited us over to their area for the unexpected pleasure of dinner. There were about 15 of them and seven of us so it was party night. Superb curries were served, pure heaven for folk who'd had their fill of kebabs and rice. Conversation never stopped with probing questions on both sides about the role of women, religion and politics. There was humour aplenty and mutual respect for each other's traditions and beliefs, although the girls put up a good fight for females being the superior sex! Despite getting home late that night, and knowing we were back on the bikes for a long ride, Sarah made Nic a pineapple upside down cake for his birthday breakfast. It meant we girls got up at 6am to put on the slow cooker, but who needs sleep? Needless to say, Nic was delighted with his present, especially as we even allowed him the biggest piece. Does our generosity ever end?

We had time to hang around the lorry park as our escort was getting ready. The lorries are so beautiful I had to go and compliment a few of the drivers. One of them told me I should become Muslim and marry him; apparently already having a husband I adored wouldn't be a problem. We had a great banter and then he said I could get into the driver seat, hoot the horn (serious horn, not just any old horn) and wait for it... start the engine! I was in heaven but even that wasn't enough to make me leave Phil, change my religion and marry him.

Our first escort was Mr Aswad who jumped in Martha armed with his gun, as Dickie jumped on his bike. Ro and Dickie had been getting some limited time on the bike due to their priorities of getting food, making lunch, finding accommodation and fixing Martha! So our time in Pakistan started off well for them as our guard wanted to stay with the cyclists the whole time. We were going to stay in army or police compounds until we got to Quetta so there was no need for them to go ahead. Dickie didn't start the trip as the fittest of people, but had already lost weight and now Nic was about to become his personal trainer. Both Dickie and Ro had aspirations of getting to the North Col on Everest and cycling as much as possible would be a big help. Ro was already reasonably fit, but Dickie was ready for support and guidance and Nic was there to offer it. He did his first 100km ride and was really chuffed. As the trip went on, Nic and Dickie became a better and better team and it was great to see how Nic motivated and encouraged him.

Meanwhile Ro preferred Jamie to train her on the art of truck surfing and became a natural.

The terrain in Pakistan was hugely different from Iran with neither hard shoulder, nor lanes and lots more dust on much rougher roads. It was hot and dry and we were flanked by high mountains which, with the aid of a vivid imagination, were full of bandits ready to jump out. I let my mind wander a few times and rehearsed what I would say to my kidnappers: "I am really poor and not worth much; I am also by far the oldest, worth even less; I am a woman, worth even less. Take the men - they are much more important and you'll get more!"

Our first stop was at a police checkpoint – well, more of a shack with a man in an old uniform and a rope across the road. We stopped for some food and to check the book each person crossing has to sign. We saw the name Gerry Winkler. He had been here a couple of weeks ago and just seeing his name triggered that spirit of competition in all of us, especially Jamie, who took great joy in pretending some poor rock was Gerry and throwing it and stamping on it.

No matter how remote the places at which we stopped in Pakistan, people emerged from nowhere and, within minutes, our one policeman had two or three colleagues. This was perfect territory to get the football out; the boys flaunted their skills, then the true star came past, took the ball and scored a goal under the rope, shouting 'England 1 Pakistan 0'. The match was born. We made two teams and the fun and slapstick that emerged was fantastic. Final result was England 7 Pakistan 5 with lots of goodwill all round. The cricket bat, football and hacky sack were our natural social accessories for the rest of our trip in Pakistan. Sport is a superb way for people to interact without having to speak the same language. It was also the best way to enjoy Pakistani people.

Football at a check point made bureaucracy fun

Cycling through bandit territory, we took time to enjoy opportunities like dune jumping. By the road were some stunning sand dunes and Jamie, Sarah, Ro and I did our best flips and dives – all trying to outdo each other's gobsmackingly vulgar attempts at gymnastics. We did 127km before reaching a police compound where we stayed for the night.

Another great day of cycling lay ahead but our 114km fell short of our initial target because Dom was feeling a bit off. He didn't whinge but we knew each other well enough now to know when someone was struggling. It was a blessing we stayed in a Government house with a huge lounge and some of the mankiest beds ever – I preferred the roll mats. Quite literally, it hadn't been cleaned for years, with clouds of dust erupting from the settee as you sat on it and even from the floorboards. When the proprietor

Girls showing our dune jumping skills

of the house asked with a big grin if we liked it, Dom's face said it all and made us just laugh out loud: "Yes, it's perfect!" he said.

We weren't allowed to camp but the upside was a huge football pitch just over a big wall. All but Dom and Ro climbed it to watch local football training: it was a full-sized pitch and great to be the ones staring instead of being stared at. It wasn't long before the ball was passed our way and Nic and Jamie and Dickie were on it like a hot rash ready to flaunt their skills again. Sarah and I knew we were in a country where women wouldn't be seen joining in but there was no harm asking. They had no problem whatsoever and soon another match was in the making. From playing netball and hockey at school, I'd learned the first rule of defence is to stick with your opponent and guard them at all costs, so they don't get the ball. I applied the same tactic and went in like a raging bull; this guy with no trainers couldn't get away from me but still got the ball and completely outskilled me. Never mind, it was great fun. The only person I fouled, ironically, was Jamie – he probably deserved it! Dickie was huge in comparison to these guys and they loved him in defence. Nic and Jamie did themselves proud especially when Jamie scored the goal of the match; enough to live off for days to come. Sarah and I couldn't have given more of our 'bish bash bosh' style if we tried. They were all very forgiving without losing the true feeling that it counts to win. We had an absolute blast and took some great team shots just as a magnificent sun started to set in the most all-encompassing pink sky we had seen to date. We were all fit but came in feeling we had had a work out. We shouldn't have been too hard on ourselves as we had also cycled quite a way that day too. Ro turned into my 'fix it fairy' again. My 'gel' seat was on its last legs and looking incredibly sad for itself. We had chatted about it at lunch and I was selling the glorious time it had given my bum on this journey. When I woke up next morning, I went to my bike and my battered old gel seat had been to the surgery and had a serious Botox job – it looked more like a saddle of beef with string on it, but you get the point. Ro had stayed up and done an amazing job of rescuing my seat. What a girl!

Next day was Valentine's Day. So what, I hear you say? Even though I don't like to over do this commercialised day at home, I couldn't help but have warm and mushy thoughts about the one I love. I had lots of them all day while on my bike; Phil was never far from my thoughts but I also know I loved this journey so much that, even if it meant upsetting him for a short while, it was the right decision. I knew I was also feeling more and more grateful to him for supporting me rather than just sticking to his guns and objecting to the bitter end.

Playing football was a great way to interact... if we could keep up

It made the whole thing so much more of a pleasure when the one I loved was with me rather than against me.

The day was a short one of just under 60km to another army compound in the middle of a small town called Dalbandin. Ro and I went shopping and had fun with men making bread and showing us how they cook it in these oven-like things in the ground. I also had some fun with the children hanging over the top of the compound walls trying to stare at us. I stared at them and started singing 'Doe a Dear' and they duly gave me their version. Kids are another great way to integrate as they are always prepared to come and interact when fun is involved.

Temperatures were really high and we were grateful for having filled the van with bottled water. We were advised by our guards not to leave the compound; there were street protests about the shortage of water as the area (Baluchistan) appeared to be neglected by the Government in terms of water and mains electricity. After a couple of hours we were told we could go but cycling to within 200m of the compound we stumbled on a rather excitable crowd waving their arms beside a blocked road of burning tyres. Dom immediately turned and told us to hot foot it back to camp with a sense of urgency in his voice and face we hadn't witnessed before. We were soon back in the compound, although it took time for Dickie to turn the van around and we had left him behind... oops. He arrived very shortly after and all was well. We had a bit of a team chat with our armed guards and agreed to take the ring road around the town. This meant a longer day but, at least, we could get going and avoid any trouble. We had the hottest day yet and a strong head wind to fight with. Bring it on... again!

It turned out to be 187km of amazing scenery, including real desert scenes with camels. The road often disappeared under sand, just adding to the charm. At one tiny village, an older man was at work on an archaic, yet effective water well system. I offered to give him a break and do the pulling. Although quaint and great photo material, it really drives home how lucky we are to live in a country with constant running water. Every local person was welcoming, curious and, as far as we could see, happy. We really grumble far too easily in our world of NHS, social services and convenience shopping.

It was late by the time we arrived at our next commando dessert guards outpost camp and the only thing they could offer us – as again camping was deemed a big 'no, no' - was a huge empty garage. This was great as it was flat and like camping under a tin roof. We mustered enough energy to get creative with apple crumbles and risottos. Food is important and we were never lax

Some amazing landscape that went for miles on end

in cooking each night, plus Ro and Dickie always did us proud at lunch and snack shops. Our new guards for the night were intrigued and kept coming and shining their torches at us but we didn't have the energy or inclination for any bonding.

Spectacular scenery is a huge motivation to get out of bed early to get the miles in. There were undulating sand dunes, flat plains, an oasis with palm trees and rice paddies with mammoth mountain ranges as a back drop. The occasional camel caught the eye as the only 'wildlife', apart from the odd bandit we hadn't yet become acquainted with….thank God! The women we had seen in Pakistan were so refreshingly colourful. There was a pick-up truck with about 15 women and girls in the back singing, playing a flat drum and waving at us. I stopped to have a bit of a chat – well, more like a series of gesticulations followed by my half-a-dozen words of local lingo. Anyway, they all laughed (hopefully with me, rather than at me) before suddenly turning and running away squealing. Ro had pulled up with a camera and their reaction said it all. Ro immediately put the camera away and they all returned unperturbed - but point made.

Lunch was in the shelter of a deserted shack in the middle of nowhere. As ever, a crowd appeared and Jamie spotted potential footballers or cricketers. Our bike maintenance shop (Dom and Nic) often opened over lunchtime and they managed to mend spokes, change tyres and generally save the world whilst eating their lunch in the allocated time slot. Ro often disappeared to get good footage and this was no exception. She even chased the occasional mini tornados or whirlwinds, worrying us that she would go too close and be whisked off to meet Dorothy!

We arrived that evening in yet another official residence, a prison. We were given our very own huge room overlooking the courtyard with three very traditional barred cells across the other side. The men inside didn't look in the slightest bit scary; perhaps because they were behind bars? Sarah was particularly pleased as she'd always had a warped wish to spend a night in jail. Yet another dream fulfilled on Everestmax!

A superb day took us 148km along mountain passes to Quetta. There was not much traffic as Pakistan was having a national day of protest against the Dutch cartoons. That probably wasn't good for us but we had received absolutely no hostility whatsoever so far. We had stayed in official compounds but shopped and played sports with locals who couldn't have been friendlier. We knew not to be paranoid, although the media would probably have regarded us as reckless.

Sarah did not look proud of her white shirt for much longer.

Nic was in his element with hills to race up. He was the role model although all of us were getting strong enough to enjoy rather than endure steep hills; perfect training for Everest. The route took us through three mountain passes starting in the Sarlath Mountain Range and finishing in the Central Brahu Range. Lak Pass was the high point at 1,950m and provided views of more than 50 miles over the plains below.

We arrived in Quetta, the biggest city in Baluchistan. Our next challenge was to see whether they would let us continue with Martha. We ended up spending two days almost hotel-bound as our security was more questionable than ever as we sought advice from local police, the Pakistani home office, and British Embassy. Their first response was that we shouldn't cycle; obviously not an option for us. After a long day of negotiations, Dickie and Nic returned victorious with the promise of further escorts across the country with a planned itinerary so the police and army stations would expect us. The Pakistanis did absolutely everything

It was always fun to cycle into the town mayhem and be part of it

My previous army training came in handy when demonstrating how to treat guns with respect

possible to help us complete our journey and to do it safely. We were blown away with their generosity, although not enough to refuse the black market offer of a few beers in the privacy of our hotel room. Dickie got hold of them and, having been alcohol-free for so long, we all had two sips and giggled like teenagers experiencing the evil fluid for the first time. Needless to say, after one large beer each we had a great night and slept well.

The next day involved meeting our new set of escorts consisting of two armed vehicles – Sarah and I were even escorted to the loo at one point. They weren't too precious with their menacing weapons, allowing us to pose for photos and brandishing them to our hearts content. As the day wore on, the escort range reduced until we were left with one chap on his motorbike/moped more interested in shooting local foxes than guarding us. This didn't really matter as we never felt under any threat and everyone was really friendly. We were offered two games of cricket, invited for tea and spent lunch with a group of friendly locals - all in an area populated by people who supposedly don't like westerners!

Cycling towards more mountains, we passed though chaotic villages, testing our skills by negotiating our way through busy market streets where a wide range of goods were being sold, including an eagle! It was hot and dusty and the road became less and less forgiving, leading to a bone-shaking couple of hours before arriving at Ziarat. Then we were welcomed on our approach by the local police who had been looking out for us. We were pleased to see Ro and Dickie, who had been held back to do some paperwork for Martha that had taken much longer than anticipated.

Great hills were just what we wanted. We wanted steep and long... yes, masochism had hit its peak. Dickie was stuck with Nooradin, our customs escort, and looked about ready to cut his wrists by the end of the day. Ro had been on the bike all day so he had no real respite from being talked at, apart from during food breaks.

We got in our daily game of cricket and Ro and Sarah stole the show with some superb batting against a seven-year-old bowler – they take no prisoners. I left the crowd crying for more with a few magic tricks and a bit of a song and dance. Let's face it, there's not a huge amount of variety going on in the villages so a bunch of westerners on bikes who think they can play cricket, sing, dance and do magic tricks are a big attraction. Pakistan and India proved to be the biggest crowd pullers and we tried to please.

Our next camp was in the middle of a police family compound on a smallish grass area surrounded by a moat-like trough. We set up camp to the obvious interest of the local residents and it wasn't long before the cricket bat was out and we were fully immersed in a match. This led to another invite to the school enclosure area for an even more intense game with the older boys.

Jamie and I flaunting our football skills during our lunch break

At least 50 younger children followed us over like a gang of Pied Pipers. The boys were in bat and doing Britain proud while I tried to entertain the younger ones and girls with yet more song. It was a good job there was lots of room as the circle grew and grew to about 60 kids. The dash to the middle for the chorus of the 'oh-key-koh-key' was carnage and I was on the edge of needing crowd control. The hyper energy was positive apart from crushing one poor little toddler who got in the way. Fortunately, he was fine.

Making dinner back at camp was a very public affair and the small moat feature around our tent proved a good crowd barrier, giving us a few meters all the way around. We asked them just to stay outside that area as we felt like the main attraction in a zoo. The evening went on with police visitors wanting to talk about politics and religion but we weren't forthcoming. We were exposed to so much potential culture, history and politics but the thing that made everything so enjoyable was our fun interaction with people .We had lost interest in 'heavy' subjects, either through tiredness or the fantastic geography and experiences we were having already. Either way, our last guest turned up at about 10.30pm trying to talk 'heavy' and battled on despite constant efforts to change the subject to trivia. Jamie finally took the initiative, got into his sleeping bag and pretended to snore really loudly to encourage him to go: it did the trick and we were like a bunch of kids trying to hold back our laughter while our guest made his way home. All our kit was safely in the tent or locked in Martha; we were all very good at keeping our kit in order so there was plenty of room for everybody, computers and kitchen kit in a relatively small area. We fell asleep in blissful ignorance of what was about to happen.

This area of Baluchistan (Loralai) hadn't had any rain for six months... until that night! All of us were woken by a surprising 'pitter patter' on the tent that seemed to get stronger and stronger. The boys (Nic and Jamie) went into hero mode, jumping out of their bags in the middle of the night to ensure the zips were closed and computers were out of harm's way from the rain. We all fell back to sleep feeling smug as you do when it is wet outside and you are warm inside. This smugness increased as a full scale tropical storm emerged, including thunder and lightening. At 6am, a concerned guard shouted to make sure we were alright with Dom replying "all good and under control in here, thanks," as we remained in our canvass cocoon.

Then at 7am, Dickie sprang out of his bag like a coiled spring and shouted at full pitch: "Flood, flood, flood!" Obviously his naval officer days helped him deliver such an explicit message and it got a very fast reaction; none of us had ever seen Dickie get out of bed quickly before. Within a couple of minutes, six inches of brown water was invading our tent. The team went straight for the computers and transported as much as we could as quickly as we could to a sheltered veranda area just three meters away. Dom saw his phone float away with the kettle; anything that wasn't already rescued was floating. Fortunately, the computers were safe, largely due to the boys moving them in the night and their quick reactions that morning. It would have been devastating to have potentially lost so much of our image bank and our only real means of having regular contact with the UK. Ro realised it would be good to get this on film. Then we realised this wasn't flood water from a river but had so much more to offer, including rotten vegetables, human excrement and all manner of waste. We had been immersed in the full force of an overflowing Pakistani sewer!

Nic ankle deep in sewage inside our tent but with a big smile after rescuing my famous grey pants

The next six hours were dedicated to cleaning the kitchen kit, and doing what we could with our personal kit. The local crowd who watched us the night before was now back to see how we coped with this. Jamie had a chat in English with kids who only knew the phrases 'hello, where do you come from?' and 'yes'. Ro caught him on film asking the kids: "Is this your sewage we have been sleeping in?" Of course they all answered 'yes' in unison and with big smiles. It was a funny moment. Nic kept himself amused by the fact the only thing completely safe from the sewage in the tent was my pair of clean grey knickers. I constantly rotated my drying underwear in the rooms or tent we were sleeping in and my grey and distinctly unsexy, practical knickers (Bridget Jones, step aside), were often the source of ridicule. Hence the irony they survived the flood.

It was amazing to see no stress among the team at all. If this had happened in the UK, we would have washing machines, tumble dryers and clean water in copious amounts. However, there was limited running water (one slow running communal tap) and Sarah and I spent out time queuing like everybody else to fill up water bottles to wash the important things to get back on the road. The rest of the team washed, folded and hung out what they could as soon as the rain stopped. The sun shone long enough and hard enough to dry what we needed. The sleeping bags and other stuff would have to be done as and when... time to find some perfume to spray!

We were back on our bikes by 1pm and still managed to get 80km in. Nobody dwelt on the whole smelly inconvenience: your tolerance threshold for real problems goes startlingly high on these trips. However, our escort van seemed to want to keep its distance today – I wonder why? The scenery again was stunning and any thoughts of sewage and smells were soon long behind us. Spring had arrived and we were passing paddy fields and orchards with trees full of cherry blossom. Further down the road, the tarmac disappeared and we were on our roughest road yet with steep cliffs and outcrops displaying a huge variety of geology, getting Sarah very excited. Then came another thankfully uneventful night in another police compound, allowing us to get some more kit dry.

A variety of terrain, weather, escorts and bike incidents dominated the new day. We were warned by our friendly and enthusiastic police guards the road would be rough for about 10km …or 15…or 20. Detail wasn't their strength when it came to distance. What we did get was more than 40km of partly-made road. I refer to stretches of about 50m, then back to broken or mud roads with extreme degrees of consistency. It was like cycling through a mud bath in some stretches and muddy boulder fields for others. Jamie and Nic created a kind of invisible force field to protect them from flying mud and sludge but Sarah, Ro and I made up for that by getting covered from head-to-toe like mud magnets. We all had to keep the balance between going fast, negotiating mud, preserving bikes and just enjoying the ride. Jamie tried to teach Sarah and me how to jump bumps rather than 'roll' them. We were enthusiastic students and 'teacher' was within his rights to be frustrated, but we were having a great time anyway.

Mr Nic McSlick merits a mention here: misjudging hard mud for soft and managing to career off to the side at a healthy speed yet somehow doing a very credible dismount onto both feet and running with the bike. Whether he fully made up for the fall by making it look cool, I leave for you to guess. Our venerable and trusted leader Dom, who had kindly given me some top tips the previous day, became a fulfilled teacher as his student out-biked him by taking a rather technical off-road line around a truck. He then came unstuck trying himself, necessitating a full dramatic dismount. There was no room for egos on this trip!

The 'road' we were travelling was the only such route to this area from the east with endless beautiful lorries trying to negotiate challenging terrain. We counted 30 waiting their turn to take a run at what was effectively a mud slope. As we cycled past them in the opposite direction, we were hooted at and offered tea. They didn't look distressed at their task ahead; merely resigned to it. They were all smiles and probably enjoying the novelty of us as much as we were enjoying the novelty of them.

Dickie did an amazing job with Martha. The mud was up to the axle on several stretches for the length of the vehicle and we needed to push, shove and dig. He managed to get her

Ro on top of Martha with our armed escort

up mud hills with revs and swerves any rally driver would have been proud of. Ro took to the roof of the van as her bike needed repairing although we had got back onto relatively normal roads. Our escorts changed and the new ones, with their big guns, joined her on the roof, making her look like the most protected woman in Pakistan. The day started with blue sky and a tail wind and ended with thunder, lightening and rain. Variety is the spice of life!

Our next day of cycling was right up there with the highs of biking as a long switchback uphill took us to the top of the longest set of dramatic switchbacks in a gorge I had ever seen! It was absolutely stunning. Ro took footage as we disappeared with km after km of stunning gorge flanking us. Each switchback had to be taken seriously as the trucks weren't worried whether it was safe to overtake. We could see for long stretches with no fear of a crash and whooped and rode our way down this heavenly sight. The valley that followed was a stark contrast as we cycled through what seemed like a sandy gravel pit for miles.

We made it to the next police check-point to take us into the next region of the Punjab; meaning a new set of officials with new ideas. We went through the normal process of writing down our passport details and so on and, as we tried to leave with our new escort, the powers-that-be decided it was too dangerous. The next town was DG Khan, a prohibited area for foreigners, and we needed permission from the Government to stay there. We objected and they eventually said we could go before changing their minds again. They suggested driving us to Multan (100km past DH Khan). Dom tried to explain as calmly as he could that we couldn't miss one km on the bikes. He explained all about the world record, the charities and that we had already cycled 5,000km and were only 33km away from a pre-arranged destination with the authorities in Baluchistan. Still the answer was negative: even more annoying as Jamie wasn't well and needed to go to bed. This was a particularly well manned post and at one stage up to 15 policemen spoke very loudly and it felt like nobody was listening. Dom couldn't have made the position clearer and was happy to repeat it as many times as they needed. But they weren't letting us go anywhere without putting the bikes in the van.

Although they could all speak English to a point, they seemed to be missing the real one. My patience was shot and I jumped in with my now famous international body language and gesticulations. I explained and demonstrated that, instead of the bikes being in the van, we would ride beside it and it would take less than two hours. For whatever reason, this seemed to do the trick and we were finally on our way.

When we got to DG Khan, it was dark and we had cycled into the middle of pure chaos. We had no idea what the event was but everyone was involved in the mayhem-filled streets.

The lorries in Pakistan are works of art

The highly decorated trucks were just huge versions of rickshaws and bikes and cars all lit up in the dusk due to the many reflective stripes. It wasn't just a visual feast, it was an audible one; there were horns, bells, jingles, music and squeals coming from everywhere and we were right in the middle of it. Animals pulled carts, carts carried animals and people were inside and outside the vehicles; we counted a family of five on one motorbike. I have seen circus acts offer less impressive displays of balance. They were all enjoying themselves and time and time again we heard 'welcome to Pakistan'. All this was in a town we had been told was off limits to foreigners for their own safety.

Time moved on and, as our escorts changed again, we were told we were going to the next police compound. After just six km, we realised the next town was over 90km away so we stopped and refused. Jamie was ill and it was really late and dark. Negotiations ended with them promising to escort us back to the very same spot next day if we put our bikes in the van and made camp in Multan, the next town. Reluctantly, we agreed as there was a distinct possibility we would have to fight hard to get back to this spot and avoid putting our whole trip at risk. We climbed in with optimistic attitudes, tempered by the realisation painful talking lay ahead.

We arrived at Multan Police compound at about midnight and managed to pitch our tent relatively fast so Jamie could relax.

Nic and I enjoying truck surfing

When somebody was ill, the team let them have space while trying to do everything they could for them in camp. Everybody did much more than you could expect of an ill person in regular circumstances. If we had stopped each time somebody lost their 'oomph', we would never have made the deadline to get to Everest. That was enough to keep going even when individual tanks were running low.

Our escort arrived bright and early the next morning with transport for our bikes and us. To our surprise, we were on our way back to DG Khan. We had made all of 20km when they stopped. New protests in the region would continue for the next four days and we had to go back to our tent in Multan. Being used to these hiccups by now, we put our thinking caps on. Dickie called the head of police – no straightforward task - while the boys and Dom worked out how to get all our bikes into Martha so that transport was less of an issue.

Turning Martha into a bike carrier for some reason did the trick and we were off. When we got to DG Khan, we got our bikes out and peddled away feeling relieved we hadn't had to fight harder to get there.

The journey back to Multan was a meteorologist's dream. We were innocently riding along as a pack, enjoying watching the variety of water buffalos, camels and donkeys pulling carts as we overtook them, when we saw the sky become very sinister in the distance and moving fast towards us. One moment we could see everything yet within seconds there was nothing but sand as a sandstorm had taken us by complete surprise. We pulled off the main road and took refuge behind a building not knowing what was to follow. It was incredibly dramatic in speed as well as impact. I remember seeing a palm tree being bent over by the power of the wind and sand and feeling really lucky it had happened right by a building so we could hide. We were still outside in the aftermath but not getting the brunt of it as the building was our shield. It continued for a good ten minutes, followed by an electrical storm and heavy rain. We inevitably got soaked to the skin and cycled into Multan via every major puddle possible. Yet again, I seemed to be the dirtiest and Dickie described me as looking like an urchin chimney sweep from Oliver Twist. Happily, our escort allowed us to book into a hotel for the night. It felt so posh with showers, beds and TV and we fairly lapped it up.

We made our way back to the police compound next morning fully expecting a slow start from our new escorts with lots of chat before being allowed to go. With this in mind, Nic, Jamie and I passed the time practising hacky sack and, before long, we had attracted a crowd of about 30 from the compound which looked more like a training academy. Jamie, our guru of

Look at the smiles on our faces. We knew it was downhill all the way! Pakistan

hacky, had one of his proudest moments yet and the three of us managed to pass it between each other without drops. Then I did a spontaneous catch on my chest before making a knee and foot pass. I had never displayed such good skills before and to do it in front of such a good crowd was fantastic. Nic and Jamie couldn't stop laughing at how good it was. The army cadets and officers probably thought I was ultra cool and we all knew it was a fluke... who's telling?

It was Dom's turn to feel a bit out of sorts. Perhaps we had all become victims to a varying degree of the sewage night. It wouldn't have been difficult to handle our kit and manage to get some form of bug into our systems. It was going around us all slowly but fortunately nothing serious. Just call it squits.

Our escorts were ready and we managed to do 130km. The terrain changed again with field upon field of oil seed rape, sugar beet, wheat, rice and citrus fruit orchards. We had come out of the deserts and the wealth of colour was refreshing. Our lunch stop involved having boat races across a river on a couple of dug outs free to use to get to the café on the other side. Jamie and I tried our best only to be beaten hands down by Sarah and Ro. I never said they cheated... but how else could they have won?

Ro loved shopping at the local stores

We stayed yet another night in an army compound but this time were taken to the senior officer's house to be welcomed. He was a smartly-dressed colonel in his early thirties, who invited us in for tea and soon afterwards for dinner too. We accepted graciously, suggested we get washed and were shown to the equivalent of the officers' army barracks. In Pakistani terms, these were really comfortable working quarters - rooms with beds and an ensuite. Luxury may have resembled a prison cell in this instance but what they lacked in decor was more than made up for by convenience. That night we dressed in our best clothes (very similar to our everyday non-cycling clothes) and went to dinner. Before we had even sat down, he welcomed us at the door and greeted Jamie with: "You are a very good looking boy!" Nic and Jamie had both had their fair share of approaches by men during their journey in Pakistan but this was by far the most shocking. Jamie, without thinking, put his back to the wall while the rest of us couldn't help laughing out loud. The colonel made it even worse later, saying we were all welcome to stay the night in his spare room, but Jamie could stay with him - this in a country where homosexuality is illegal! We managed to laugh it off and Jamie felt safe knowing we wouldn't leave him – unless as a natural sacrifice for the team to continue with an escort. Only joking!

The night continued in very humorous vein as we sat round the table being waited on with great food and chat. One of the team told an anecdote the colonel didn't understand, so I turned to him and said in my best Pakistani accent: "Is it better sometimes if I am talking like this to translate?" Well, the jaws of my other six team mates dropped to the floor. It was fine to do the accent in fun with crowds but doing it to our colonel host was another matter. As it was, he turned to me and said: "Absolutely!" I had license to be Pakistani all night and drive the others nuts.

Then discussions turned to marriage. The colonel was engaged to be married soon but obviously very apprehensive it would tie him down. He said: "You British can have free sex, no?" This wasn't an unreasonable assessment from their point of view as all you have to do is watch MTV and we have no morals whatsoever. However, Dickie took what he said literally and came out with the instant reply: "No, sometimes you have to pay for it." We were all now on the floor as none were expecting an angle that gave us new insight into Her Majesty's Forces! As the only married woman there, I was selling the virtues of marriage and started to wax lyrical about Phil and commitment without being convinced the colonel was ready or right for it. In his world, it seemed like he had no choice. We left that night having had a tremendous insight to his world; I hope he felt a little more enlightened about ours.

Our next day took us away from rural Pakistan and onto the Lahore dual carriageway (Lahore being the capital of the Pakistani province of Punjab). This allows for a slow lane of local traffic, complete with donkeys, overlaid tractors and carts - you can't get bored as there is always something to look at and overtake. That's the great thing about biking: you smell, see, hear and touch things you can't really experience through the window of a vehicle. It was a short day of less than 90km, allowing time to give our bikes some much needed TLC, with bike-cleaning guru Nic McSlick being as generous as ever with his time and patience. Even Dom decided to give his bike a once over... miracles do happen.

Keeping our bikes functioning was not always easy when cycling such long distances in tricky conditions

A glorious sunrise put us in the right mood to enjoy the last big stretch to Lahore and one of our final days in Pakistan. The suburbs saw us go through tree-lined roads with a strong flavour of colonial England in the buildings and layout. That was all to disappear when we reached Lahore city centre; possibly the most chaotic and dirty city we had cycled in to date. This was, by now, a fun challenge rather than an intimidating obstacle. As ever, the danger wasn't so obvious due to the speed and forgiveness of traffic but it didn't stop it being really challenging.

We stayed that night in a central cheap hotel. We referred to the gospel of Lonely Planet and went to some key attractions where rides in motorised rickshaws made rollercoasters seem tame. Our driver was eccentric, to say the least, insisting on talking to us all the time – too much eye contact with us, too little on the road. How we got there in one piece was amazing. We weren't blameless as we had encouraged him to race against the other rickshaw with the rest of the team.

Our initial destination was the fort and the Mosque. We all did our own thing walking around enjoying the atmosphere, soaking in the noises and smells of a place of worship. The architecture was stunning and deserved time in its own right. Amid hundreds and hundreds of people coming and going, an air of calm made you want to whisper for fear of disturbing the peace this place created. Our next destination was Coco's Den, an open air multi-level restaurant serving amazing food in a traditional but funky atmosphere overlooking the illuminated Mosque and fort. We had a great night together reminiscing about the joys of Pakistan - the sport, people, biking and, of course, the sewage!

Next day, brought us to our next border (here's to country number six!). Getting out of Pakistan was easy enough, but going through no man's land to the Indian border brought its fair share of hassle. Dickie and Ro did their thing but all the negotiating skills in the world weren't going to let Martha into India; one reason being a ban on left hand drive vehicles. Poor Martha was to be 'junk' from that day on. We had wanted to donate her to one of the charities in Nepal as she still had plenty left to give but it wasn't to be. Our only option now was to hire a vehicle to support us across India, less of a big deal as we had come so far. Martha had already given as much as we could have dreamed of, despite her bag of bolts episodes.

The positive side of this border was an amazing system of colour-coded porters. I had seen this on Michael Palin's travel documentary but seeing it live was just amazing. Literally hundreds of Pakistani porters, dressed in bright red and green long shirts, carry loads in a very orderly line to the border where they pass them onto an Indian porter dressed in very bright blue. There seemed remarkably little confusion and it was like watching a synchronised porter display. Another positive side of the border crossing was witnessing the now world-famous huge attraction of the changing of the guard. Every day, the Pakistani and Indian armies re-enact the closing of the border between the two countries and a flag-lowering ceremony takes place here. Wagah Border is the only official land crossing-point between the two countries and separates Amritsar, India and Lahore, Pakistan. Each day, the 45-minute ceremony involves a carefully choreographed 'stand-off' between Indian and Pakistani soldiers, ending in the lowering of both flags and the slamming of the border gates.

Colour co-ordinated porters at the border with India

CHAPTER **TWELVE**

A colour fest of beautiful ladies and girls working with chillies

Who Needs Personal Space? - India

INDIA

Population: 1,103,596,000
Capital: New Delhi 295,000
Area: 3,287,270 square kilometers (1,269,221 square miles)
Language: Hindi, English, 14 other official languages
Religion: Hindu, Muslim, Christian, Sikh, Buddhist, Jain, Parsi
Currency: Indian rupee
Life Expectancy: 63
GDP per Capita: U.S. $2,600
Literacy Percent: 60
Industry: Textiles, chemicals, food processing, steel, transportation equipment, cement, mining
Agriculture: Rice, wheat, oilseed, cotton; cattle; fish
Exports: Textile goods, gems and jewellery, engineering goods, chemicals, leather manufactures

DICKIE AND RO stayed for the Wagah Border spectacular on the first night in India while we cycled off with what we needed from the van to find a hotel in the nearby town of Amritsar, just 30km away. They joined us later in a taxi with lots more of our kit and raving about the show. Sarah and I decided we would see it next day as it was too special to miss. However, tomorrow was another day.

We all went to dinner and enjoyed the fact we could have a beer legally. We had been in Muslim countries since the beginning of the journey so were ready for a bit of good old fashioned western debauchery. Dickie, Jamie, Nic and I went on after dinner to explore a bit more of downtown Amritsar and it turned into a classic late night of tall beers, tall tales and laughter. Dickie was on form and his naval stories were flowing – he must have been such a laugh to have as your officer! Our night ended up taking us to an unlikely final destination. The last place you would go after a night on the beers in the UK would be a temple or church but that's where we ended up. The Sikh Golden Temple in Amritsar is absolutely stunning and, even if you aren't religious, you would be hard pressed not to find something spiritual in the air. It was 1am when we arrived but that was no problem as it is open 24 hours a day 7 days a week. Nobody can go in without their head being covered - even the men. There is a basket of hats to choose from and whether they did it intentionally or not, the boys managed to pick the most bright and offensive ones. When I saw them wearing a variety of pink, orange and yellow mop caps, looking more like they were in a Hansel and Gretel production than entering a temple, I was in bits. We weren't trying to be disrespectful but the four of us were beside ourselves with laughter that is always harder to control in a place you aren't supposed to be drunk and disorderly.

The Golden Temple

However, we managed a very respectful walk around the temple and it really was all it was built up to be. People were sleeping and praying and bathing in the waters. All seemed calm and tranquil and we eventually found our way back to our hotel and slept like babies.

A big admin day followed as Dickie and I were set the task of finding a van to hire. We saw the size and shape of a van we thought suitable just parked in a street and which fortuitously happened to have 'tourism' written on the front. Bingo, we thought, but who owns it? There was neither number, nor contact and we couldn't just wait in the street until somebody came to drive it away. Dickie suggested I stand on the roof and shout to a crowded street to ask who owned it. I was in my element being given permission to shout - and it worked! This led to a chain of events that lasted under two hours and resulted in a van and a driver to come across India with us all for a bargain price. Perfect, I still had time to go with Sarah to the Wagah Border event.

This is a popular tourist attraction with an atmosphere of jovial patriotism pervading on both sides. The ceremony is an exhibition of force mixed with co-operation, more reminiscent of dance battles than military aggression. It even ends with a handshake between the participants; if only all our issues could be resolved that way. Thousands of people come every day to see this and cheer madly. The soldiers shouted really loud and kicked their legs really high (looked a bit painful to me). Flags were flying in the crowd and the chanting was more suited to a football match than an official military ceremony. The reality consisted of two small teams of army boys marching towards each other, exchanging keys and walking back; well worth the visit but amazing such an event could draw such huge crowds every day. What a trade Alton Towers would do here!

We went back to Amritsar which is busy, colourful, friendly and with the occasional pleasant aroma... only occasional mind. It's like walking back in time going around the small streets with horses, bicycles and rickshaws all vying for space. The Sikh community added a whole new colour scheme with their turbans, with pink and orange very much in vogue.

We were on our way next day to explore India by bikes. Dickie and Ro had the sad task of going back to Martha, collecting the rest of our kit and putting it into our new chauffeur-driven bus (the girls called her Marigold, the boys called her van). She was large, white and had flowers on her back end, patterns on her mudguards and some truly awful interior decoration, including a swirly-style carpet on the ceiling and walls with matching tassels and curtains. She was full of character and now our kit and, most importantly, she worked. Our driver Mr T was quiet, knew enough English to get by and was always well dressed and on time.

The landscape was flat with long avenues of trees painted white halfway up their trunks. The fields were full of people harvesting by hand and loading their products into carts, wagons, rickshaws and anything else that was loadable. Most were massively overloaded and many deserved balancing act awards. Villages and countryside merged into one as small roadside stores covered every mile. Oxen, donkeys and stray dogs seemed to live on the side of the roads and in towns with no natural owners or identity. The journey had started to change from remote, wilderness-like areas linked by rural villages and occasional cities in Pakistan to busy and constant in India. The best change, though, was the availability of cold drinks and most stalls seemed to have fridges. We had been drinking lukewarm water for weeks and, as the temperature was getting hotter and hotter, cold drinks proved remarkably refreshing.

The traffic etiquette in India deserves its own paragraph: drivers take noise pollution to a whole new level with their love of horns. They seem to honk them all the time whether they need to or not, going to the extreme of having signs saying 'Blow your

Horn' on their backs. There is also a distinct lack of instruction on what brakes, indicators and mirrors are for.

Our cycle journey coincided with some important Test cricket matches back in the UK. India being a nation of cricket lovers, too, you'd see TV sets on in either hotels or some stalls. The boys would rush between 20km stretches and find a stall with a TV. It was fun watching them get so excited about it all. Boys and their ball games!

The honks seemed to get more persistent each day as our tolerance grew less but the landscape never failed to entertain. There is never 'nothing' going on in India; there is always something being planted, reaped, pulled, chased or cooked. It's so heavily populated that land not used for growing crops is usually there to home, store or sell things from. Things feel faster here and, as there is no hard shoulder, when those big buses hoot and speed by you can really feel it.

Our drink stops were, as ever, time for chats and fun and our fun fights often drew a crowd. Jamie and I managed to break a plastic chair and got the teacher look of disapproval from Dom, my junior in age but senior in responsible attitude. We were often spoiled by the storekeepers and one man brought out his bed made from wood and vines for us to lie on. We must have looked particularly tired that day. Roadside food was also interesting and the hotter it got the more flies we had to fend off. But we needed to eat and our philosophy was that, by now, we had enough germs in us to fight off an army of bugs. Being clinical about food was impractical although we were always clinical about water and our drinks.

India was the place to draw a crowd. We had spent a few days in our new country by then and started to know how to manage such gatherings. If we had a puncture, we needed one person to entertain; Jamie and I were getting particularly well rehearsed at our magic tricks while a couple of others did the repairs. Children always like to be entertained by magic. I got a real buzz out of watching their faces fill with wonder as I made the yellow hanky disappear or Jamie produced a coin from behind one of the children's ears. The rest of the team spent the entire trip trying to work out how we did our tricks. I think Dom was particularly frustrated at not working it out... it's magic!

If we were having food from the van, we made a physical barrier between us and the crowd by putting up bags or wood or anything we could find. We were a big attraction and could easily attract a crowd of more than 100 within 10 minutes of stopping. Most amusing element of all this was when I told one of my long-winded jokes to a big crowd: I laughed and applauded

Crowds would gather in seconds when we stopped

myself at the end and they all joined in without having understood a word... a stand up comic's dream! This wasn't a tourist route and we really were very high novelty value for them; so as long as they made us feel welcome, why should we worry about again becoming a zoo attraction? Talking of zoos, it was great when we came across the beginning of monkey territory. They were on the road, swinging from tree to tree and generally enjoying life without a zoo to be seen. We all went a bit monkey-mad with images but how couldn't we? None of us were stupid enough to be fooled by their cute appearance into going too close.

India offered opportunities we hadn't experienced before as Nic and Dickie challenged themselves to find the most attractive pile of dung. In much of Asia cow dung is collected, splattered on the wall of a house or field and dried out in the sun before being used for fuel on the fire. They pile it onto donkeys to transport it or in yards to store it and these were some of the most beautiful piles of pooh we had ever seen – true works of art with practical value!

The most artistic pile of manure I have ever seen

We had seen many vehicles on our journey that were completely over-stacked by UK terms but India stretched the benchmark - and some. Any method of transport seemed legal (apart from left hand drive vehicles apparently – not that we were bitter!), so any amount of goods were stacked up as high and wide as possible. The only limit was the law of nature manifesting itself in the form of spills into the road. Bricks would be placed around the offending spillage and life goes on around it. There were constant displays of impressive stacking; some scary, some bewildering.

Wide loads were common and skilfully loaded

Our stretch of road to Amroha was one of the dustiest in India and that was saying something. We were enjoying India a lot but, due to the dust, noise and crowds, were all glad it was only a short time to get to Nepal. That night in Amroha, we stayed in a hotel hosting a huge wedding and the boys had a room holding a party for mosquitoes too. The girls had a smug moment but it wasn't long before we all got the joy of the 'buzzzzz' constantly in our ears and the odd nip, nip, nip. Are we sure they have any use in evolution?

We were very kindly invited to the wedding and witnessed the parade as it arrived through the streets. The fireworks, music and display of the parade were amazing and that was just for the groom arriving! We joined the party for a munch on the buffet and even had a dance but we were all pretty tired and some mildly sick. We managed to sleep through the 'buzzzzz' and loud Indi techno music that kept going until 6am!

Negotiating the traffic was enough to wake anybody up next day and we made the first 50km in under two hours. The day's entertainment revolved around Nic trying to pacify a policeman when he accidently ran a toll gate in the wrong direction. Nic's diplomatic smile and endearing tone won the day... what a smoothy! Sarah's offering was to cycle away after a drinks break with a trail of toilet paper hanging out from the back of her shorts. We did tell her eventually! I got the crown

A school bus

by pulling out after lunch, turning left instead of right and cycling back to Pakistan! They did stop me but, of course, there were jokes in my and about my directions for the next week.

The bikes were all doing well, thanks to the careful maintenance programme led by Nic. It was always much funnier when something happened to his bike such as when his chain snapped. He said it was because of the immense force he exerts - we put it down to over cleaning. Star attraction was a very large group of several hundred women and girls smiling and chatting away while sorting through red chillies. They made a mundane task look fun. We stopped and, although they were all a bit shy at first, it wasn't long before they were comfortable enough to let us take some photos. The rich red chillies and their sarees added up to a colour fest.

We arrived in Bareilly in the state of Uttar Pradesh to hear about bomb blasts in Varenessi, a popular tourist destination. Also the bird flu problem meant chicken was off the menu. Although we took notice of these newsflashes, they were background knowledge rather than things to worry about. We only had four weeks before we were to meet the climbers in Kathmandu – and my reunion with Phil. We had come too far not to at least get there.

The slickly-oiled Everestmax team was back on the road next morning with 160km to go to a bigger town and the hope of finding something resembling a hotel. Camping was out of the question in this part of India for several reasons: firstly, any patch of land not used to grow and sell simply had to be a rubbish dump; secondly, we would need a rota for crowd control. It was bad enough stopping for a drink so, if we piled out the whole tent and kit, they would think the circus had come to town.

The sights of the day included two red headed cranes turning Jamie into an ornithologist as he jumped off his bike to get a picture. Sarah's highlight was a Holy Man wearing a blue loin cloth with a colourful combination of white body paint and yellow and red spots on his head. He was making holy hand shapes and smiling widely next to a very colourful Hindu statue. Our threshold of weird and wonderful had got higher in India due to sheer saturation but the Holy Man got a high score. This was also the first day for a while when the whole team was fit and healthy with fully functional as opposed to over- functional digestive systems... what a relief! It also allowed for race tactics to kick back in - I would creep up behind the boys and boom

The most beautiful camel I have ever seen

off into the lead and they had to combine chasing hard to catch me with spouting a ream of excuses. At one drinks stop, we saw some vines hanging down from a tree: a gift of a Tarzan swinging competition. Dom, our inspirational leader and father figure, kept his troops entertained by trying to emulate their style. He did a very good act of not being able to catch the next vine while swinging, preferring to improve team morale by allowing them to think they could do better. How selfless of him.

I was cycling with a young lad and his mates on their bikes. When kids rode bikes, they were always adult versions so they really had to stretch over each side to maintain contact with the peddles. Some of the smaller boys mastered the art of being able to peddle putting one leg through the main frame and skillfully balancing in a constant standing position below seat level. My new play mates were obviously after a bit of a challenge so I obliged with mini-spurts before really going for it. We went for ages until he finally conceded defeat, having had fun throwing antagonistic gestures at each other all the way. I'm all for giving kids a sporting chance but how would losing have made the Brits look? I got the crown for my country!

Ro and Dickie continued to be a very matched couple even sharing one puncture each. They ended up having to bargain for the best stretches of the day as heavy traffic was now considered fun rather than scary. The only thing I can compare it to is a living version of some computer game as you duck and dive between cars, carts, donkeys, lorries and rickshaws. Nic showed a chivalrous side by not boxing me in between an ox and a lorry as we all attempted to become King or Queen of the Dodgers.

Our hot clammy weather broke into rain next day to settle the dust but the down side was we needed to give lorries more space as the spray of dirt and skid factor had risen considerably. Just ask Dickie. We left our town through the usual smog of a hundred tiny bonfires used to burn rubbish. Each household or storekeeper took pride in their area by carefully sweeping their rubbish into a tidy pile, yet there appeared to be no organised rubbish collection. Some gets burnt, with the rest getting passed on down the street until collecting in corners for dogs and scavengers, including children, to feed off. Humbling.

We passed an industrial-style of agriculture in the form of brickmaking. Thousands of bricks were hand-made in the field and transported down the road to be fired (heated into harder bricks) to the tall chimney standing out with its height and belching smoke. We saw a boy of about seven years of age with a cart of bricks. How many of us would allow a child to work, never mind let him drive a heavy cart and ox with bricks on the back? Very humbling.

Poverty was also more apparent on the outskirts of the bigger towns where shanty-style shelters were built between stores and under bridges. Children and toddlers stood by the side of a main road inches from fast cars and lorries, their survival chances seemingly only marginally better than the dogs sharing their dens. Consider me well and truly humbled.

On a positive note, we were back to 'mud magnet' cycling and some were almost as muddy as me by the end of day. Nic McSlick defied nature by somehow staying clean despite the conditions. Sarah bust a gut to catch up and keep up with Nic only for him to casually pull out and peel an orange while maintaining a pace that kept her panting. How irritating! My moment of the day consisted of discovering a new hacky sack move by accident while Dom demonstrated his ability by flailing his way through the passes and landing on a thorny potted plant.

Naturally we were all sympathetic. Jamie maintained his status as the undisputed master but knew we were hot on his heels.

We had a rest day in Lucknow as we were in a hotel that gave us space to chill and update on some much needed kit admin. The day was bright, sunny and perfect for giving the tent a thorough clean for the first time on the trip. The girls got our legs out: actually, I was the only one and that was only because we were in a closed compound-like area. The jibes began as the team got out their sunglasses and started to scream at the blinding brightness of my legs! Satellites had to take cover. Their only mistake was poking so much fun at me too close to a hosepipe in a country free from drought. In the absence of a smart retort, I resorted to my best form of attack and drenched the lot of them hook, line and sinker.

That night we celebrated Ro's birthday with a surprise huge chocolate cake. She was delighted but her best present came from Sarah who got somebody to write down 'no coriander please – I am allergic to it' in local lingo. So many dishes seemed to revel in it that Ro developed a habit of studying the menu and talking us grumpily through the strictly limited coriander-free options. Then when her food arrived, she would look, sniff and poke it like a child before giving us a running commentary on her hate of coriander. We all hugged and thanked Sarah for her fun and ingenuity.

Jamie paid the classic chocolate cake price riding out of town the next day when his seat quite simply sheered off. I had never seen anything like it and his replacement shorter stem, happily for us fun seekers, looked pretty ridiculous.

Next day, we cycled over the Ghaghara River in Faizabad, a perfect balcony to view river people go about their daily routines. Their homes were made of a mixture of cane, rope and tarpaulin. Each house was neatly partitioned with bamboo and their yards ran almost into the river where they did their washing, bathed and swam. Not the most hygienic but that's life in India. The rest of the day saw us cover 145km towards the Nepalese border, including 120km on appalling roads. Our bikes got a full hit of bone-shaking territory and Premier League potholes.

Soon we were at the border of our next country, Nepal. We said a very big thanks to our driver Mr T and goodbye to Marigold; both had been loyal, reliable and professional. Mr T, who had slept in the van each night, was quiet but seemed happy to be with us without really understanding the attraction of hot and sweaty cycle rides. We reflected over breakfast on our India experience and yet again we left with positive and inspiring feelings of the people and the country. Mind you, we wouldn't miss the overcrowding, incessant horn blowing and lack of space.

We all had a bit of a moment thinking we were now so close to our first milestone of Kathmandu. I was incredibly excited to be going back to Nepal. I had called this country home for four years and, like anybody who'd been there, held a special place for it in my heart. I was also really looking forward to catching up with Mahendra, Rahsmi and Sharda and saying 'Namaste' (the traditional Nepalese greeting meaning 'I salute the God within you'). Ro and Dickie went to the border fully expecting some kind of delay… but no! It was the easiest crossing yet particularly as we didn't have a vehicle. Hey, had someone switched off the 'horn' switch? No vehicles, relative calm, just rickshaws and people in the streets – we were in Nepal heaven.

CHAPTER **THIRTEEN**

The team take a moment to enjoy their first sight of the Himalayas

NEPAL

Population: 25,371,000
Capital: Kathmandu; 741,000
Area: 147,181 square kilometers (56,827 square miles)
Language: Nepali, English, many other languages and dialects
Religion: Hindu, Buddhist, Muslim
Currency: Nepalese rupee
Life Expectancy: 59
GDP per Capita: U.S. $1,400
Literacy Percent: 45
Industry: Tourism, carpets, textiles; small rice, jute, sugar and oilseed mills; cigarettes; cement and brick production
Agriculture: Rice, corn, wheat, sugarcane
Exports: Carpets, clothing, leather goods, jute goods, grain

Himalayan Dreams - Nepal

WE CHECKED into a hotel which even had a bath! Sarah was in heaven as one of her personal luxuries she had brought with her was a bottle of Radox bubble bath. Now, after several thousand miles, she could finally use it. Hands up all of you who would have thought of that for your one luxury item? The lack of moving vehicles was explained next day: there was a potential strike lasting several days due to Maoist problems in Nepal. Yes, we'd ticked off bandits, bird flu, Taliban and nuclear unease on our hazard checklist, now for the Maoists!

The Maoist problem had been a recurring issue when I lived in Nepal. They represented the poorest part of Nepal and had started with humanitarian goodwill. As time moved on and the group became bigger, some leaders remained true to the cause but others began to wield more fear than respect in certain areas. There had been stories of Maoists hurting and even killing locals who disobeyed although tourists avoided the horror stories, merely being asked for money for their cause. Anyway, you get the point: when the Maoists declare a national transport strike and penalties for those who disobey, only the foolhardy fail to take notice.

We needed to make contingency plans in case we couldn't hire any transport for support. We started going through options and asking around to find out how long the strike would last. The variety of answers roughly equalled the number of people we asked – anything from two days to a full week. It was only a four-day bike ride to Kathmandu and the option of flying Dickie and Ro with the absolute essential kit now pushed the sensible button.

Despite the transport problems, we managed to have a fantastic first day in Nepal. We arrived on the festival of Holi, celebrating a very bad goddess being killed by a very good one. I had always enjoyed this day. Traditionally, people place coloured thumb marks on the forehead of relatives, friends and others they see. However, as the years have gone by, it has turned into carnage in the streets and some people daren't leave their homes now for fear of being covered from head-to-toe in multi-coloured paints. Our first Holi experience came when Dickie walked back to the hotel having popped out to buy something. We were all in the yard and all we could see was a body with a very pink face and green hair. There was no need for any further incentive as we had bought our stock of paint in India the day before. All of us except Dom went out into the streets looking for trouble... and we weren't disappointed. We tried to ambush some kids trying to ambush rickshaws. We started softly as they were only children but it took no time at all to learn they were more than our equals in the art of paint fighting. Ro's hair was a particularly good

Colours day in Nepal saw Jamie and Nic take the hits

target as it holds so much paint in its wild bushy consistency and, each time I turned to look, it changed colour. A woman and four children came in to attack the boys and, charging to their aid, I became the perfect target for a bucket of water. Such perfect comic timing kept the boys amused until they were attacked seconds later. Pure pantomime.

As our tour of the town continued, we came across a bunch of adults who had obviously been enjoying the Nepalese 'spirit' of the event. Dickie moved straight onto the dance floor closely followed by yours truly trying to pull some 'moves'. Jamie generously described it as my attempt at Nepalese break dancing. When we eventually made it back to the guest house, Dom illustrated great pride in his team's appearance, taking photos from the balcony whilst sensibly refusing to come near us. It took a serious amount of shampoo to remove the evidence and even then we all had sporty shades of red, blue, green and black in our hair for days to come. Dickie's beard looked particularly becoming with a new shade of red. To be honest, I'm not convinced he tried that hard to get rid of it. Too much time in Pakistan!

Jamie had been liaising with our charities and arranged for us to visit Practical Action, based in our current location of Bhairahawa. Practical Action makes projects happen in countries that need practical solutions. In this case, they were funding the construction of bike ambulances. The beauty of the project is it was designed and built in Nepal, keeping costs down and money in the local economy. The project itself is a tremendously important aid to those who live in areas desperately short of motorised transport and provides an essential service in rural communities. I would encourage anybody to support them (please visit *www.practicalaction.com*).

Practical Action bike ambulance

It was time to leave Ro and Dickie to try and get themselves and our essential kit to Kathmandu by plane or transport while we got on our bikes. We agreed to meet in four days time in a hotel near Thamel, the throbbing heart of the tourist region of Kathmandu. Although the Maoist strike was bad for Nepal – and now Dickie and Ro – it was fantastic for us cyclists. We had been cycling along the flat for ages in India and our altitude had gone as low as 200m above sea level (a little lower than the altitude we reached on our first day in Jordan!). Now we were into the hills and the scenery was about to blow us all out of the water. Our first 30km continued as flat and normal but then we turned a corner and entered a narrow gorge and the majesty of the Himalyan kingdom appeared in earnest. The road wound its way up past small villages with kids running out into the street shouting 'bye bye'. The English teachers obviously needed a lesson or two themselves. The children were

Digital cameras are a great way to share moments

Dom enjoying superb roads with no fear of any traffic due to the strike

all smiles and energy and seemed so much healthier than the street urchins we had left behind in the cities of India. We stopped in a small village for a drink of Nepalese tea, the most delicious drink in the world – as long as you like sugar.

Nic and I saw a football and started to flaunt our skills before the more talented Jamie, threatened to steal our show. That's when I tried an ambitious 'over my head' trick; the idea was great but my skills were awful as I accidentally kicked it over the roof of one of the houses with sheer drops of several hundred feet directly behind. Fortunately, the ball bounced into a recoverable area. It became the source of much hilarity and cue for me to sit and enjoy tea and company. I tried out my pigeon Nepalese, which is always appreciated. I loved the look of these villages; thatched houses lined the small road with banana groves as the back drop; people carried their loads in woven baskets hanging from their heads, looking constantly happy. It is an incredibly welcoming country with a population world famous for an ability to smile and laugh at life.

That night we made it to a village called Bartung at 9.30pm where we stopped for some food and were invited to stay upstairs by the hospitable café owner. His daughter Tara, who was 21 and very good at English, stayed with us for most of the evening. We got on very well, chatting in broken English for ages together. We went downstairs and had our first plate of dhal bhatt, a traditional Nepalese food they eat two or three times a day. It usually consists of rice, dhal and vegetables and, sometimes, a meat stew. It is gorgeous and the great thing is you pay one price and they keep topping up your plate until you have had enough. The family basically vacated their lounge for us so we could all sleep together. Nic and I still managed a bed fight despite being on the floor. We bade very fond farewells to our incredibly welcoming host family next day and were off on the bikes again for another memorable day enjoying no traffic on the road.

It wasn't long before we reached the show stopper for us: our first sight of the Himalayas. The Annapurna mountains and Mt Machupachu (the famous and holy Fishtail Mountain) were there in all their splendour and glory. As we stopped, I had a bit of a moment and had to ride off and have a few minutes to myself with confused emotions going through my head. I was missing Phil to share the moment, yet really happy we had made it this far. Being back in Nepal reminded me I'd left there before I was ready. Jamie cycled up to me, saw my eyes were welling up and offered me a hug. He had never seen me look distressed in the whole trip and was a bit stunned. I had no control over what my head and heart were doing: emotions one, Pauline nil. He handled me well and, once I had purged whatever I needed to purge, the gang turned up and I got back to enjoying the amazing ride and sharing the excitement of seeing the mountains. It was particularly special for Sarah and Jamie as they had never been to the Himalayas before. Everest had started to creep into our heads a lot more over the past week or two. By seeing the Himalayan range, we gave ourselves reason to believe we were going to make it there. It felt great.

We were all very excited about reaching Pokhara, a place I knew personally and the guidebooks rave about. It is a town based on the shores of a large lake overlooked by the Annapurna range of mountains. One area had been developed purely on the back of tourism, hence the tempting promise of cafes and restaurants serving sheer delights from steaks to apple pie and custard. The boys, especially Jamie, had lost a huge amount of weight and hadn't been feeling 100 per cent for a while now. The last thing you should do is get used to feeling unwell as that becomes the norm and you don't deal with it. The other good thing about Pokhara was we could get to a doctor and have some blood tests to see what little germs we had picked up on our journey so far.

We only had about 20km to go but the rumbles of thunder and menacing sky said it all. It was now a race against time to get to Pokhara and there were obstacles. First was Sarah's brakes; she wasn't confident they would hold on the predominantly downhill journey. The boys did some reassuring tweaks and off we went. The lads raced off loving the adverse conditions, but we all had to go steadily as random blockades appeared out of nowhere across the roads - some of stone, others wood and one in the form of a burnt-out car. Dom and I waited for Sarah to make sure she was happy. She seemed fine so off we went again. The boys were ahead but stopped to help at an accident scene where a man had fallen off his roof and broken his leg. They took details and said they would cycle to town and get an ambulance up to him. As they were cycling off, they missed being hit by lightning by only a few feet. This turned out to be the coolest part of the day for them and prompted the killer line: 'We are so hard; not even lightening can stop us!' They bigged up their bravado image so well, I almost think they started to believe it. It was a good job we were there to keep them grounded and realise they still had a long way to catch up rock-hard Pauline!

The weather got worse and worse as the rain fell harder and harder in full monsoon-style. It was dark by the time Dom and I rode into town and found Nic and Jamie in a tea shop but there was no sign of Sarah. We would give her 20 minutes as she was very tentative on those untrustworthy brakes. After half an hour,

Jamie and Nic got back on their bikes and braved the dark, wet and cold to ensure Sarah was ok, meeting her a couple of hundred meters down the road. She had lost the use of her brakes - bad enough when going downhill in the dark with hairpin bends and big drop offs, yet to make matters worse she had two punctures. She had started to run with her bike and got to a village where the locals were helping her to mend both punctures when all the electricity was cut off (very common occurrence) and they finished in candlelight - another lovely gesture by local people seeing a westerner in distress. Sarah was completely unfazed as she knew we would be waiting somewhere obvious when she got to Pokhara. So a short 20km turned into an eventful long 20km.

The rain refused to relent and the dark made distinguishing between potholes and puddles a hazardous challenge. Our own sound effects were the best indication and kept us entertained for the next 20 minutes as we rode into the heart of Pokhara and found a guest house. Rain never stops play in the Everestmax world! We had a quick shower, stuffed ourselves senseless in the nearest restaurant and still made it back with enough energy for a bed fight. Another fantastic day.

We had arrived in Pokhara at night in a thunderstorm and during a power cut. Imagine the joy of waking up to a blue sky, snow capped mountains and a stunning lakeside view without even a hint of a hooting horn or lorry. Dom did a really early 5am walk (he gets excited and can't sleep, bless); the boys did a pre-breakfast walk (although they claimed it was a 10-mile run around the lake); Sarah did the same and met them going the other way; meanwhile, I conceded to the mature and relaxed approach to life and had a full blown lie-in.

Pokhara proved the perfect place for the bulk up breakfast as we spent two hours eating. I had managed to lose about 2kg over the cycle ride so far yet Jamie and Dom had lost over 20kg! Dom had a bit to lose but Jamie was now looking too skinny so we found a medical centre and got some blood tests done. The results came back that night and he was on a collision course with antibiotics straightaway. Sarah did the same as she, too, hadn't been 100 per cent. It was a good move as you want to start Everest strong, not fighting off tropical bugs. We made time to hire a boat to go on the lake and show off our best diving moves. Definitive tan lines were displayed and my shockingly white legs attracted still more verbal abuse.

March is normally one of the five busy months for tourists in Nepal, but not during our visit. The Maoist problems had a huge impact on tourism, despite there being no record of malice directly against tourists. I felt very sad for the traders, knowing they had five months a year to make their money and this was one of them. The disruption couldn't stop Dickie and Ro however. We got news via email they'd got a flight with cargo space and were due to fly that day.

Jamie arranged for us to visit an SOS Children's Village. This was one of the three charities we were supporting and it was so good to see it in action. We cycled into a garden area with an SOS Children's Village flag hanging from the mast as a centrepiece for this pristine collection of homes. This village of homes cares for Tibetan orphans of Nepal and we were each greeted by the village director with a Khata. This is a silk scarf with auspicious symbols woven in and is often used as a sign of recognition and respect. The atmosphere was instantly warm, friendly and very welcoming. The grounds and building were immaculate, yet homely and we were shown around a typical home. The head of the family was a mother figure who cared and looked after six

SOS Childrens Villages Nepal. A superb charity

to eight children with a monthly budget provided for by sponsorship and fundraising. We were also shown around the primary school which was clean and tidy with the children smiling and well dressed. Naturally, we lapped up the opportunity to play with them. Football started the ball rolling, followed by table tennis and posing for photos. I was really impressed by the level of love and care I felt. This wasn't a sad orphanage but a real community home that had already made the difference to hundreds of children's lives. I would again encourage support of this great organization (*www.soschildrensvillages.org.uk*)

Purely by chance, Mahendra, my old buddy and business partner from Equator days, was in town and we arranged for a bevy and catch up. It was fantastic to see him looking so well as we spent several hours just chatting and becoming a mutual admiration society. I thanked him for the great time I had working with him and he thanked me for introducing the trekking company to Equator, saving the company during testing times. We had always been partial to rum and coke and, by the time I left him to find the team, we had revisited what a bottle of rum can do! I had no idea where they were so went along the street full of bars and restaurants shouting: "Everestmax... where are you?" in that tell-tale tippled tone. Jamie popped his head over a balcony and shouted back. They saw the funny side as I poured myself into a seat and joined the team for a meal. For some reason, they seemed even funnier than normal.

I convinced them to come and meet Mahendra who was hosting an end-of-trek dinner at a restaurant with some live music. I wanted to show him off to them and vice versa. However, the team was all polite but not really the fun-packed bunch I had described to Mahendra. That judgement may have been a symptom of my particularly gobby, excitable mode but I was still proud and Mahendra obviously thought they were all very nice. I cracked on having a good time and dancing with Mahendra was great as I hadn't danced to live music for so long. Without sounding too corny, time is never an issue between real friends. We had picked up where we left off four years ago.

Our goal was to get to Mugling only about 100km away. We heard the strike was off for now - great news for the local traders and Nepal, in general, although we would need to be more traffic aware. Although I had spent years in Nepal, I had always seen the road from a bus roof or inside a car/bus. It was as different seeing it on a bike as it was going trekking or kayaking down the rivers. You have more time, senses are more exposed and you have the opportunity to stop at points of interest. I was really enjoying my new take on this country. We stopped to have a chat with some very happy and smiley

Ladies stopped to chat with us while working in the rice paddy

ladies picking rice while the men were ploughing with their oxen in the field next door. There were constant glimpses of children, women and men carrying large loads in head baskets and still with the energy to smile and give a wave or call 'Namaste'. We have it so easy, you know.

At one stop, Jamie was flirting with a 55-year-old larger-than-life woman which was good entertainment for the team. If nothing else, his magic tricks and charm acted as a good PR move for the team. The older woman loved him although I couldn't really see it going anywhere. Sarah entertained us at a couple of the drink stops by going off without her rucksack. So the boys did their chivalrous thing again and enjoyed the self-awarded hero status. Now and then I felt it necessary to keep them in place by putting a few rocks in their sacks. I'd taken the blame for a phantom rock loader earlier, so decided to enjoy the title.

We got to Mugling in good time and found a curry house near the guest house with Dom following later. We were all sitting enjoying a drink and then the very, very, very loud local music started inside this relatively small room (ps did I mention the music?). We knew exactly what Dom would say when he walked in as it was his catchphrase for any occasion that didn't suit his fragile, conservative, grumpy old man disposition. Bang on cue, he blurted out: "You are having a laugh!" Naturally, we insisted there was no other place in town and had just ordered, so had no choice but to stay and soak up the atmosphere. My digestive system wasn't exactly perfect, so I took it easy on the food and bust my guts with laughter instead. I'm not sure what I enjoyed more - the banter about Dom hating it, or watching Dom enduring it. Both in equal digestible portions, I think.

Next day felt pretty special to all of us as we were to arrive in Kathmandu, the place we had earmarked as the end of phase one. It was nearly in the bag! We left nothing to chance and didn't even talk about celebrating until we were actually there.
We had a suitably classic day to finish on with a 2,000m climb going up and down and a 113km ride in stunning scenery.
On the last steep ascent, we rode switch back after switch back taking us to the top of the valley bowl and then down into Kathmandu. Nic said it was his favourite day of the whole ride.
I struggled as I was a bit low on energy and it was a hard and steep ride up to the top. We found time en route to stop at another Practical Action project we had been told about.
The 'gravity lift' linked a remote village 2,000m up a hillside with the valley below. It was a small, manually operated cable car system in which loads of up to 120kg were sent down from the village. This meant produce such as vegetables could be delivered in four minutes whereas the villagers carried it for over two hours - another example of how Practical Action was, helping people to help themselves.

As we were getting back on the bikes, a western man in a jeep pulled up and said hello. He looked at me and I looked at him: "hi Tony!" was followed by "bloody hell, Pauline!" Tony Jones had been in Nepal as long as anybody I had known. He maintained a distinctly British air, but loved Nepal and had done huge amounts for the locals he worked with to ensure they benefited from tourism. He was a thoroughly decent chap with whom I'd got on very well as rivals when I worked in Nepal as he also ran a trekking and rafting company. We shared respect and a common approach to ethical tourism, except he lived and breathed it all year, every year and I was merely a visitor compared with him. It was a great chance meeting: I was starting to re-enter my old world and hopefully the stories I had told the team were becoming a lot more real to them.

Nepal is still one of the poorest countries in the world which is why tourism is so important. There are many subsistence farmers and a good presence in tourism and industry but far too many folk have no education and are forced into child labour. Witnessing children as young as four working in small groups with a hammer chopping small rocks into stones is heartbreaking. Seeing the children at the SOS village highlighted that education is a ticket out of this world for them. So much more could be done but thank goodness for organisations like SOS. Our support for both Practical Action and SOS was reinforced that day by seeing the gravity lift and children working in jobs you wouldn't ask life prisoners to do in our country. We felt very proud to be supporting both.

We all regrouped at the top with Nic and Jamie waiting for the rest of us as we weren't as fast. My engine wasn't running on full but I loved cycling down into the valley and through the busy and familiar streets of Kathmandu. I was useless at guiding the team to Thamel as I had only ever travelled in rickshaws, buses and taxis, but we eventually pulled into the hotel where Dickie and Ro had made a huge banner draped from the balcony saying 'welcome to Kathmandu EVERESTMAX'. It was a great sight and great to see them both again. Absence makes the heart grow fonder and all that. They had had a tough time dealing with the cargo and strikes but were there with big smiles. They laughed at the chaos which was now synonymous with the logistics of Asia. Both parties were dying to exchange stories but decided to have quick showers before enjoying a big meal to celebrate the end of phase one.

It was now March 26 2006 and the climbers (Dr Andrew, Patrick, Nigel, Seb, Chris, Andre and Tarqua) were due to join us over the course of the next week. Phil had come out three weeks previously and was up in the Everest region with two friends, Martyn, our Lake District buddy, and Bruno his brother-in-law. Phil was a reluctant participant initially but, once on board, was going to do it properly so came out early to acclimatise and get mountain fit. It was a great opportunity for Martyn to finally experience the place we had talked about so much. As we had arrived in Kathmandu on time, I had arranged to meet up with Phil in Lukla where you fly to do some high altitude trekking for five days. I was now only a day or two from seeing Phil! I was very, very excited. I would look out for Martyn and Bruno who were intending to fly down to have a couple of days of rafting before they flew home. This would also leave Phil alone, so there were no distractions when I got to him.. way hey!

Our team met in the lobby having taken only 20 minutes to shower and change as we were keen to get out and celebrate. We were all in high spirits without having had a sniff of a beer yet. I had told them all about the Fire and Ice restaurant having the best pizzas in Nepal and waiters who even looked Italian. I was just recounting how this was Phil's favorite place in Kathmandu when I glimpsed a familiar face out of the corner of my eye: it was Martyn and, before I could let out a squeal of excitement, Phil stood up behind him! Well, you can only imagine how my heart missed a beat. Before I took my next breath, I was over the other side of the restaurant with my arms around Phil's neck, kissing the living daylights out of him. I remained attached to his neck while he said hi to Dom and Sarah and introduced himself to the rest of the gang. I eventually let him go and jumped on Martyn too. I was already on a high and this was just icing on the cake. Why had he come down? Answer: he didn't see the point of missing out on a couple of extra days with me for the sake of $150 when we had already been apart for so long. Good answer! Needless to say, it was a good night and Phil's arrival marked the beginning of the new, extended team.

Sonam our Sirdar and 5 times summiteer with Dom and Nic in Kathmandu

The next couple of days were spent doing admin for the mountain: we needed to find gas for cooking at the higher camps and all the necessary odds and sods. Dom, Nic and I made our first visit to Thamserku, the Nepalese company which was to be our mountain support team. They were going to be responsible for running Base Camp and Advanced Base Camp with cooks, food, tents and loos as well as a support team to set up our tents and take oxygen to the higher camps. The rest was down to us as we were self-managing as opposed to a commercially-led group. The difference is significant both in terms of cost and management.

Thamserku was an impressive outfit with large offices and, to our surprise, there was a big banner welcoming Everestmax. This was a good first impression to make us feel they cared about each team they worked with. We were invited into a posh office and met Mr Rai, who was well dressed and every inch a businessman. We were treated like respectable business people with cups of tea and documents and plans. It was a far cry from feeling and looking like a rough traveller and the novelty was fun. The meeting highlighted lots of areas that needed clarifying and we left the office feeling reassured we had good support. We were introduced to Sonam, who was to be our Sirdar (boss of the Nepalese support team). He had been to the summit of Everest five times himself and had been part of Everest expeditions in various other roles on an impressive 23 occasions. As he walked over to us, he was already half bowing with a greeting of 'Namaste'. He was about 50 years of age with a smiling, welcoming and quite simply adorable disposition. His English wasn't great, but his wealth of experience was going to be something we would turn to on the mountain and his charm and ability to manage his team an invaluable asset. We left happy.

Phil and I with Mahendra Rashmi and their children

Phil, Martin, Bruno and I went to spend the evening with Mahendra's family. All the kids were there which was great to see as they had grown so much since I had last seen them. Rashmi was as lovely as ever and the rum was out just like the old times. The poor boys had to listen to us reminisce but were very much part of the banter as they gave their first impressions of Nepal.

The next six days were free and we all had family and friends with us. Nic and Dom were joined by their girlfriends (now wives) Siobhan and Becky; Sarah had her parents and Jamie had his dad and good friend Chris; Dickie and Ro enjoyed visiting a family whom Dickie had sponsored over the last few years; Phil and I flew to Lukla to take the opportunity to walk at higher altitude for a few days. Jamie did the same with his dad and we crossed paths in the bakery where naturally we were still trying to eat as much as possible for the sake of Operation Bulk Up.

Never again will I enjoy bakeries as much as in this build-up to Everest. How often can a girl go in and eat as many cakes as she wants without feeling guilty? Consider it a joyful sacrifice.

It was great that Phil and I had some time to ourselves to catch up before immersing ourselves into the group culture. I wouldn't pretend it was all plain sailing between us initially but, by the time we returned to the group, we were back to normal, having talked through petty niggles that had arisen due to the long absence from each other. I fully expected a hard transition as Phil had been living in the van outside Glenmore Lodge. He had been working full time and his evenings were spent researching everything there was to know about Everest. Meanwhile, he would read our daily blog and discover I was having a ball with a bunch of people he didn't know. His emotions were bound to be a bit mixed; good thing was we could be honest about it all and talk as opposed to sulking or being moody.

During the later part of the biking trip in Nepal, Dom suggested that Phil would be a good number two on Everest. I initially thought this would be great and accelerate Phil's role in the team, so chatted with him about this on the trek. Phil made some very good points -the main one being he was there to make sure I came back safe and he would be unable to focus on this if he took a leadership role. He was more than happy to run sessions on skills the team needed to learn, like working with jumars and generally managing yourself on a mountain. I thought Dom should know asap so I sent him an email from Namche whilst we were still trekking.

The trekking did me so much good: I slept loads, ate loads and went high enough to boost my confidence I was going to have a good time at altitude. Phil was already fit and acclimatised. It was also really good to have some solo time, especially in

Seeing Everest and Ama Dablam from the north side in Nepal

Tengboche, where there is a world-famous monastery overlooking some of the most famous mountains in the world, including Everest. I had been here several times before but never with the knowledge we were about to attempt Everest. It is very sociable in the tea houses as you always end up talking to other trekkers about their route, plans and life. I loved telling people I was up there to climb a mountain as it generally drew admiring comments of 'wow' and 'amazing'. You could indulge adventurous aspirations as if you'd already succeeded. But this was different: I had slight reservations about mentioning we were attempting Everest if only because I didn't want to annoy the mountain by trying to be a bigger celebrity than her. She was listening and would help those who respected her.

When we got back to Kathmandu, Dom had gone for a break with Becky and left a list of jobs for us. This involved another visit by Phil, Jamie, Nigel and me to Thamserku where we were ushered into a grand boardroom for a meeting with Mr Rai. All very grown up and serious again and I fell straight back into corporate mode and led the meeting. I find it very easy to be a bossy woman when surrounded by men.

Dom was back that night and I reported in like his PA. There was lots of kit and food to organise but it was all pretty well done. Phil and I had dinner together that night as, from the following day, we were in group world again. I had ordered a special 40th birthday/thank you cake for him, having missed his birthday and wanting him to know how grateful I was to him for coming. He had made lots of sacrifices to do something he had no inclination to do. I knew he wasn't going to really enjoy it, but I was going to help him try!

The last day in Kathmandu saw the arrival of the last of the climbers and we all had dinner together that night in a traditional Nepalese restaurant. A western team of 15 and a six-strong Nepalese team joined us which meant a huge change. There were a couple of speeches to toast the success of the first phase of the expedition and celebrate the start of the next and the new team. Jamie's dad has the most contagious laugh and is a larger-than-life, happy character, but nothing could hide his anxiety about his blue-eyed boy going to Everest; Phil and I reassured him we would always have one eye on him, as he was now like my little brother. It was a good night with a good vibe between the new team of climbers and bikers, none of whom I'd met before. They were all Dom's friends and the rest of the team had met them at build-up events I wasn't around for. It was going to be fun getting to know them all.

Next day saw the cyclists, minus Dom, back on their bikes. Dickie and Ro shared the spare bike and Phil and Chris went in our support vehicle whilst the rest of the climbers stayed in Kathmandu and were going to start their journey in a couple of days. We would all meet up again at the border between Tibet and Nepal at Friendship Bridge. This gave Phil a couple of days to get to know the team as I knew them, rather than as part of a big team. He could see the rapport and team spirit and could finally be part of what he had read about for the last three months. It also gave the team the chance to get to know the man I had constantly talked about. They were all a bit disappointed he didn't have that strong Glaswegian accent I had constantly associated him with. This insight gave him time to build confidence in characters he would be happy to be with on the mountain. He took no time at all to see that running alongside the humour was sound common sense. This wasn't a team who would be reckless or put anybody else in danger. They had respect and self-awareness in abundance. Fantastic, he might even start to enjoy the journey!

Cycling out of Kathmandu was fun, but the smog and pollution in the inner city was hideous. Some of us wore face masks making us look like a cross between paranoid Japanese tourists and Star Wars extras. Only an hour into the ride, we were out into the foothills, climbing towards the border, then descending again. We were expecting a huge uphill and got an average one but the huge down certainly didn't disappoint. Bring it on! Jamie became entertainment manager at a lunch stop by trying to carry a traditional basket (strap around the head). Knowing he likes a challenge, we put a five-year-old child in it who clearly loved it. Not sure Jamie could say the same, but he was never one to disappoint a crowd.

Our home for the night was Sukete Beach Resort, owned by Equator Expeditions. Mahendra's grandparents lived on site and, as soon as I had parked the bike, I went to their home where they greeted me like a long-lost daughter. It was sensational to see them and I felt very proud to share the Equator experience with the team; they had heard so much about it and were now living it themselves. The resort has a fantastic grass roof eating area with a pool table, bar and dining area. There is a pool where you can swim and also learn to roll a kayak as the Equator kayak schools run from there. The Bhote Kosi river also runs alongside, so who could wish for more? We had a great night with a few beers as we knew there were going to only be a couple more nights over the next six to eight weeks when we could do this. The crack was good, food great and sleep simply superb, all safely cocooned from the city traffic and horns.

Next day, we used the opportunity to go rafting and Dom joined us at Sukete. Equator also uses this resort as a base camp to run its two-day rafting trips. Again, it was fantastic to share what Equator was first famous for. Mahendra was one of the first-ever Nepalese raft guides with Tiger Tops. They respected him so much that, when he said he was going to leave and start his own company, they gave him a raft. How many companies would do that?

The Bhote Kosi river is a fast, technical descent and we all had a blast. It doesn't have huge wave trains but fast rapids between large boulders which a skilful guide can negotiate with an obedient novice team. It is amazing how obedient even the most maverick person can be when faced with the choice of swimming or being in a boat in grade 4 /5 rapids. Between squeals and shrieks from the girls, there were what can only be described as manly calls from the men. Dickie, being of the larger frame, nearly squashed me on one of the rapids when we all had to jump onto my side of the raft. Being a gentleman, he tried to do it courteously. It must be one of the few 'extreme sports' where you can take complete novices. If you haven't given it a go, you really should. That night was Jamie's birthday and Chris's last night. There were toasts, jokes, cake and laughter which was a great way for Chris to spend his last night with Jamie. The electricity cut out, so pool by torchlight was fine but we also knew we were back on the bikes the next day. Dom had arrived and we were ready to go.

We reached the border town of Kodari, a steep one-street village, by 11am. We had to wait for the climbers and the trucks with all the mountain kit. We needed to go through together and waited and waited. Waiting always feels longer in a border town, probably because they are always the worst place in the whole country. They always seem dirty, unsafe, soulless places and this was no exception. The worst part was looking down into what was once a pristine river. The last 50 years has seen the introduction of plastic and non-degradable rubbish that all seems to be thrown into the river. Each year the monsoon rains come and wash a proportion of it away to cause harm further downstream. It looked and smelt disgusting. However, the people in our border town were as lovely as ever, apart from the child in the tea house we had found to spend the night. He was about six and the first child on our travels who behaved like a spoilt brat and always got attention when he wanted it. Even ever-patient Nic had to get up and walk away. He didn't bring out any maternal instincts in us girls either and merely increased the need to leave town. We knew we were going to be there for the night when the climbers turned up late in the afternoon as the border closed at 5pm. Our supplies truck arrived later that night.
We could all breathe a sigh of relief as the Moaist problem could come back at any time and hold us up for days. This would have really jeopardised our Everest attempt as we couldn't afford to arrive late and lose precious acclimatisation days.

Jamie and Nic used their time well, teaching Ro and Sarah how to win at pool. Meanwhile, Dickie teamed up with the local pool hustler in an attempt to outshine the boys, even if twice potting

Porters demonstrate organised chaos at Friendship Bridge

the black too early didn't help. At least, he was in with the local cool gang. Our kit arrived eventually and it proved to be a reasonably uneventful border crossing. Dickie was able to hold onto all his diplomatic patience and skill. The biggest challenge was transporting all the kit from one side of Friendship Bridge in Nepal to the other side in Tibet/China. This was all of 200 meters but, because no vehicle is allowed to go over, everything had to be carried across by porters. This is big business for the locals and when they saw the truck they thought it was Christmas. Literally hundreds of men, women and children formed a mob at the back of the truck while Sonam, our sirdar, organised who carried what. The mob became an orderly line as they got their goods and went across the bridge and piled them in a big heap on the other side. Organised chaos, but it worked. We were all a bit sceptical about how safe everything was as there was lots of trust involved. Anybody could have just taken their bag and walked off, knowing the contents was probably worth more than most would earn in several years. What if the bag with the oxygen masks went? We couldn't realistically have replaced them at this stage. We should have known better: we lost nothing and they all went away happy.

Having fun rafting the Bhote Kosi with Equator Expeditions

CHAPTER **FOURTEEN**

Prayer flags on high passes were always an uplifting sight in Tibet

TIBET/CHINA

Population: 2.62 million
Capital: Lhasa
Area: 1 228 400 square km
Language: Tibetan
Religion: Tibetan Buddhism with minority Muslim and Christian
Currency: Yuan
Industry: Solar energy and tourism
Agriculture: Subsistence agriculture

Who Turned The Wind Up? - Tibet

AMAZINGLY, we were now in Tibet, our final country. The cyclists carried on ahead of the climbers and had to cycle slowly as we were now approaching the world of altitude. We had gone up over 1,000 meters the previous day and today was to be another 700m. The ride started in spectacular fashion with amazing views over the gorge. We were nearly there. The whole team stayed the night in Zhangmu, where everything was very Chinese. It was in stark contrast to the Nepalese and Tibetan-style of house. It had an old-style Communist feel to it with calculated, bland, positively frills-free architecture. However, it was perfect for such a large group and kit and our Chinese liaison officer tried his best to make everything run smoothly.

We had time to meet our Nepalese team who were now travelling and eating with us; we were finally one big team. I was given the fun task of interviewing them so we could introduce them on our blog. I asked all the basics, plus one profound question: "What is your dream?" I thought it would provide an interesting contrast to us westerners. I started with Sonam: he was 43, married with one son, had summited Everest four times from the south and once from the north and been on Everest expeditions no fewer than 23 times. He had also climbed Ama Dablam, Lhotse, Pumori and Makalu among many others. His dream was to retire at 50. The Sherpa climbing team included Sonam's son,Thering, who was 21 and would be making his first ascent from the north side of Everest. He had already summited on the south side and was living his dream by climbing in the mountains. Then there was Karma, aged 31, married with children, aged eight and three, who had summited Ama Dablam but missed out on an attempt on Everest in earlier years. His dream was to summit Everest; Dorjee was 37 had summited Everest once from the north side and Ama Dablam. His dream was to be able to continue climbing mountains. Then came the all-important cook team; Njatembe (Nat) was 32, married with two children, aged four and two. In his seven years as a cook he had been on Everest six times and was already living his desired life by cooking on large expeditions. Last and by no means least, Pemba was aged 36, married with two children aged 12 and nine. He had already spent eight years as a cook on high altitude expeditions and had been on a French cooking course. His dream was to become a climber.

That evening, Dr Andrew Sutherland, general all-round hero and fab person, explained he wasn't only a climber in our team but a doctor to help with any medical problems. He was the kind of doctor any expedition would want; an endearingly eccentric character who obviously knew his stuff, completely unassuming at the same time. He was to prove one of the biggest assets to the team on the mountain, both socially and professionally.

Whether because I was suddenly surrounded by a hareem of men or Phil was there, I decided to wash my hair in cold water knowing I couldn't dry it properly as there was no fire nor heating and the temperature was very low. Despite an enthusiastic towel dry, I went to bed with half dry hair – not a good idea as I woke up feeling on the verge of a cold. I was apprehensive because I knew from experience that, if you get ill at altitude, it takes much longer than normal to recover, if at all.

Ro decided to cycle with us with Seb performing the support role for the day, taking our drink and warm clothes and meeting us at regular intervals so we could adjust to the temperature and take it steady. Rab, part of the British army expedition attempting the west ridge of Everest, went with him. He was joining his army team late and became an honorary member of ours the previous night when we'd shared a good banter. It was only a 35km day but with 1,500m of ascent. We would be cycling slowly as we were limited to how high we could go each day for the purpose of acclimatisation when over 3,000m. Textbook dictates no more than 300m to 500m per day and every third day to be a rest day. Cycling at altitude is draining so every 10km felt more like 30km.

The scenery was yet again stunning and changed dramatically from a steep gorge with precarious drop offs from the road to wide open snowscape. One section involved cycling through high banks of snow either side of the road. We were lucky as sometimes there is too much snow to clear this road so early. Altitude started to affect us after a few miles but we were in no hurry and hoping to see Seb. It was too cold to just stop and relax as we needed clothes. We were sure he wouldn't be too far away. I kept thinking positive thoughts about my head cold, willing it not to take root. We kept going and made jokes about how funny it would be if we all ended up getting hyperthermia because one of the climbers had forgotten about us. Morale was high but the temperature low. One of the Toyota landcruisers passed us with Phil inside. I got him to give us some of their drink as we were now thirsty, cold and hungry. They hadn't got much with them that was accessible as everything had been packed in other vehicles. Phil said he would get to the destination and make sure Seb turned back to give us our supplies. It was obvious he must have forgotten us or presumed 35km wasn't a problem. We hadn't taken anything with us as we thought we would have the support vehicle with us all the time. As it was, Ro and Dickie had their crown of top support team well and truly confirmed. Phil got to the next town of Nylam, found Seb straightaway and explained we all needed our kit, drink and food asap. Everything physical is exaggerated at altitude so, although only 10km from our destination, the sight of Seb and Rab brought shouts of joy. Seb thought we were going to kill rather than hug him. Rab was particularly impressed; thinking even army boys would have lost their sense of humour over this one.

The landscape is overwhelming

We arrived in Nylam and made home in another basic hotel. However, due to local knowledge, we were told about hot showers down the road and Patrick, our base camp manager, had a hairdryer! I think Patrick deserves a formal introduction: the fact he had a hairdryer was no indication of his ability to adapt to his surroundings. Patrick was absolutely essential to the success of our mountain experience. He was a complete extrovert complete with neck ties and an almost bouffant hairstyle. He was also one of the kindest and funniest people you could hope to meet. Patrick was the reason Everestmax was a coffee house and a social magnet at Base Camp. He wasn't interested in climbing it, his focus was on making new friends and helping us get the most from what he considered to be a very privileged experience. An example of his ability to integrate came in Nylam where he heard some children singing and went over to the source. It was the local school and he was invited in by the teacher to give the children an impromptu English lesson. He was like a sponge for Tibetan culture and constantly flaunted his linguistic prose by quoting phrases from his book and making every waiter, porter or child in the street listen. Every expedition needs a Patrick.

Our rest day in Nylam consisted of lots of tea, chat and Everest talk. I did several head steams to stem off the cold that was neither getting worse nor better. Dom gave a great team talk to re-enforce we were all one team now and how he saw the mountain going. He addressed issues that were obviously big to the group such as who would go up the mountain first. The strongest, most experienced climbers were the criteria he would look for and he wouldn't make special allowances for the cyclists. This was received well by everybody and accepted without question. We were all mixing well and the banter was flowing.

Doctor Andrew (The Doc) was also doing pioneering research into how the eye can be an early detector of altitude sickness by measuring the thickness of the optic nerve as we became his guinea pigs. He was using high tech, radical measuring techniques to test us at different altitudes. We discovered later there was another team doctor at Base Camp doing similar research and another version happening on the south side of Everest. So three docs were in a race to gather data and produce results and it was great to have the Doc with us so we could be involved. Between them all, they could create some really good research into early assessment and save lives.

Climbers and cyclists split next day; the climbers carried on ahead of us in the landcruisers and we would meet them in a few days at Base Camp. I had to say goodbye to Phil again but this felt nothing like the last time. What is four days compared with four months? He was very much part of the team and it was all smiles as the two teams went their separate ways.

This was also going to be our first night under canvas with Thamserku. We had a jeep and truck with us, a tad imbalanced compared with just Martha. We now had a full set of tents each as well as a dining tent; we were going posh! It also meant we were going to be fed much better as the Chinese options were limited in the morning to plastic jam and chapattis with green-looking eggs. Soups were good but there never seemed to be enough rice and low content curry. We were all struggling to eat enough. Ominously, Patrick learnt the phrase 'more food, please' on his first night in Tibet.

Luxury camping with a tent each

Cycling was hard and distances that previously took us an hour, now took three or more, including breaks. However, the scenery was becoming ever more spectacular as the road undulated with steep ups and downs. At the top of every steep section, there was always an array of prayer flags: square pieces of cotton with the Buddhist script printed in black against colours of blue, yellow, red, white and green. The belief is that, as the wind blows them, prayers are said. You see them in every aspect of Tibetan life, hanging from homes, pony and carts, the tops of high passes, anywhere the wind blows. Even if you aren't Buddhist, they add to the sense of spirituality associated with the wonderful people and landscape of Tibet. Passing through villages, children ran after us with smiles, snotty noses and rudimentary clothing. We stopped to do magic tricks, sing songs and generally enjoy their company. I had no such love of the notoriously infected dogs that appeared from nowhere; if scratched or bitten, we would have to get ourselves back to Kathmandu for a Rabies injection despite having had the inoculation. The inoculation just gives you time to get to hospital for a three-week course of further injections, so once bitten our attempt at Everest would be all over. I kept a weary eye out for all canine movement!

Biking in the vast dry plains of Tibet

We cycled another 35km, with a 630m height gain taking us to 4,240m. We hadn't planned to go above 4,100m, particularly as we had the benefit of camping in this vast area. But it was all set up by the time we cycled into camp, so we decided to stay and, touch wood, no headaches. Ro and Dickie had uncharacteristically left us for a long time without support, hence we were higher than we had agreed and I needed some more kit. I was still fighting off the head cold and was anxious. I explained to Dickie and Ro how things stood: they were no longer just our support; they were also responsible for our welfare. If we got a cold or flu, the likelihood was we wouldn't recover. I could feel my voice wobble as I was explaining. They saw my distress and really, really listened and promised to stick more closely with us. I don't think even I'd realised how much I wanted this next stage to work.

For the first time on the trip, I was actually worried about the mountain. I didn't want to arrive under par after working so hard to get there. A stupid cold brought out my underlying ambition and fears. Ro and Dickie couldn't have handled me better; not treating me like a drama queen, they respected my opinion based on my experience. Although not attempting the summit themselves, they were as much a part of the Everestmax attempt as any of the cyclists. No more needed to be said. That was the joy of having a team you could be honest with; we just learned together and move on.

Dom had been on Everest and other high altitude mountains and always had problems adjusting in the early stages. He was particularly disappointed with the height of the camp but the energy to reset it seemed greater than the potential headache to endure. He made it through the night without too much unrest - but all of us were feeling the effects.

Wandering into a local village, we found some men playing a rather gregarious game of dice. It looked fun so Jamie and I offered to be their pupils. Jamie flung the dice with admirable gusto to do westerners proud and I was equally as forceful in a lady-like way. Lord knows what we were saying but, yet again, just through interaction with sport or games we all had a great time. We gathered some spectators before long and had children dancing before they knew it. There is also now a small group of Tibetan children growing up thinking the phrase 'oh you bandit!' is very cool.

Tibetan kids are full of smiles

Next day was a beauty! We had to cycle over the Thangla Pass, an impressive 5,050m with an 800m climb before lunch with a further 400m and 5,000m to follow. We had all slept remarkably well and had a hearty breakfast, knowing it was going to be a big day. We all kept the pace slow, even Nic who became my little guardian for the day. My cough had become a hacking, chesty, noisy demonstration to gain me loads of sympathy even though I was feeling much better. However, it only took a 200m climb for my headache to kick in. If your chest is bad, you will not optimise on oxygen. Nic offered me his iPod, dosed me with Ibrufen and stuck close. What a sweetie. All the team was great and supportive of each other.

The top of each pass was absolutely stunning and the landscape had taken on an even more majestic form with snow-capped mountains to the north and vast expanses of undulating barren hillsides. There were eagles and wild horses as well as butterflies that must be the hardest in the world as we hadn't seen anything resembling a flowering plant for them to live off in over two days! We were able to stop and take respite from the cold and uphill in a local Tibetan tea shop offering us hot, sweet, milky tea. We were all tempted to stay for the night in domestic smoky bliss. Carpets on the seats, a hot dung fire iron stove in the centre of the room, with a constant supply of tea being boiled on top while the daughter used her traditional wooden churn to make butter in the corner – just wonderful. But, no, we needed to cycle up another hill in strong wind at altitude and get some more photos taken with the prayer flags while pretending to look comfortable!

We managed nearly 60km that day before spotting a yellow tented campsite in the near distance. We could almost smell the sweet tea and biscuits waiting on the table, courtesy of a smiling Pemba, our cook and camp co-ordinator. It was a great way to

Our first sight of Everest

end the day and chat continued over dinner. We knew there were only a couple of days to go before our small team would become one big team. We were all becoming nostalgic about biking already and, although excited about the mountain phase, would have been happy to carry on cycling all the way to Australia! Whatever we had, it worked: we knew when somebody just needed space or needed boosting; everybody pulled their weight and the overriding positive energy made every day a good one. The mountain was a bonus, not a necessity. Getting to Everest Base Camp was going to be success in itself; one of us getting to the summit would be phenomenal. Otherwise, we had still enjoyed an amazing journey we could be proud of forever.

Next was another landmark day as we all were stopped in our tracks by the sight of the big lady herself. We had just cycled for a few hours along the valley floor (4,400m) before we turned into a new river valley and stopped. We saw Mt Everest as a team for the first time after three and a half months and 7,800km. We took photos, talked about promised cups of tea at the top and general nonsense, but underlying it all was a huge flutter of nerves. We were nearly in a position to take the mountaineering phase seriously... oh boy!

We cycled on through a village called Tingri, the nearest proper village to Everest and a hell hole renowned for rabid dogs. I cycled through with a stick in my hand to make myself feel brave in case any snarling frothy-mouthed canine came near. I had heard too many stories about the dogs from this village and couldn't get through fast enough. We made it several miles outside town and turned off down a dirt track where we saw our camp set up and ready. We were really starting to feel like colonial gentry as nothing was too much trouble for our Nepalese team. All we had to do was cycle, eat, drink, sleep and let our bodies adapt to the altitude. It was hard but we were all doing well. There was a stream running by our camp and we took the opportunity while the sun was out to have a good old fashioned wash. The water was still freezing and it was fun to listen to the different squeals and guess who was washing. Even our macho team of men let out a little whimper or two.

Then came the hardest day on bikes we had experienced in a long time. Starting full of optimism with a wonderful sunrise, this was meant to be the penultimate day of cycling. We had been told it would be about 40km max, traversing the mountains and then a slight ascent before the big and final climb next day – technically accurate but not taking into account the weather.

We started in mild wind and sunny conditions, then, from nowhere, the wind started and with that came the dust and sand. We all had to wear our buff scarves, hats and glasses to stop the pain of the sand on our faces and eyes. We were cycling so slowly it didn't really matter if we closed our eyes. We took nearly one and a half hours to cover eight km! Finding a broken down wall, we all took refuge. We boosted each other's love of pain and adverse conditions and managed to get back on the bikes. The wind was getting stronger and I can't really put into words how uncomfortable it was - which is a shame as this is a book so I'd better give it a go! Imagine yourself on your bike cycling into town but stuck behind a vehicle towing a wind blaster on full speed with a pile of sand in front of it blowing into your face; add in the fact it is winter with super cold temperatures; on top of all that, altitude didn't help as we were exerting all our energy to peddle as well as being in a sand battle. Does that sound like fun?

Much needed Tibetan tea house that gave superb shelter from the wind and great tea

We saw a local home in the middle of nowhere. The prayer flags drew us in and again we took refuge in another wonderful and welcoming Tibetan home. No sooner were we inside than we had hot sweet tea in front of us. We were worlds away from the outside and loving it in a Tibetan tea house accustomed to hosting western groups on their way to base camp. Two ladies were on a traditional loom making blankets and we went into the kitchen to enjoy the heat from the fire and the smoky atmosphere that tends to take you back in time.

There was a young man with his young son: he was a proud man in his twenties but looked more weathered and had the classic male headdress of a ponytail braided with red ribbon neatly circled up on his head. They reminded us we were visiting a country where people lived from the land in some of the world's hardest conditions and didn't see it as a problem. Cycling for a few days in these conditions was hard; living there full time much, much harder. These people need very little: they were historically predominantly yak herders, living from the milk and meat and skins. They would grow anything they could in the short summer months at this altitude. They didn't wash much because of the freezing temperatures but are incredibly hardy to the elements. Life was a game of survival, yet they had their religion, festivals, family and healthy approach to life to make it a place I felt privileged to visit.

We prized ourselves away from this comfortable cocoon back into the wind. We started well but the wind and sand were relentless. We weren't on roads but dirt tracks and sand. Our support truck had gone ahead so we had no choice but to press on to the point where Nic and I were blown off our bikes. We all ended up having to push our bikes the last five km into camp and Ro and Dickie were out there shouting support. We were absolutely exhausted cycling 28km in eight hours! Snow started to fall as we

A Tibetan man with the traditional hair style

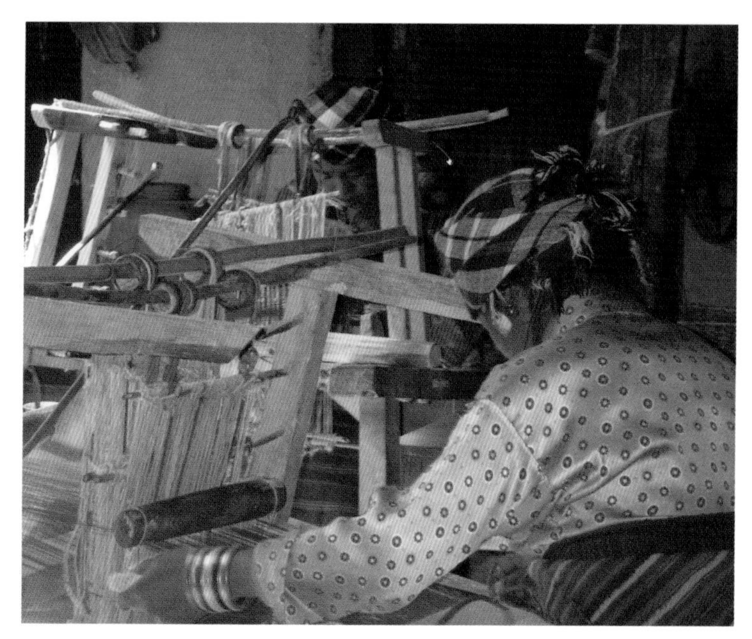

Traditional weaving is very skilful and beautiful

The higher, colder and windy final stretch made cycling harder than ever

were tucking into our first cuppa so we were lucky. The Nepalese team decided it would be safer to sleep in the truck rather than a tent. They had re-enforced our tents with heavy stones but it would have taken an earthquake to stop us sleeping.

We were ready for an easier day; well, as easy as it gets at over 4,700m in Tibet. We woke to sunshine, clear skies and low wind and, even more importantly, no more snow had fallen. The first half of the day was uphill, with a head wind and breathtaking scenery (no pun intended). We had to cross several flowing streams, knowing wet feet in these conditions is asking for trouble. Nic McSlick led the way with a clean run and set the standard. Due to a mix of pure skill and desire not to fall in, we followed suit to impress our Tibetan liaison officer and Nepalese team. They still couldn't quite get why we were insisting on cycling the whole way. Come to that, did anybody?

There were also frozen fields of ice on which I managed to do an elegant dismount. However, a four-ton truck took the limelight by getting stuck in soft mud with a bit of ice for good measure. Fortunately, the Everestmax super hero team came to the rescue and, with a dodgy tow rope and brute force, we managed to pull it out. These challenges keep the days interesting. Another point of interest arrived with Jamie claiming the highest puncture at 5,050m... another record for Everestmax?

To our surprise and immense pleasure, we were given 15km of off-road downhill. Fantastic! At lunch we were struggling to eat, never mind be energetic. However, with the wind behind us, adrenalin and some big 'yee haaaas', we were off. Sarah had never really done off-road and took to it like a duck to water. The boys flew off and told me they were awesome and I allowed Dom his manhood by letting him overtake so I could have the route to myself... how kind of me.

Dickie, ever the communications Guru even in Tibet, went off to Base Camp to update them we were running a day late and get some more gas for cooking. We camped less than 30km from Base Camp…so close! The final day's cycling was suitably hard but it would have felt wrong any other way. The first two kilometers were straight back into such strong headwinds we were again forced to push our bikes. It was bizarre that the only time any of us pushed our bikes throughout the whole trip was in the last 60km. The wind eventually relented to the point we could ride again and we made it to Rongbok Monastery only eight km from Base Camp. We had a photo session with a backdrop of Everest and the spiritual landmark of Buddhism in the foreground and a bunch of westerners trying to look like we belonged in the picture. Posing felt great, but exhausting.

After such a big ask, we had to go and have lots of sweet tea while Ro and Dickie went ahead to warn the others we were coming. If it wasn't for it being the last eight km of our epic journey, we would have all voted to stay much longer drinking tea in our very cosy tea house. However, history was calling. We mounted our bikes and rode the last stretch of switch backs. First person we saw was an enthusiastic Doc, who was the look out. We all closed in so we could ride the last few kilometers as a team. We were all in a pack when we saw the climbers holding the Everestmax banner and Dickie and Ro. Dickie gave the welcome speech as we were coming to a stop. We were emotional as we got off our bikes and all the bikers and Ro and Dickie hugged each other in turn before moving onto the welcome committee, including Phil, who respectfully stood back until we had had our moment.

What a moment, too, after 8,000km, 112 days on the road and eight countries. We were still a superb team. As we walked into Base Camp, I asked for one more team photo before we merged into the bigger team. It was a great feeling to like everybody so much and finish this part of the journey wanting to do more with the same people. That is a big compliment.

I had often contemplated why our team was so successful and always came up with the same reasons. We were all so different and there were no egos or sense of oneupmanship in anything other than biking at a fun level. Otherwise, everything was a team goal: whenever anyone did something particularly well, it was celebrated; if things went wrong, lessons were learned and we moved on.

A dominant 'we can do' attitude drowned out any moments of doubt and bolstered much-needed courage when the going was tough. We allowed for each others' quirky differences by dealing with them at a personal level and never allowing them to become a team issue. We all had moments when individuals were winding us up but not once did I see any tension being brought to the team as we all had such mutual respect. The magic of a range of different strengths and personalities should never be underestimated.

Dom was a superb leader: we all supported his approach and hard work and he knew he had a team to rely on. None of us were shy of hard work, made a drama out of a crisis or, more importantly, a drama out of trivia. The result was a superb team and a successful end to stage one of an overland epic.

The next two big challenges were upon us, with Mt Everest being the obvious one. The other was to incorporate new members with different personal goals into our team with the common focus of an expedition journey.

CHAPTER **FIFTEEN**

A yak herder and his yak

Two Teams Become One - Everest Base Camp

EVEREST Base Camp (BC) was to be our headquarters for the next six weeks. We would be going up and down via Interim Camp, Advanced Base Camp (ABC), North Col and Camp One to try to acclimatise before making a summit attempt. We would then come back to BC to recharge at a relatively low altitude of 5,400 meters. This was pretty much the same for all expeditions.

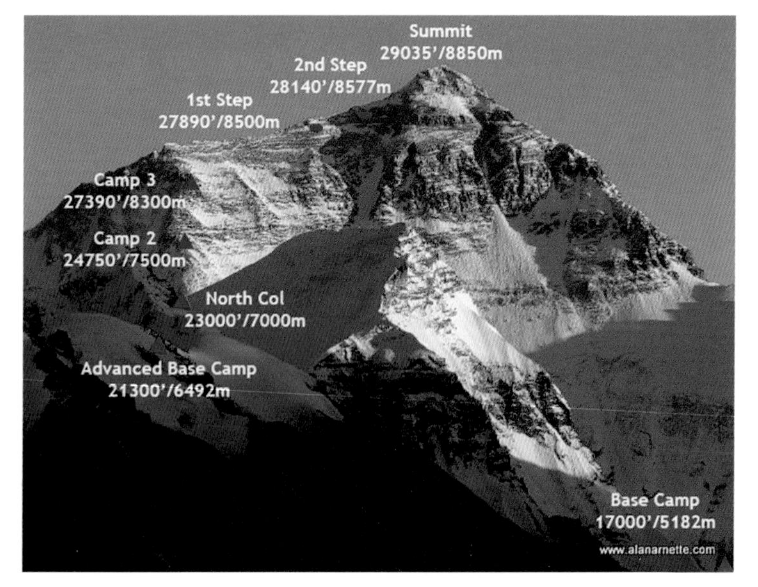

Everest Route Map courtesy of Alan Arnette (Reproduction prohibited without permission).

BC was well and truly established by the time we cycled in. The scene was, if you forgive the pun, very 'tents': a great dining tent to seat us all at one long table. Thank goodness for the kitchen tent where Nat and his team created fantastic food in ridiculously rudimentary conditions; three cheers for The North Face tent allowing each of us to sleep in what felt like luxury even though the two drop hole toilet tents and shower tent were more practical than beautiful. You knew the toilet was engaged if the shovel was lying flat.

Our team base camp

The shower tent worked by boiling a bucket of water with a tap at the bottom and hanging it from the top of the open air tent; oh and nearly forgot - the 'chill out' North Face dome tent was the best of all. In here, we watched movies, played cards, read books and generally chilled and chatted. Our green tent we had used on our bike journey became the communications tent with the generator and satellite phone as well as bike storage. That night we all ate together and toasted the end of the bike journey and the beginnings of the climbing team. We were one big team now. The cyclists made a conscious effort not to be bike bores and integrate. I had Phil as my new focus so it was even easier for me.

The next six weeks were so different. We were no longer on the move every night, seeing different views every day or doing lots of daily aerobic exercise. We did, however, continue our weekly weigh-in and heart rate checks. Jamie, Dom and Dickie had lost lots of weight on the bike ride; Sarah and I had obviously taken the 'bulk up' advice to heart and managed to put weight on cycling over 8,000km! How wrong is that? The chart below gives the key stage weights of the team including their final weight at the end of the expedition.

Who Lost Weight	Dead Sea Weight (Kg)	Base Camp Weight (Kg)	Finish Weight (Kg)	Total Lost (Kg)
Dickie	111	103	88	23
Dom	99	88	74	25
Jamie	80	76	67	13
Nic	89	88	86	3
Ro	60	58	55	5
Sarah	69	72	64	5
Pauline	64	65	57	7

Phil and I had time to catch up and share feelings and ideas. At this point, we had no plan how to approach the mountain from the point of view of 'us' as a team. We hadn't discussed it with Dom either. As far as he was concerned, the most experienced and well acclimatised were the criteria to pick who went first and when. This was fine with us. However, the whole point of Phil coming was to ensure I came home as well as giving him a good crack at the summit. We decided that, as long as he was on the mountain and in contact, we shouldn't be shy of climbing separately if the event arose. We couldn't plan any further as neither could guarantee we would be ok above 6,800m as that had been the highest we had climbed on Ama Dablam. Phil had spent time with the other climbers now and, although he liked them as individuals, was more aware than ever of the lack of experience. Many had been guided up mountains or winter climbs; not a problem in itself, but being guided means you don't have to make your own decisions.

This wasn't a guided trip - people had signed up to be part of a team who could make their own decisions. Who went with who was therefore very important.

Phil was alarmed at how little some knew about the route. One of the climbers asked who he was going to rope up with. Phil replied: "Nobody. It's a fixed line to the top." How could he have no idea about such a basic fact? In contrast, Phil had researched every step. He had talked to people who had done our route in detail, bringing with him top tips and having read all the information available. He couldn't understand how anybody could do this without having the same level of self preservation. Alarm bells were ringing louder than ever. He voiced his concerns but wasn't going to make any judgements until he had time on the mountain. Meanwhile he had been nicknamed Tigger as he had acclimatised well due to coming out early and trekking in Nepal. He would go off and walk the ridges around Base Camp and ask others if they wanted to come but the new arrivals were finding it hard enough energy-wise just to make it between tents. He was pleased he had taken the extra four weeks in Nepal, although that wasn't an option for many of the others due to family or work commitments.

Our first full day in Base Camp was a great way to start. The local Lama, from the Rongbuk Monastery, had been booked to come and join our team at our camp to perform a pujah ceremony: a Buddhist service to ask for the blessing of the gods on our expedition. The Sherpa team wouldn't have felt comfortable doing the mountain without this very important ceremony. They had spent time preparing an altar by our camp with offerings and incense. Offerings covered a wide range of needs for modern worship such as Bells Whiskey and Coca Cola as well as axes, crampons and mountain equipment. We all gathered

Our superb Sherpa team Pemba Karma Dorjee Thering, Nat and a guest

The Puja ceremony is very important to the Sherpa team. It gave us time to reflect

around the offerings as the Lama chanted and rang a bell whilst throwing tsampa (flour made from barley) over the altar. We all used it as a time of private reflection on things to come. An agnostic would have found it hard not to feel something spiritual. We were all in our own worlds but together at the same time. The sincerity of the ceremony was followed by a party of drinking the local fire water chang (barley beer) and the Lama smearing tsampa on our faces. The Sherpa team definitely saw this as a final blast before their work really kicked in and, although they did us the courtesy of staying for a drink or two, it wasn't long before they were off to their own private area to enjoy the rest of the day together.

Our Base Camp was one of many. We reckoned there must have been about 1,000 people altogether in this large flat expanse of sand-coloured dusty nothingness, flanked by hills of equally barren nothingness. It was an international gathering of varied abilities and climbing styles. The British army had made Base Camp with the rest of us, although they were attempting the West Ridge rather than the North Ridge route. Rab came and saw us when he was down and we made friends with another couple of lads too. We wouldn't see them other than in Base Camp as their route meant they split from our trail and made their higher camps away from us all. I knew some of the team personally: Dave, my ex, was one of the leaders as well as Dave Bunting, who had come and attempted Pumori with his army team when I was working in Nepal. We had organised his support team. Unfortunately, I never got to see either of them although we sent a couple of emails. In one, I asked a favour as an ex-military person, ex-girlfriend, ex-support co-ordinator: could they give us the weather as they had the means to get it straight from the best teams in the UK? The answer was disappointing as it said they were happy to give information as long as we reciprocated with equally good information. I was a bit thrown by this. We got the feeling that maybe it was protocol and outside their control, got over it and maintained good relations throughout. The Doc even went and visited their camp one to do some more research on their team and was made very welcome.

One of the most important teams at BC was Himalayan Experience, a firm owned and run by Russell Brice. Nic had managed to get a meeting with him in Kathmandu where he had agreed to help us with oxygen if we ran out. That was really reassuring to know. Russell was famous for his company and had a Discovery team film crew with him, making a documentary on the commercial ascents of Everest. He has a huge success rate and follows fairly strict criteria before he allows people to pay him obscene amounts of money to guide them to the top. I don't think there is anything wrong with commercial climbing up Everest, as long as people like Russell are running the company. His clients accept they have to have been on at least one big mountain (over 7,000m) and that he makes all the decisions on Everest. This helps people who have the determination to do Everest but lack the technical knowledge to climb without putting other climbers in danger by making mistakes that force others to come to their rescue. The danger comes from outfits which let anybody pay them to do the ground support so they can go up 'at their own risk and in their own style'. These are the people who cause the biggest problems; they make mistakes and the Sherpas and sensible climbers have to deal with the consequences. The moral has to be: if you don't have the skills to do it independently or be with people who will make the right decisions for you, pay somebody to make those decisions for you! Our team didn't have a great profile of technical mountaineering decision makers but enough to make judgments for the inexperienced – yet we were far from ideal.

Russell Brice was also the man who every year sent his Sherpas to fix a line[13] of over 2,000m from the bottom of the first wall to the summit of Everest. Russell has summitted Everest five times up various routes that make the North Ridge route look like a walk in the park so he gets respect as a mountaineer, not just a commercial guru. He asks for $100 per climber from other teams to use the lines. It is hard to believe some people don't pay yet are quite happy to use them as $100 is nothing compared with the overall cost. We had no hesitation in going over and thanking him and paying our dues. He was so well established he had fixed water pipes into his camp for running water to the kitchen. He was also a big employer of local Tibetan people and treated them like his other family. Sounds all warm and cuddly from this, I know, but he had a bit of a frosty reputation. Fortunately, this was a feature I never saw.

Some other teams in the camp were French, Irish, Russian and Spanish. Patrick, our red coat rep, went round introducing himself and making friends. The Everestmax chill tent was open house and the Doc was another reason we were so popular. The Doc never said no and helped so many people with varying degrees of AMS[17], coughs, colds and eye problems. The Everest Circus, as it is sometimes called, can get a bad reputation but people like the Doc and Patrick help you see the best in people. Friendships and casual acquaintances forged at Base Camp with other teams were to pay dividends for everybody later in the expedition. What you put in is what you get out, as they say.

Phil had promised to run a workshop on how to use jumars,[12] work on fixed lines and give top tips on high altitude

Doctor Andrew Sutherland our medical hero and entertainer

Patrick Worthington our Base Camp Manager and social guru

There would only be a couple of days for the whole team to be together from now on. This was the only opportunity to get a team photo with Everest in the background and would act as a 'before and after' image. None of us knew what was coming and who would be coming back fulfilled, frustrated or elated. We wanted to capture the excitement in a team shot. As we cheered for our photo, the first of the yaks were arriving, ready to load up our gear to transport it to Advanced Base Camp (ABC) at 6,400m.

mountaineering. The whole team gathered in the dining tent as the wind was a distraction outside. Many of the team had never seen a jumar; never mind used one so this was invaluable. It also gave Phil the chance to say he was there to help if they had other questions. He was very approachable which made it easy for people to go and ask questions and get tips. He proved very useful throughout the expedition and was definitely marked out as the one who really knew what he was talking about when it came to mountaineering. This was good for him and the team as he felt acknowledged and they felt they had a help point. The only limitation to this was that we would all be splitting up to take our own time to acclimatise at different camps and wouldn't see many members of the team for long stretches at a time.

The yak looks like a long haired, stocky cow with horns born to carry. They live more comfortably above 3,000m and all have bells around their necks. Although charming at first, this can really get to you when they are dinging away outside your tent at night. Their Tibetan handlers look just as hard and weathered. They drink the now notorious Tibetan tea which Phil is convinced makes them as hard as nails as there is no way you can drink it without being completely insensitive to taste, smell and after-effects. Their skin is like a wrinkled leather no amount of moisturiser could repair. Their dress is even hard with some wearing yak skin trousers and everything is thick, old and dirty. They make us look like wimps in our duvet jackets, gortex and everything else. This is their home and they survive by being self sufficient in adverse conditions. They are inspiring in their simplicity and seem to have a good crack as a team when driving the yak train (term used for a group of yaks carrying kit). They look after their yaks well and don't load them with any more than 35kg, which is good for both business and welfare.

We had taken time to pack everything back in Kathmandu so everything was labelled for ABC or Base Camp (BC). The fragile kit was packed in blue heavy plastic barrels so the yaks couldn't cause damage as they bumbled their way along. Karma, one of our climbing Sherpas, called me over and said: "Small problem didi." We were about to do our first yak haggling. The yak handlers insisted we needed nine more yaks than we had paid for. It was like being party to a trade union talk. We called Mr Rai having agreed to the extra yaks after an hour's haggling. This should have been covered by Thamserku but we had to do our best to make sure nobody was getting ripped off. However, we soon learnt that yak business is big business now and they have set fees and ways of working that are in fact reasonable and predictable. Hats off.

When the yak team was ready, six of our team were also ready to go to Interim Camp, halfway to ABC. The journey between BC at 5,200m and ABC at 6,400m was too big a jump in altitude and was also 22km away. So the practice was to go to a makeshift camp where there were no cooks, just a few tents and a rough tent where the team could cook themselves food and boil water. The yak train was going all the way to ABC with the Sherpa team to set up ABC camp. Phil was one of the team going. There was excitement in the air as they went off with the yaks as this was the beginning of the approach. We watched them off and were looking forward to how they would get on. Their intention was to go to ABC and come down again or see how they were getting on. They would also set up the satellite phone from ABC so we could be in contact. Although I had lots of mountaineering experience by then, the ABC was a personal unknown. I hadn't seen any pictures so it was all down to imagination. Most of the Everest pictures I had seen had been from the south with the Khumbu ice fall. It now seems weird to think how naïve I was. What could be so different to any other mountaineering camp?

All the Everestmax team had stayed at Base Camp with Patrick and the Doc. Dom had taken a turn for the worse. He always knew he would struggle in the early stages of acclimatisation but had hoped our approach would help. The Doc was paying close attention to him and the moment of truth came in the chill tent. There was just Dom, the Doc and me in there as the Doc said that Dom was too ill to stay at this altitude. He was developing pulmony oedema[11]. Dom wasn't surprised and handled the news with his typical self-contained sarcasm, trying to make light of it. He said it was disconcerting going to sleep and hearing every breath gurgling in his lungs. I knew he was gutted and this wasn't good news for the man who had conceived the whole expedition. He could still attempt the mountain but the odds are already against you when you are fit, never mind having to recover from a serious lung condition.

I needed to organise a jeep to come up to our camp and collect Dom to take him down as he wasn't strong enough to walk. He could barely make it from his tent to the chill tent. I had bumped into Anil, the camp manager of another team who had been a trekking guide for me at Equator. I had heard he was in town and went to his camp as Sonam wasn't around and I needed some local advice on how best to get a jeep. He couldn't have been more welcoming or more helpful. It was great to see him and he treated me like a VIP in front of his team saying I was 'the best boss'. We had got on very well in Nepal. We both went down to the 'Tented Village'. This isn't an official village; but literally a 'village' that comes to life this time every year to service the needs of the Everest expeditions and tourists who now come to visit BC. There are lots of tents selling things like hats, gloves, socks, beans and noodles and with hot sweet tea, beer, soft drinks and Tibetan tea for those who can stomach it. They have makeshift cafes with carpets on benches and dung burning stoves, plus horse and carts for the tourists coming up from Rongbuk Monastery. Anil took me to the TMA (Tibetan Mountaineering Association) and they said a jeep would be there. I thanked Anil and walked the 20 minutes back to camp to tell them it was on its way. After an hour it still hadn't come so I jumped on my bike and cycled back down to the village. They told me it had already gone but another one was soon available. I was familiar with this style of approach ie say what she wants to hear, even if it isn't the truth. I explained in more emphatic body language than ever I needed a jeep as my friend was very ill. They could see I was now getting upset and it worked; being a girly is sometimes just what it needed in this environment. The jeep arrived and Dom and the Doc went down to Rongbuk to settle him in for a steady recovery. The Doc left him and came back up for the night.

That afternoon, Ro and I went for an acclimatisation walk up along the ridges surrounding camp as we could get as high as 5,600m. I didn't want to go to Interim Camp until I had done short and high walks more productive than doing 11km going all the way to Interim for the same height gain. Ro and I always have a laugh and it was good spending time with her again. I always took the mickey out of her and Dickie getting on so well and making her promise Sarah and I would be her bridesmaids. He had now lost loads of weight and cut quite a dashing figure!

The tent village and tourist pony and carts just below Base Camp

When we got back to camp, Ro, Patrick and I went over to Russell's again and asked for some tips on measuring our oxygen tanks and attaching the regulators. Russell was great and did a couple of demos for us on our bottles, discovering one was faulty. It was going to be worth testing all of them before sending them up to higher camps. Patrick fell in love with Russell's camp and also got pally with some of the camera team. He is such a 'darling' anyway, fitting in easily and bringing back tales of dining tents and video rooms to keep us enthralled.

That night Patrick, inspired from his time with the celebrities, brought out his guitar to the chill tent and had us in stitches as he started a sing-a-long, making one up as he went along. Alan, from the army team, joined us with his guitar and his songbook they had compiled for their team (I still use a copy). I was able to bring out my harmonica again and play along in a raw kind of way. Much to Dom's distress, it was filmed and made it to the final cut of the Everestmax DVD. He hated my harmonica and now it was captured on film and audio for posterity. You can't keep a good thing down.

Doc went down to visit Dom next day and the news wasn't good: it had started to affect his eyes and he needed to go further down and have a bottle of oxygen with him. Dom went as far down as Tingri and stayed in a small dingy room with his bottle of oxygen unable to do anything but sleep. We were all worried as we wanted our leader back and well. There was a very mellow atmosphere over dinner that night as we all recognised Dom might not be able to recover enough to climb or even come back. We didn't give up on him but kept realistic so we could help him cope if that was the end of his expedition. He was the first one to be seriously ill from altitude but was he the first of many? Nobody had even made it to ABC yet.

I went to bed wondering how Phil was as I wasn't feeling 100 per cent myself. I was trying to drink the recommended three to five liters of fluid a day and not rush around but the body tells you when it isn't happy. We hadn't heard from them. He had planned on staying at Interim Camp for two nights, although the others only wanted to stay one. Having heard nothing, we presumed they had opted for the second night. They didn't have to all stay together; we were at the unpredictable mercy of open planning.

I was stirred from my sleep by the gentle sound of a yak bell. As consciousness dawned on me, the bell got louder and louder and I realised it was Dickie using Patrick's newly acquired memorabilia as a wake-up call for those of us at Base Camp. Oh, the sense of humour. The Doc had energy to spare and cycled down to the village where he made a new Tibetan friend by letting him have a go on the bike. He was a bit surprised when the man offered him a silver ring to say thanks and tried to explain a handshake was enough. He was reading Seven Years in Tibet and was finding it hard to distinguish between genuine cultural generosity and custom described in the book and exploitation of Everest 'visitors'. It isn't wrong for the Tibetans to think all westerners are loaded. They know how much the flight ticket costs just to get from the UK or USA. That cost alone is more than most of them will see in a lifetime of working. You can't blame them for trying but, in this case, it was a genuinely kind gesture. They exchanged gifts; a bracelet for the Doc and a pair of gloves for his new Tibetan friend.

Jamie, Nic and the Doc left for Interim Camp next day but I wasn't feeling ready to go yet. There was no rush and I hadn't felt good the day before so was happy to wait another day or so. Sarah, Dickie and Ro were the same. Patrick was enjoying himself far too much at Base Camp to go anywhere. Not long after the boys had left, Andre and Seb arrived back from ABC looking like they had just been through a big and not necessarily good experience .They had the look of 'glad to be alive'; exhausted from having walked for more than six hours over broken and challenging terrain from ABC that morning. We gave them lots of tea, food and emotional support and it looked like they'd had a traumatic experience. They had all stayed at Interim Camp for the two nights as they were exhausted after the walk and were definitely struggling to adjust to the altitude and even colder conditions. They had also experienced their first periodic breathing which often happens at altitude when you go to sleep. Typically, three to five deep breaths will be followed by a couple of very shallow breaths or even a complete pause in breathing which usually lasts around 5 to 15 seconds. This may end with a gasp that wakes the individual or their sleeping companions! This had obviously scared them. They were both fathers, with Andre having had his second child only weeks before leaving for Nepal. Their remote, precarious location meant help couldn't come fast; helicopter evacuation wasn't an option and the back of a yak the only ambulance. On their way out, they had already seen one American climber on the yak ambulance due to a really bad chest condition. They needed a morale and security boost by coming back to BC. They were also brother-in-laws and felt the bond of family.

That night, we had our first contact with ABC on the satellite phone. Phil sounded a bit low but it wasn't the medium to explain why. He was going to come back to BC next day. Tarqua wasn't well and was resisting encouragement to go down. We had already seemed to hit lots of mental and physical obstacles and only half the team had made it to ABC. This was totally normal. This was altitude and, if you are ready for it, you are less scared and better prepared. Many of the team hadn't been at real altitude before and it was bound to be a scary experience. This was totally normal and we had all willingly signed up for it.

It snowed all that night but I slept really well which was good as sleep cures so many ills. I knew Phil was intending to come down but wasn't sure when. We had started a routine of a 9am and 5pm check-in via the satellite phone. Phil's morning call sounded much happier but Tarqua sounded like he was having problems. He had a chat with the Doc and was pretending he wasn't as bad as he looked. Maybe, they would stay another day.

BC had completely transformed from a dry sandy environment to a snow-bound winter scene. Ro and I joined Patrick on one of his social visits and we met the French team of Caroline and Jacque Letrange and their friend Rudolph. They had a small and well kept dining tent with a table for about six. How perfect. Caroline was everything people don't imagine a mountaineer to be: beautiful, petite and elegant even in a duvet jacket. Husband Jacque was a larger-than-life character who was tall, slim and athletic and again had that French chic about him. Rudolph was their friend and obviously part of their extended family. We had a ball for several hours as Jacque insisted we all spoke in French. They offered us cheese and biscuits and Caroline, a professional photographer, set her camera up in the tent to capture the atmosphere. I only wished Phil was here to benefit from this kind of time - just meeting and enjoying people without focusing totally on the mountain experience. The people were the mountain experience. I had also just met the only other married couple climbing together so we could share our own unique emotions.

Back at our camp, Jamie, Nic and the Doc returned from Interim Camp exhausted yet in good spirits. Ro and I decided to make flapjack for the team as a boost and good energy food. The food from the Nepalese team was fantastic but taste buds have specific needs and just don't find certain things appetising. Flapjack hit the spot for everybody.

We got our 5pm call and Tarqua had a more serious chat with the Doc. He needed to come down. Then we were told Phil had already left to come down on his own at noon. I was shocked as we had agreed not to travel between camps on our own. He was breaking our own rule. Why? I became unsettled and wanted to go and meet him but didn't know if he would stop at Interim due to the weather. Also it was getting dark and conditions weren't exactly friendly. It was too big an ask for someone to come with me. I totally trusted Phil in the mountains - he would never do anything stupid and would be even more careful walking on his own. He does worse walks in the Cairngorms all the time. I went into the chill tent with everyone after dinner and decided to leave it another hour before having a team chat about whether we should go and look for him or presume he stayed at Interim. Andre and Seb had taken six hours and Phil should be about the same or even less. He had been gone five already.

We were all watching a DVD when the door rustled and there was Phil. I jumped up and couldn't get outside fast enough. Sarah grabbed the camera and I grabbed Phil. He hugged me with one of those heart-felt hugs. What was wrong? Phil didn't want the camera on him so I asked Sarah to stop. We had a hot cup of tea and got him some food from the kitchen.
He confirmed Seb and Andre's words that it was much colder and more uncomfortable at ABC without going into detail. When he had warmed up and settled down, we went back to our tent for a chat. He was quite emotional about it. He said: "I was up at ABC with a bunch of people I don't know. I was thinking I don't want to do any of this without Pauline. Why am I here and she is down there? We go together or not at all." That was great for me to hear. There was no other person I would rather be on the mountain with than Phil but it took this for us to accept we weren't going to compromise ourselves. If Dom sent one of us up first, we would say no thanks and wait for a later slot, so we could go together and not compromise the other team members' opportunities. Great.

Being surrounded by a group of people not coping emotionally or physically had really made Phil question the point of his trip. Seb, Andre and Chris had been freaked out by the periodic breathing. Chris woke Phil up in the middle of the night in a panic as he thought he was going to die. Also, Andre and Seb were disgruntled at Interim Camp that Phil had only boiled enough water for them to have a couple of liters of water each. They hadn't noticed he had been up since the early hours just boiling water for everybody. Their approach to the mountain was very different to his. He was coming on a mountaineering expedition and they were more used to being guided and catered for. They weren't bad people, just inexperienced at this style of mountaineering. This was frustrating. If we (Phil and I) were together, we would work well as a team and be able to help the others. As two singles, you would have missed our strength. That was a turning point for us and we were inseparable from then on. Phil had a lie-in as he was tired physically and emotionally. Altitude certainly highlights emotions for whatever reason. The snow was deeper but that didn't stop Nic and me who were developing a routine of early tea in the tent.
I enjoyed our chats but that morning we had a more sobering one. I explained Phil's conclusions and we agreed the team was lacking emotional and technical preparation. However, we also agreed this was all surmountable due to the team's willing and agreeable nature.

Base Camp was basically a slow way of life: We did normal everyday things but did them all slowly. Let's start at the beginning of the day when you are told to drink lots to stay hydrated in this dry and oxygen-strapped environment. The only negative is the night-time toilet expedition which tended to be my first wake-up call. In the dark, I would reach for my pee bottle and (turn away now, boys) my 'she wee'. This is a fantastic device designed to allow women to pee into a bottle and, having mastered the art, write our names in the snow! It was fantastic because it meant we were spared having to get out of our tent and get fully dressed and booted just to make it to the toilet tent. This was enough to interrupt the best sleep in the world.
Once snuggled back in your sleeping bag, you dose off for a few more hours and refuse to get up until the sun hits your tent and

starts to warm things up. At night in early April, the temperature dropped to -15 C. That meant everything in the tent that wasn't next to your body froze - toothpaste, water, socks et al. However just 20 minutes of sun and you could happily get out of your bag and simply add another few layers that could be peeled off during breakfast as it warmed up. Once in the dining tent, we would start with hot Tang (powdered orange juice), chocolate, tea or coffee. Nat offered a cooked breakfast of porridge or omelette and toast, depending on your appetite. We needed to eat and drink now as the mountain would test all the energy reserves we could muster.

After breakfast we got ready for the 9am check-in with ABC which was always good for a discussion. There weren't always many constructive things to do afterwards so we had to find ways to entertain ourselves between acclimatisation walks. Our skills were developing with Patrick becoming the undisputed master at card games as the others just looked on. I practised the guitar just enough to avoid alienating the rest of the team. We all did some reading and somehow managed to keep the chat going on all sorts of topics, a good proportion of which didn't involve climbing Everest. There were always emails and photos to sort and washing from a small tin bowl was a full half-day activity. Nat boiled water for us which was a job in itself, then it all came down to timing. Clothes froze if you hung them out too late; you needed to capture the height of the sun or the wind would turn them into coloured pieces of board. Ro decided the washing line should be hung inside the communications tent as the tents would heat up during the day without the wind. Bingo, a drying room. Having a shower had its distinct limitations if you wanted your hair to dry. It was also rather a chore, so we had them out of necessity rather than a way of filling time.

Nat and his Tibetan kitchen boy, Kamala, actually a father-of-three, would create a lunch for us of bread and beans (not Heinz) and various attempts at pasta or yak cheese. We couldn't fault them for effort. In the afternoon, we continued our efforts to amuse ourselves whilst not getting too excited in case our heart rate increased too much. We had to limit Patrick to how many times he could win! Then, before you could recite The Bible backwards, it was time for our 5pm check-in call with ABC, which gave us something to talk about as we made the seamless transition from communication tent to the dining tent for dinner. The temperature would drop dramatically again so our evening dress consisted of duvet jackets and hats. We got ready for our 'guess the soup' quiz. Sometimes, we were stunned with what they produced, such as steak sizzlers one night, complete with chips. Was there no end to their talents? We generally managed to talk about food from home regardless of how good the fayre was in front of us. Toilet humour was also part of our British rapport. How many funny stories are there about wee, poo and diarrhoea? They really get you going. The Doc offered more than most and in such style. After the pleasantries of the dining table, we would adjourn to the chill tent and either watch a movie, play cards, read, chat or do the guitar thing. Then it was back to the tent to take a couple of layers off and allow our thermals to double up nicely as pyjamas. So endeth a typical Base Camp day.

Back to what was happening in the world and Chris, Tarqua and Karma walked into camp. Tarqua had gone from being a tall, well-built young man to a skinny vulnerable one who needed help walking. Chris and two of the Sherpa team (Karma and Thering) had done really well to help him get back to Base Camp in eight hours. Nigel was still on his way and had found it hard to keep up but it was still light. He was Sarah's uncle and she started to feel worried he had been left alone. We decided to focus on Tarqua for now and, if and when there was cause to be concerned about Nigel, we would turn our attentions to him. The Doc immediately assessed that Tarqua was suffering from cerebral oedema[10] due to his inability to walk in a straight line. He told us to get the gamoff bag out: a big sleeping bag-like capsule that can be pumped up so that the person suffering can be put inside and the pressure simulates going down in altitude. It isn't a cure but aids recovery for a period of time. We were all in the chill out tent with him trying to make the moment less stressful. I played the harmonica which was considered a big enough distraction. The Doc called a high altitude consultant in the UK on the satellite phone and did an international consultation confirming what the Doc already knew. He needed to go down and it would be the end of his attempt on Everest. He broke the sobering news to him while he was in the bag. We were about to officially lose the first member of the team as well as being still without Dom - and it was only week two.

The Doc breaks the news to Tarqua who is in the gamof bag, that his Everest attempt is over

Chatting to Nic early next day, it became clear how hard it was for him as he was Tarqua's mate on the trip and felt really bad for him. So he decided to go down with him as far as the border to Nepal to make sure he was ok. This was beyond generous as Nic was potentially risking his own acclimatisation schedule and therefore his attempt on Everest by doing this. Who knew how long it would take to get down and then back again? This was a big decision only he could make. I was full of awe for him and also concerned it was the right thing to do. Karma was around to help organise the jeep. Tarqua fought the decision and the Doc had to have another chat to convince him he had no choice. He couldn't rejoin this expedition but it didn't mean he couldn't attempt Everest again in a couple of years. As he got into the jeep with Nic, we all waved our goodbyes and moved on. We were already anxious about Nic making it back in time to make his own attempt.

Phil and I joined Patrick and Andre in the village for some sweet tea and entertainment as Patrick did a fashion show in a local fur hat that suited the flamboyant showman perfectly. Patrick and I constantly took the micky out of Andre who had a superbly posh accent. We would ask him questions about art in our best Liverpool accents as he is one of the art experts from Sotherby's in London. We promised to turn up outside his office, dressed in shell suits and bling and ask for him by name. Now there's an amusing thought!

I was so pleased to see Dom when he arrived back that afternoon.

This whole expedition was his idea and the new arrivals, Phil apart, were all his mates. It seemed very wrong for us all to be carrying on without him. He looked great and was smiling from ear to ear as he really felt better than ever. I had been holding fort on the admin side, emailing Thamserku about concerns with our oxygen bottles and some other minor things that needed addressing. I could now happily hand it back to Dom as that was the role he wanted and seemed to enjoy.

That night we watched a movie, all tucked up in our sleeping bags feeling safe and warm. Then, through the door of our chill tent, we saw Karma looking very concerned. Pemba, our ABC cook, had just been brought down on the back of a yak for the last 10 hours with a bad case of AMS and was in a really bad way. The Doc immediately got him on oxygen and then into the gamoff bag. We all waited in the chill tent while Doc took control in the kitchen tent with Dom, Jamie and the Sherpa team. The Doc gave us an update: if he hadn't been brought down, we would have lost him. This only went to prove that nobody, not even Sherpa folk, are immune from the effects of altitude, a warning made very clear when we heard the news that Russell Brice had lost one of his favourite cooks to altitude sickness only days before our team had arrived. There is a tendency among the Nepalese team not to be honest about how they are feeling because it is deemed weak or fear of losing their job. This wouldn't be the case at all, especially with Russell or Thamserku. However, they could leave it too late to share their symptoms. We read the riot act to Sonam and the team about being honest with us. We had the medicine for nearly everything and a great doctor; all they needed to do was to trust us. Despite these warnings, Pemba still carried on as if nothing was wrong for too long. It was only thanks to the Doc he is still alive and kicking today as he recovered within a couple of days of being sent lower. He came back and worked as Base Camp cook and Nat went up to ABC. Another welcome returner was Nic, who had been gone for a day longer than he hoped due to the bad weather. He was in good spirits and never dwelt on the fact he had been a hero for his mate. We did dwell on it, as, if nothing else, it gave us something else to talk about apart from the mountain and the food we were missing.

The next few days saw everybody apart from Dom and Patrick leave Base Camp for Interim, ABC and the North Col. Phil and I left with Sarah, Nigel, Chris and Nic for Interim. Wow, how can walking that slowly be that hard? We were obviously carrying quite big packs including an extra tent for ABC between Phil and me. We could have carried this for miles at sea level but we were walking to 5,800m just to get to Interim camp. The terrain was like I'd imagine the moon surface - lots of big and small boulders and very little vegetation. Yak trains passed us while their herders sang, laughed and joked with the energy of children. We felt pathetic in their presence. When we finally reached our camp, it was even more rudimentary than I was prepared for. We had just been camping in positive luxury with chill tents, dining tents, kitchen tents, cooks etc. Now we had merely a shared tent to sleep in and one battered old scout tent with a cooker for us to melt snow and cook noodles. We had oodles of noodles as they weighed so little and were easy to eat and cook. However, the positive was that we were camped right next to the most spectacular geographical wonder of giant penitentes. They take the form of tall thin blades orientated towards the general direction of the sun. Penitentes look like huge pyramids of ice that have broken away from the glacier on its descent down the mountain. Some were well over 100ft high and looked like

Me relaxing at interim camp

jewels coming from the deep frozen ice. They were stunning and crying out to be climbed with some good ice tools and crampons. As it was, we were doing well to take our boots off, never mind kit up and be energetic. There really wasn't a huge amount to do apart from sleep, melt snow, chat and wonder at your surroundings so that is exactly what we did for two nights.

Our next stretch of low energy, slow pace walking was to Advanced Base Camp. Nigel and Chris had gone ahead but Sarah was reluctant to carry on and needed another night at Interim. She was struggling with unfamiliar and scary acclimatisation, having seen Pemba, Tarqua and a few others come back down to BC in a less-than-healthy state. She wanted to be sure she was ready and her head was full of doubt. She was confident enough to walk with us for the first 10 minutes and then explain she was going to stay another night, even if she was on her own. I had a real conflict of loyalties here: I know that if Phil hadn't been there, I would have stayed with Sarah as a friend but Phil and Nic looked at it from a more mountaineering perspective. If she was safe and happy to be on her own, we needed to go to ABC to stay on top of our acclimatisation. We were already the last group to be going high. The practical argument won - a fair point even if, in a girly way, I wanted to stay. Sarah convinced me she would be fine and Phil and Nic were ready to move on, especially as there were only so many noodles left at Interim. So, with a guilty conscience, we said our goodbyes and carried on.

The next stretch of heavy breathing/walking became more and more spectacular as a valley of penitentes marked our way up to ABC. It must have taken us about five or six hours to scramble 11km! How slow is that? We couldn't even talk enough to make it interesting or was I just suffering from being iPod-free. Happiness at our first glimpse of ABC was tempered by the

A spectacular valley of penitentes - walking to ABC from Interim Camp

realisation we still had some way to go, although it did put a tiny, weeny spring in our step. Each and every set of tents we passed was like a false horizon. Surely our camp was next?

Phil knew where he was going: when I saw him shake hands with somebody, I knew we were there. Thank God! Every step was now not only hurting my legs but my entire being. We were now at 6,400m; it wasn't going to be easy. I fell into the dining tent and good old Nat was there with a cup of tea. Nic and Phil were right there with me for the tea break. You had to question why on earth we put so much time and effort into putting ourselves through such hardship. Ridiculous hobby! There is lots of retrospective pleasure in the world of mountaineering but much camaraderie comes from extreme adversity. Next day saw Sarah arrive at Advanced Base Camp full of the joys of spring. She had had a good night and joined Russell's team for the evening. Her walk up had been strong and it was the right decision for her. I was really glad to have her with us again.

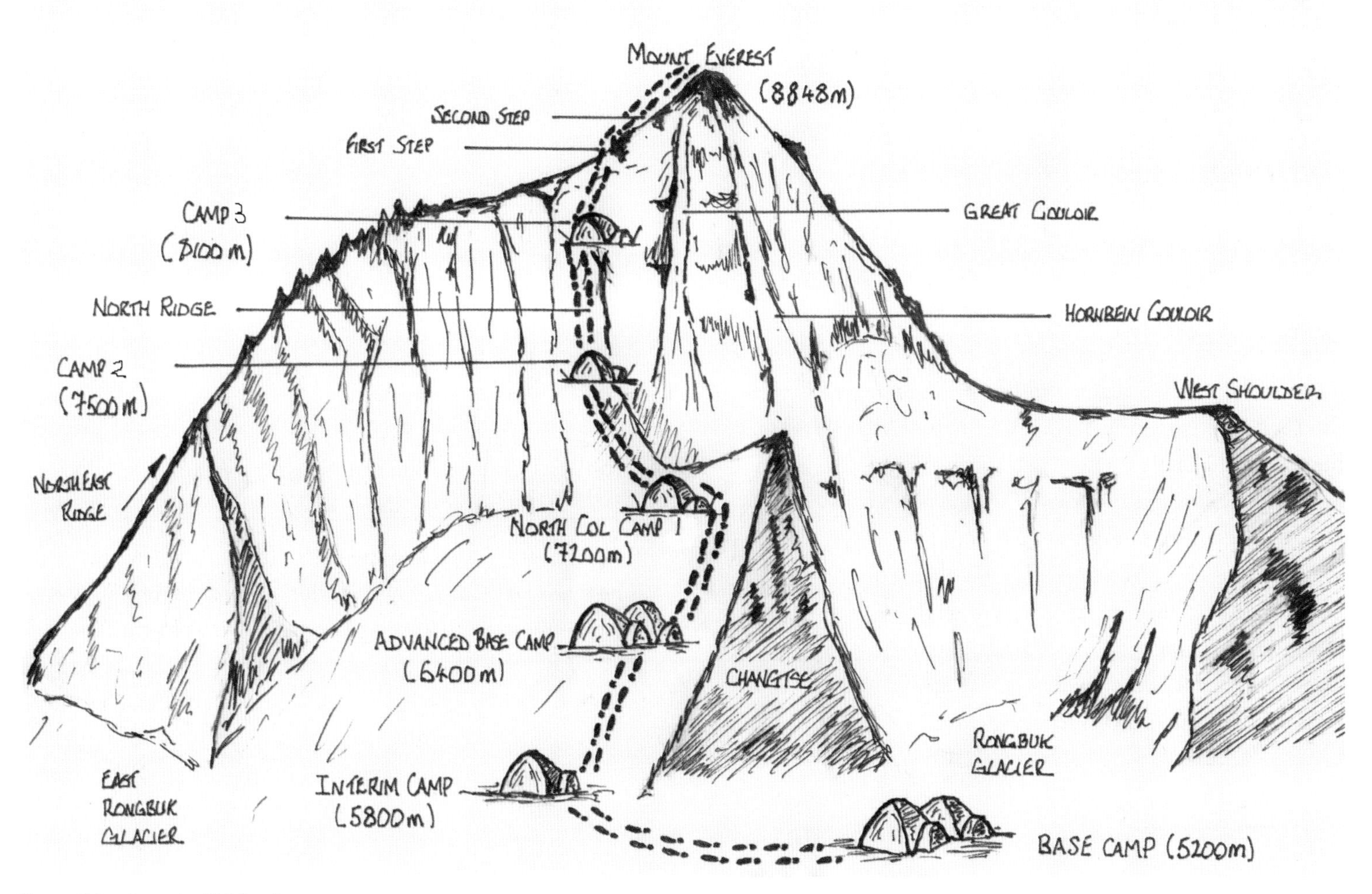

Everest Map drawn by Phil Sanderson

CHAPTER **SIXTEEN**

Jamie, Nic, Dom, Patrick and the Doc promoting Buff neck scarves with Everest in the background

Let The Pain Begin - Advanced Base Camp and North Col

ABC WAS very, very different. The thousand or so people down at Base Camp were sprawled over a huge area of about one square km. In ABC, we were tightly packed like sardines as different teams struggled to find areas flat enough for all their tents to be together. Our kitchen tent opened into our dining tent to maximise on shared heat and space. Our toilet was about 50m away, suitably solitary and almost like a big outing at this altitude. The other big change was the temperature; the sun was really strong during the day when you would quickly burn without cream. But the temperature dropped as dramatically and inevitably as the sun. We would all end up sitting on our down suits and summit boots around the dining table, looking remarkably over-dressed and trying not to go to bed before 7pm. Yes 7pm! It meant a long night in our sleeping bag but, at least, we were warm and didn't have to do much apart from keep turning over so parts of our bodies didn't go to sleep first.

Phil and I chatted for ages about everything and nothing. The nights seemed long but we didn't want to get out until the first rays of sun had hit our tent and started to thaw the zips out. We would also be woken by the freeze forming on the hood edges of our sleeping bags or the need to use the pee bottle due to the inordinate amount of water we were having to drink. Pemba and his team had the extra job of collecting ice and melting it all - never ending, but absolutely necessary. Just being at ABC was draining; breathing felt like a big effort, let alone the extra demands of walking, going to the loo or eating. Getting ready for bed was a seriously big event, just managing the change from down suit to sleeping bag without getting exhausted or freezing was hard enough. Making sure we hadn't left anything in the dining tent and assuring ourselves the toilet really could wait until morning as long as our pee bottle and bowels were empty

ABC where we are all cramped into a small area

kept mind and body busy. Multi-tasking at its supreme best! We also had to be more diligent with any kit left out as it would freeze even faster than down at Base Camp.

Appetite is also affected at altitude; your body expends more energy so you need more food. Yet you don't always feel like eating and, if you do, your desires tend to be very specific. In order to help people stay on top of their weight and keep the bulk up, we had a table in the dining tent full of goodies for people to eat. It had chocolates, boiled sweets, biscuits, spreads and a whole range of things we had brought from Kathmandu anticipating this problem. Pemba did his best to cook hearty food like omelettes and porridge, garlic soup and pasta but it all depended on your unpredictable palate.

The Doc and Seb made their way up to the North Col (7,200m) on the day we arrived. They came in shattered amid descriptions of exhaustion, breathlessness and having to look at one man's backside for hours on end. However, they were elated and strong. Their successful experience was a good boost to us all as they were definitely proud of themselves and felt they had ticked the next box and done it well. As a group, we were in almost celebratory mode. It's good to be excited about each stage as you never know if it will be your last! We all started talking about how strong we were feeling and that there was a good chance we could all have a go at the summit. The problem was the oxygen supply wasn't geared for everyone to do so. The group therefore agreed to talk to Dom to get to the next stage with Russell and find out whether his offer of oxygen would be on sale or return. Each bottle was $400 so it was a big deal to bring in more as each climber would need five. If we were to offer our Sherpa team a chance to summit, they would need about three bottles each. Our supplies were for five summit attempts based on Dom's theory that on average less than half of the team would make it past camp two (7,600m).

This seemed reasonable at sea level although Phil had questioned this even when we met in Scotland. Our tent was buzzing with success and optimism and there were 12 climbers left in our team and three Sherpas who wanted to summit. We wanted to be ready for all of us to have an attempt without the heartbreak of having insufficient oxygen. If Russell was happy to do sale or return it would be perfect, then we'd just have to ask Sonam if we had time to ask our Sherpa team to take up more oxygen to camps two and three. Even if we geared for nine attempts, it would be building on an optimistic and positive attitude in camp. We knew that Dom had a harder battle given his recovery from pulmonary oedema and retina damage. There was also a high chance a couple more of us would drop out. But why plan for failure when we can plan for success? Doc and Seb said they would go back down to Base Camp and explain our discussion to Dom. We all wanted Dom to be there but the satellite phone wasn't good for conference calls and it was incredibly expensive. It was such a positive vibe; it would have been good for our leader to share it.

The next day saw our very supportive Sherpa team see the next batch of us take on the first real part of the mountain. Phil, Andre, Jamie, Nigel, Chris and I left together and were all in good form, talking like true mountaineers... for the first 10 steps at least! It wasn't long before we realised this would be a day of few words. Our packs were light as it was just a day trip. Next time, we would be taking, sleeping bags, food and overnight gear. We walked out of Base Camp and past many other camps. It wasn't far off the land of the Zombies when it came to the westerners. The Sherpas with their heavy loads were still able to talk and laugh to each other as they shifted tents, oxygen, food and general supplies for all the teams. Amazing.

It was about two km from our camp and a 250m ascent to the start of the North Col wall. After 20 minutes or so, we were out of the camp and walking through a stretch of lateral moraine which are parallel ridges of debris deposited along the sides of a glacier with a path, flanked by snow banks making a natural line to the main glacier. After about an hour, we came to some large blue plastic barrels that various teams had left, including our sirdar Sonam. This was where we were to leave our crampons[4] and axes when we came down ready for our next attempt. This meant reducing the amount of time we were carrying the heavy hardwear. It was also a natural break spot and a place to put on crampons. Wow, we were already exhausted and the steep section hadn't even started!

Looking up at the 1000ft North Col wall

At altitude, you can feel tired even when you are strong. Each step feels like somebody has glued Velcro to the bottom of your boots and you have to fight for every inch. Once we had negotiated an obvious path through the start of the glacier blocks, we came to the flat stretch of glacier. It looked like we were about to walk across a frozen lake. On the opposite side, we could already see lots of people at the base and en route up to the North Col. It was like watching ants. The human train was tiny against the giant wall of snow that rose steeply before them for about 1,000ft. The ants were barely moving. The prospect of getting to the top of the wall seemed incredibly uninviting, even after only a couple of hours. This was endurance at every level: slow, boring and completely exhausting with hours more of the same to look forward to just so we could come back down again - all in the hope we could do it all over again another couple of times more. Ridiculous hobby!

We plodded on across the flat glacier, avoiding looking up as the wall didn't come closer very quickly. It was better to look at your feet and sing at least two songs in your head before looking up to feel if any progress had been made. When we eventually got there, it was time for the harnesses, helmets and jumars[12]. I went after Phil. We clipped our jumars onto our harness and then onto the fixed line. There were three lines, two for those going up and one for those going down. Let the plod commence!

Our plod was in the middle of one of the most majestic mountaineering venues in the world but the plod itself didn't feel majestic, exciting, glorious or, in any way, pleasurable. It was hard, slow, uncomfortable and a bit thankless. We were going up for hours, just to come down again. I couldn't stop thinking we were going to have to do this all over again and then again! Negative attitude doesn't help so I just kept singing songs to myself as there wasn't a lot of chat going on. Funny enough, they were all slow songs, even if I was only singing them in my mind.

En route up we had a couple of small crevasses[7] to negotiate. Russell's Sherpa team had put in ladders for us which sounds easy enough but was still a balancing act over a bottomless hole. It was enough to make your heart beat even harder and you think twice about each step. There were two ladders at about halfway that were only 10ft or so each. In a funny way it broke the monotony but at least monotony was easier on the heart, lungs and head. Sounding fun yet? There was one last ladder at the top of the wall: this was a steeper and bigger crevasse. The ladder was about 20ft long and it felt like 100ft as it was the gateway to the North Col village of tents. You knew you could sit down and think about going back down when you had got over the ladder and walked about 20 meters.

Phil on the top ladder of the North Col

Our group had stayed relatively close together. There was no fast lane; some people were going even slower than me and there were times where we had to overtake as they took a break on the side. The Sherpas made us all look like lightweights. If they overtook, which they did a lot, they would clip onto the 'down rope' which was less busy and then get back onto the up rope when there was a decent gap. We saw our Sherpa team on the top set of ladders. They gave us their cheery support and delivered more oxygen, food and tents to the North Col, ready to take it to the next two camps. As they waved their goodbyes, we were on our last few meters up and probably looked as out of our comfort zone as a fish in a dessert. We all made it to the top so we took a team shot – just in case this was as high as we got. The picture said it all: I couldn't raise a little finger never mind a smile or the energy to perform to camera. We were all exhausted.

Tired at the North Col. Andre, Chris, Nigel and me looking exhausted

The way down was hard but my legs were strong. As we moved down, it was easier than going up yet equally exhausting as the wall was steep and each step needed placing. It was a bit of a staircase now, as so many people had been up and down, but for me they seemed like big steps. Crossing the wide lake-like expanse at the bottom seemed as long as when we came in, as we were still moving slowly. We all got back to camp totally exhausted but happy we had ticked another box. I can honestly say that, if somebody had given me an excuse to go home, I would have taken it at that point. There was absolutely nothing enjoyable about that day: no spare energy for chat and fun, it was all about focused endurance. Dinner time was full of mutual admiration and funny stories about how exhausted we could be. We all slept well.

Next day, Jamie and Andre went back down to Base Camp. We had been joined by Dickie and Ro which was fabulous. Their goal was to get to the North Col: if they made it, we would be celebrating our first proper goal success on the mountain. Nic and Sarah were going for their attempt on the North Col together. That left Chris, Nigel, Phil and yours truly at ABC, deciding what to do next. The others had gone back to Base Camp to recharge and come back up again to sleep at the North Col and then walk up to camp two. I really didn't fancy going back. The thought of walking 22km down and 22km back up, knowing it would really hurt beggared the question 'why?' The big question was: would we recharge enough at ABC to enable us to go back up to the North Col, sleep there and carry on up to camp two? Phil and I were both feeling strong and so were Nigel and Chris. They had already done the trip to ABC twice and weren't keen on a repeat. We decided to give ourselves a couple of days rest and go up.

Dom called that night from Base Camp and I could tell by his voice he was upset. He was annoyed about our discussion on oxygen, feeling he had been undermined and disappointed he had been written out of the potential summit team. This is where distance and phones are never as good as face-to-face. He obviously thought Phil and I had instigated unrest in the camp about the lack of oxygen as we had raised concerns as far back as our first meeting in Scotland. It couldn't have been further from the truth. If he had been there, he would have seen the enthusiasm for oxygen was based on the optimism and confidence of the team around the table. He also raised the point not all members of the team could find more money for more oxygen. This, to me, was a bit of a weak argument and showed he was upset. Having come this far and invested so much time and money already, all of us, even students, would gladly have found another $1,000 each to make sure we had a fair crack at the mountain, especially if we could get sale or return.

At the end of quite an emotional chat, I felt let down. How could he even think I would undermine him? I was his team mate and there had been no evidence of anything but support in all our time together. I was gutted he obviously felt less of me. I wanted his approval because I respected him as our leader over the past five months. Maybe he was feeling a little less in control than he had on the bike journey. He had only ever been as high as the North Col on his previous trip to Everest with the army. This was new territory for all of us and he knew that there was a lot more at stake on the mountain than on the bikes. Perhaps the pressure of leadership in an environment where he had no more experience than us, made him feel unsure of his authority. I had no idea but I was upset. We were talking with experienced heads, not novice mountaineers. We were representing a team discussion that was misinterpreted by him for some reason. My pet hate in life is injustice. Somehow I felt that Phil and I had been dealt an injustice by his interpretation of that meeting. How had the others failed to convince him it was a positive meeting rather than an undermining one?

Despite the underlying tension in our call, he agreed I could go to Russell and establish the details on the deal for oxygen - was it sale or return and would it be available from Base Camp or Advanced Base Camp? This would make a big difference to the cost. Russell and his team were as helpful as ever: their camp was just breathtaking and luxurious and life seemed very comfortable but then, if I did as many months in this environment every year as him, I would want a certain level of comfort too. It wasn't so much the tents that were posh; it was more the style of chair, abundance and variety of refreshments and the level of technology.

I spoke to Phil and Nic about Dom's reaction and both reassured me he would come round once we spoke face-to-face and got the full facts. Telephones, whether in a house in the UK, in conference meetings or between camps on the highest mountain in the world, can't do justice to feelings, emotions and misunderstandings. Nic was going down to Base Camp and promised to explain to Dom how I felt when he went down next day.

We had now spent about five days at ABC. Phil had been a great help to various team members by answering lots of questions on technical as well as medical aspects of the mountain. People recognised he had the mountaineering skills and experience to succeed as long as the elements were with him. A few of the team told me they were most confident about Phil and me making a successful attempt because of that. I had to agree as he is the safest mountaineer I know. He is also keen to share his knowledge, as that is why he became an instructor in the first place. However, neither of us had been into the 'death zone' (over 8,000m), so that would be new territory and nobody could predict how we could do.

We packed for our overnight on the North Col; I dreaded every step before we had even finished packing. Chris and Nigel would share one tent and we would have another. There were three tents at the North Col, so that wasn't a problem. This time we had heavier bags with all our overnight kit in. I wouldn't say my second time was easier, but it wasn't harder so that was good. We also took a considerable amount of time off compared to our first ascent, although I can't remember how much. However, as we had just got into the tent, Phil threw his body forward into the outer area and threw up into the corner. I was shocked and suddenly very concerned although he reassured me he had been feeling ill for 10 minutes and he felt better almost as quickly. We carried on as normal getting straight into melting snow for water to drink and eat. We were in radio contact with ABC to check in. All we had left to do was eat and sleep until the morning which was more than enough for me. It was my turn to have a turn as I went from feeling strong and fab to so weak I couldn't even get my sleeping bag out. Phil had to do everything for me, including continue to melt water. There wasn't lots of chat coming from next door either. I was asleep and out of it very quickly. Thankfully, sleep was my cure and I woke during the night feeling fine. I had probably dehydrated a bit on top of maybe pushing it a bit too fast that day. Lesson learned: I needed to slow down even more!

We woke early and felt strong and keen – weird. Nigel and Chris were taking a more leisurely pace. We knew the winds tended to come in more in the afternoon and wanted to get the hard bit done as early as possible. We were up, dressed and out by about 7.30am. We started off with nobody else around, stunning views and the summit in sight …so far away and yet so near. It was far away when you consider how slowly you move; but near because we were now actually on the route. The next stretch of plod was up a reasonably steep slope but still very much a plod with no technical climbing required. We could see the summit horizon for camp two which was at 7,600m as we were walking from 7,200m. For those of you who know the Cairngorms, this would be like walking from Glenmore Lodge to the Meill of Beuchille. It would be a stroll. Phil kept telling himself it was just Meill of Beuchille to keep himself motivated.

We started off steady, with low winds and a blue sky, then the wind started to pick up. As we got higher, we looked back down to our tents and saw the full glory of their location. North Col was a busy place and space wasn't easy to find so we totally understood why our tents were the furthest ones away from the top ladder. On a positive note, they were the nearest to the start of the camp two plod. Looking down, we got a better idea of why nobody else was there. They really were on the edge of the Col, pitched on a cauliflower-shaped cornice hanging above the East Face. Just to emphasise: they were pitched on the part of the cornice that was very deep with no mountain underneath! We decided although the cornice was well established and strong, it was still a cornice with no mountain underneath! We didn't want to undermine Sonam and his team by moving it and it would have killed us as it was full of provisions like oxygen and food. We would ask Sonam if the team could move it once the oxygen had been moved on to the higher camps. I was sure he would understand our health and safety issues.

Looking down on the North Col from our route up to Camp 2

We carried on plodding up until we got to the point we couldn't stand up because of the wind. This was good practice for handling adverse conditions at altitude; you can't afford to drop a glove as it would be gone in a second and that would mean frostbite. When you are mountaineering at this level, you need to be prepared for all conditions, not just the ones you started out in. It was a healthy reminder of how dangerous this mountain can be if the elements turn against you. We made it to about 7,400m before Phil suggested we turn back and conserve our energy. We were strong but 200m more may have taken us another couple of hours in these conditions. It was the right move for us as we had enough energy to get back down to ABC with no problems and feeling strong. On the way down, we saw Nigel and Chris on their way up. Nigel did the same as us at 7,400, but Chris did an amazing job and got close to 7,600 before turning back. They stayed an extra night at the North Col.

Our tents looked a bit precarious over this Himalayan sized cornice.

The four of us celebrated our attempt the next day together and decided to go back down to Base Camp the following day. We all got on well together with Chris being particularly entertaining; tall, athletic and in his late thirties, he had a face as talkative as his words. He was an eye expert which was great when Dom had issues with his retina. Nigel was the oldest in the team being his mid-fifties; he was Sarah's uncle and, although they didn't seem to know each other at a close family level, they got on well. His big USP (unique selling point, for those who like acronyms) was that he had an artificial left leg from the knee down, having lost it on a climbing trip to the Alps many years previously. He was one of the more experienced mountaineers in our team and the loss of a limb never stopped him doing what he loved. He was also never short of one-legged jokes, much to his credit. It always made us smile when we saw all the shoes lined up outside the chill tent... plus half a leg to boot!

We all got excited about the prospect of a bucket shower at Base Camp; wet ones are great but pouring water is just amazing! Never take a power shower for granted. On the way back down, I was dwelling on the Dom issue and how he would have reacted to Nic. Then we spotted the Doc, Jamie and Dom walking towards us. I felt my heart going faster, not because of the altitude but because Dom's reaction would determine whether he was back onside with me. We all gave big hellos with big smiles and I felt good again. We chit chatted for five minutes before I ventured: "Dom, I really think you got the wrong impression about that meeting." He replied in a corporate tone that he had chatted with Nic and we would probably have to agree to differ. It wasn't the time or place to keep the discussion going and, in a true male way, (sorry to generalise, boys) he moved the subject on. In a true female way (same apology) I wanted it sorted so we parted with me feeling just as frustrated.

We arrived back at BC and it felt like the season had changed inside ten days. We had left the camp in snow only to return to a feeling of spring. The days and evenings felt hotter, making life very comfortable. The creaks and cracks of the glacier had been replaced by the sound of running water and stepping stones were required to cross small streams of glacier melt on the way down. There was also a barrage of birds we hadn't seen before. Our team had spotted eagles souring high and the more plentiful Tibetan Snow Gog, a form of partridge.

We caught up with the multi-cultural antics of Patrick, who had dined on parma ham with the French, eaten sardines with the Spanish, refused dog from the Koreans, borrowed a heater from the Irish and discovered untold gems in Russell's camp. Nic had taken him under his wing, to lead him out of BC and actually go up to Interim. Everybody was delighted to see him go but Patrick himself wasn't too bothered. He had been enjoying his time and was fit, healthily acclimatised and acquainted with loads of great people. Why did he need to get uncomfortable, battle with acclimatisation and not be able to talk? He had a point although, deep down, he admitted he would like to get to ABC to experience what we had all been talking about. He had lots of Scottish winter climbing experience so it wasn't the mountaineering that was putting him off. He just enjoyed Base Camp. When he returned, he was fulfilled and happy to resume his role of entertainments manager. He did a great job of describing how hard it was in classic amateur dramatic fashion, having us rolling about with laughter as he imitated himself fighting the elements at altitude in a somewhat camp style.

The team had discovered fun ways to promote one of our sponsors while we were away. The Buff company had kindly given us neck scarves for summer and winter conditions which I found invaluable. Jamie, Nic, the Doc, Dom and Patrick all agreed to model the Buff scarves with Mt Everest in the background. They decided to make it an eye-catching poster by modeling the scarves in the 'buff' (nude, for those of you unfamiliar with this slang). We now have superb photos of five men backs to the camera, facing Mt Everest wearing only their Buff neck scarves, boots and, in Patrick's case, knee high socks. Bottom line: the pert buttocks were outstanding. Ro kindly offered to photo shop Patrick's butt so he fitted in a bit more. Doc decided it was spring-like enough to go for a swim in the small tarn above our camp area. Wow, what a brave man. Apparently, he came out looking more like a boy than a man, if you know what I mean?

Our team was still spread out with Andre, Seb, the Doc and Jamie attempting to go and sleep at North Col, while Dom was happy to get to ABC and return to BC. I organised a quiz night at BC with me as quizmaster (surprise, surprise). I was fighting mountainous odds to get it going as 'lethargic' easily defeated 'motivated' for anything other than food, sleep, toilet, washing or cards. However, with Patrick as my number two, we had a great night. Even Phil and Dom, who would have happily just watched a movie, joined in to humour me and against their better judgment actually enjoyed themselves.

I got an email whilst at Base Camp from Simon Hawkins, VP of Reebok UK and good friends with Martyn and Penny. He had heard about our adventures and was completely inspired by the story. I had offered myself as a motivational speaker for a £1,000 donation on my return in a circular and Simon had taken up this offer. He had faith in our adventure, whether or not we managed to reach the summit. This time he would make a further donation for me to do a live link to a conference he was hosting for about 1,000 Reebok employees. He would call at a certain time the next day to brief me, then we would go live. I waited dutifully by our satellite phone and his call came bang on cue. I jumped in with: "Ok Simon, if this stuff is going live, you better make me look good and manage me as I could just go on and on and on." He answered back: "Pauline, I am here live at a Reebok Conference..." So much for the warm up! For brief, read non-existent. Fortunately, I hadn't been rude or sworn or anything and Simon and Reebok continued to offer support to the end.

In a few more days, the whole team, with the exception of Sarah, was together at Base Camp again. Everybody had slept at the North Col, apart from Dom and Sarah, by this point (May 8th). Only Jamie, Chris the Doc, Andre and Seb had made it all the way to camp two. Dom had surprised everybody, including the Doc, by coming back stronger than ever from ABC. Next time the majority of us went up to ABC would be for a summit attempt. We were now party to the waiting game: traditionally, the jet stream winds sweeping across the summit of Mt Everest drop before the onset of the monsoon. This is the famous 'weather window' that can give climbers a chance to reach the summit in relative safety.

CHAPTER **SEVENTEEN**

I am on top of the world and loving it!

On Top of The World!

AS A RULE, a climber needs a five-day window from ABC. The first day is going to the North Col (7,200m); second to camp two (7,600m); start using oxygen to sleep on and continue up to camp three (8,100m) by about noon on day three; then sleep, hydrate and relax before starting a summit attempt that night. The goal would be to summit on the morning of day four and get back down to camp two for that night. Day five would see us safely back at ABC which by that time would feel like no problem at all. Piece of cake, eh?

That, of course, was if everything went perfectly. Ideally, you should always plan in a floating day for unforeseen consequences, such as weather or kit problems. At this point, camps two and three had two tents each, meaning they were ready for four climbers at a time. We had 12 climbers so would have to stagger the ascents and need a 12-day weather window or hope for a second weather window later in May, as was often the case. However, our official leaving date from the mountain was May 27. We either needed luck on our side or more discussion over the logistics if the weather window didn't happen.

Dom had the unenviable job of hosting the next all-team meeting in the chill tent to tell people who would be going in the first summit team. He knew Seb and Andre had family/work commitments making them keen to be first up and first home. He had already said his choice would be based on experience and how well they had adapted to altitude. We all went into the chill tent knowing someone was going to be disappointed. This made the X Factor look like child's play: some could probably never afford to come back if they missed out; others may have been unable to get the time again due to work or family commitments. It was a bigger deal to some but all were keen to try. Jamie had gone up to Dom in private and told him he was happy to go in the last group, a very noble thing to do. He had spent enough time with Dom to see this was becoming increasingly hard for him to be both leader and friend to a team he had put together. I got the feeling the cyclists were the least anxious to be in the first team. We had already enjoyed such a wonderful experience that had meant so much. The team joining us just for the climb had nothing else to fall back on so little wonder there was tension in the air.

Dom started by repeating the criteria for his choice and reassuring us we should all get to have a go. Then he announced the teams: he chose Nigel, Chris, Phil and I to go in the first summit team. There was no point in going onto the second team. Someone queried why we were being picked as we hadn't made it all the way to camp two. Phil spoke up before Dom could answer explaining his experience counted for so much more than 200m more of height gain. Nigel, Phil and I had the most experience and Chris had gone high and been in a team with Nigel. Dom ruled that discussion was over as we had all agreed his decision would stand. Friction filled the air but chatter drowned out any potential heated talk. As a team, we had opinions but were prepared to discuss things. We knew there would be some disappointed people... and this had proved it. We were glad Dom had kept Phil and me together. This meant one of us wouldn't have to step down and agree to go at a later stage as we definitely wanted to be together. How could we not? We were a team both in marriage and on the mountain. We were excited and nervous to equal degrees and eagerly scrutinised all available weather reports. When was that window coming?

Dom left next day to join Sarah to go to the North Col and get away from it all. Phil suggested we should go soon and be ready to react to any weather window. It takes two days to walk to ABC and, although you don't relax as well up there, it would be better than before as we were better acclimatised and the weather was warming up. I wanted to wait another day whilst Phil was impatient to go; Chris and Nigel wanted to wait until there was more news on an imminent weather window so they could maximise on the recharging at Base Camp.

I could see Phil's point, too, and we decided to go. We spent that day getting all our kit packed for our summit attempt. Phil was in focused rather than sociable mode, putting all his attention into what lay ahead. I have learned over the years to understand this isn't him in a mood but taking responsibility for the gravity of the situation and challenge ahead of us. I meanwhile strive to enjoy the journey and keep things in perspective. In this case, he really was in the lead as, if we forgot anything, the consequences were either frostbite, injury or death. His 'focused' was worth far more than my 'enjoy the journey' at this point.

Leaving BC, there was a definite sense of 'this is it' from the team. Frustrations were left behind and it was all goodwill and good luck as we walked off towards Interim Camp. I was so pleased I was with Phil: it wasn't that I didn't trust anybody else; I just didn't want to have such a big experience without him. We had had most of our mountaineering laughs in the tent trying to amuse ourselves with trivia and naturally there is a large amount of retrospective pleasure in mountaineering. The mountaineering itself was when we wanted each other to concentrate on the mountain. We knew each other so well and would be able to see in an instant if one of us was walking abnormally or acting strange. This would be important at altitude as hypoxia[18] affects many aspects of your body and mind.

We reached ABC while Dom and Sarah were on the North Col. They both had a great night sleep and felt strong after a good trip. Don't forget that 'good' on Everest means so much more than normal: alive and well as opposed to ill, injured or dead. Dom surprised everyone, including the Doc, with how well he had recovered. Maybe, he would be able to attempt the summit after all. We all wanted him to.

The news of the weather summit day window coming on the 15th was circulating among the camps. Russell pays thousands of pounds for his forecasts and wasn't about to give them away for nothing to a bunch of cling-ons from any other camp. We totally respected that but everyone was watching his camp for their first movements towards a summit attempt. If Russell was sending up his team, it must be good to go. In BC, Patrick worked his magic with other camps and exchanging information. The French team was particularly helpful, having some mountain guides on their team and being happy to share information from the Alps. As a thank you, we let them use our generator to charge their phones and computers as theirs were having problems. We also had a visit from our French friends Caroline and Jacques at ABC. He was as bubbly and enthusiastic as ever and I was glad to introduce them to Phil as I had talked about the 'other married couple' who seemed to be really enjoying their journey on Everest. We compared weather information and tactics as well as sharing tea and biscuits. This was the atmosphere I was proud to be part of on Everest. We weren't in a race with other teams but all wanted each other to succeed. We just needed to be aware of each other and the obstacles so many people on a mountain can cause. We had all signed up to this Everest circus and had to be sure we weren't the clowns Nigel and Chris joined us at ABC on May 11 ready for action. We all compared notes and talked about our medical packs.

Phil was king on this, too, as he knew all an amateur medic could know about high altitude drugs, having been responsible for people when leading trips in Nepal. The most famous drug is Dexamethasone (Dex). Phil and the Doc had talked about what to put in our first aid packs for the climb and had agreed everybody should take Dex. Our friend had used it on a friend in his team on Everest the previous year. It is a steroid you inject or take by tablet if you are becoming hypoxic and losing energy and combats the early stages of cerebral oedema. You should never continue climbing up after taking it. It treats the symptoms for a period of time, therefore taking the pressure off the brain. This, in turn, gives you more ability mentally and physically for as long as the drugs effects last, giving you enough in the tank to get you down. If you continue going up, you risk the symptoms returning but at a higher altitude. This would make the condition worse, putting you and those with you in great danger. Anybody who has seen the fantastically bad but entertaining film, Vertical Limits, may remember the constant reference to the 'Dex'. We watched it at least twice at BC on movie nights. It's so bad, it's good.

I had been talking to Sonam about the oxygen and tent situation. If we could get more oxygen up in the next few days, we could have three people in each tent and therefore have two sets of ascent teams rather than three. There would be a strong likelihood of a couple of people dropping out as 100 per cent would be fantastic but unlikely. If it was the Full Monty, we could still do it in two attempts with six in each party; if some needed more time to be ready and a later window happened, then we still had the original idea of three summit teams. This idea meant more people could try earlier which added to safety at the small price of being very cosy in a tent. Sonam said it would be possible despite the fact the rumour of the weather window had come forward to May 13. I called down to Dom and suggested he send two people up to join us. He agreed and chose Andre and Seb. Chris agreed to come with Phil and me so that Seb and Andre could climb together and have the benefit of Nigel, one of the more experienced mountaineers in our team.

We planned to leave in three days to miss the rush on the 13th from the rest of ABC. Being in a queue would ruin the experience but, more importantly, could potentially wreck hopes of a successful attempt and be dangerous. We agreed that, providing they could get here in two days, we would leave from ABC on May 14. The four of us, together with Dickie and Ro, spent the next day talking and preparing for our attempt on Everest. Dickie and Ro kept their enthusiasm for our attempt as strong as if it was their own as I was representing their Everestmax team too. It was great to know they would be on the radio to keep us informed and be our point of contact should anything go wrong. It felt a bit unreal that it was finally coming to a head. We were almost impatient to go as we saw other teams on their way up. Should we be going now? No, the decision to wait for a strategic day was crucial to avoid getting caught in the masses and being forced to wait our turn. There was no way of telling exactly how many had gone up on the 12th and 13th. There could be many people thinking the same as us and hoping to miss the crowds. We got rumours that the majority had gone. The mountain would be busy at different stages and we were bound to have to make judgement calls on the way.

We sat in our tents and in the dining tent trying our oxygen masks on and making sure our medical kit, spare gloves and general personal admin were all second nature when on the move. We would need to focus on what we were doing and have

everything we needed easily accessible and ready. Our faces had to be completely protected with our goggles, balaclava and mask as any exposed skin would potentially cause frostbite. Think and prepare for the worst and you will be ready for it.

Time can go slowly when you are waiting to go somewhere. Seb arrived on the early afternoon of the 12th, having walked from Base Camp that day rather than go with Andre the day before. Seb had done this twice before, was very strong and had adapted to altitude well. When he had got his breath over one of Pemba's superb cups of tea, he explained that, having passed him on his way up that day, Andre wasn't feeling well. Andre had stayed overnight at the Interim Camp and been sick. He hadn't been 100 per cent when he had left BC but hoped it was just an overnight stomach bug. Later that afternoon, Andre walked in looking like death. He was pale, exhausted and wanted to go straight to bed.

He got up later saying he was feeling a bit better and wondered whether we could delay our attempt by one day for him to fully recover. Phil and I had no hesitation in saying absolutely not. We had a weather window for Everest and nobody could guarantee how long it would last. Some said six days, others 10 and still more warned it would be impossible to guarantee anything. Each day we delayed the first team ascent, we risked cutting the safety and opportunity for a successful climb in good conditions as well as cutting short the window for the second and third team ascents. The next team would be following us three days after us so Andre could have found himself in the second team with just four days to recover. The reality is that, if you fall ill at altitude with a gastric problem, you will be very lucky to get well enough to attempt an Everest summit. It was a no-brainer: Chris and Nigel quietly agreed, and Seb didn't really comment; Andre argued he would be better in two more days and felt we should wait.

I explained the situation to Dom in our daily check-in with BC that night and he didn't hesitate either. He had spoken with Andre earlier and thought we should wait. The rest of that phone call cost us $180. We were all sitting in the dining tent and Phil was getting frustrated as he could tell from my conversation that Dom didn't agree. He took the phone and politely, yet firmly, told Dom it would be reckless to lose a day on Everest for a sick man who could go with the next group. It was heated, frustrating and left us all feeling uncomfortable. We all hated confrontation but this wasn't about catching a later bus; this could be life and death. Why shorten the safety opportunity for one person feeling ill when five were ready to go and maximise on the perfect weather and therefore the safest conditions? What if we needed an extra day on the mountain while we were up there? The result of the conversation was that Dom said we should do what we felt best as a team. That was all well and good but we would have all preferred to have made this decision with his blessing.

We had spent very little time with Andre and Seb and not owing particular loyalty to them as people meant we could make a pragmatic rather than an emotional decision. We knew that Andre had wanted to climb Everest since he was just seven years old. The point was he still could by waiting for the next team and giving himself time to recover. He had been sick for more than 24 hours, his energy reserves were low and he still wasn't 100 per cent. He wasn't in any condition to climb the biggest mountain in the world. Andre was obviously disappointed but said he would stick with our timetable by going with us and seeing how he got on. I got the feeling that Phil and I were making the decision and Chris, Nigel and Seb understood our reasoning but didn't feel in a position to explain it to either Andre or Dom. This could be a conflict of interests due to friendships. We stood our ground, confident our view was based on experience and sensible safety criteria. It was time to focus on the climb ahead.

We were ready next day soon after breakfast. I had to force myself to eat as the butterflies were now filling all the space in my stomach yet I needed all the energy I could possibly get. The six of us posed as a group in all our kit before we set off. The photos show confused smiles: nervous and excited is a hard expression to show in your face. Andre and Seb decided to set off after lunch together to give Andre more time.

The two km walk from ABC to the foot of the North Col wall seemed to come a bit easier this time. We had left our summit sleeping bags and other summit equipment up at the North Col on our last trip, so our bags weren't as heavy. When we reached our camp, one of our three tents was so full of kit nobody would be able to sleep in it. We had hoped to be able to use all three for that night. Phil and I used one tent and Chris and Nigel the other, so nobody was alone. Andre and Seb would join Nigel later and Chris would come to us. Their tent was only 20 metres away but, for communication purposes, it may as well have been 20 miles. We had our radios and agreed to check in with Dickie at 6pm each night and 7am each morning, saving our rechargeable battery. Phil and I called in to get an update from Dickie and Chris had already called in to explain Andre hadn't made it. He had turned back and was at ABC. Seb was with Nigel and Chris.

Next morning was a slow one for us. We watched outside to see a steady stream of people moving at a snail's pace towards camp two. We had done our morning check-in with Dickie. Seb and Chris were standing outside our tent and were on their way. We had a short chat in which they explained that Nigel was on his way back down after feeling unwell and not strong enough to continue. They said they were going up to camp two and would see us up there. We said our goodbyes; talking took energy so there was no real chat - just practical information and warm wishes of good luck and take care.

Phil and I got ourselves ready with our heavy bags again as we were back to carrying sleeping bags, food and overnight kit. The Sherpas had carried all the food to camp two and we just needed to take our quota from there. Jamie and Nic had done a great job of sorting out the food into bags so it was easy to take our allocation. Dom had sourced lots of army boil in the bag food which was delicious. We had really enjoyed it but Phil and I had brought dehydrated food to carry to camp three. There was a bag of extra army food too. We decided to take what we needed and then three extra bags as emergency food to leave at camp two. There was no reason why it was three; just that was as much as we were prepared to carry as extra weight.

We set off about one hour after Chris and Seb. The sky was blue and there was no wind. It was perfect but there were a lot more people than we had expected. We got ourselves clipped onto the line and started our upward plod. We expected it would take about five to six hours - hideous. I was ok at the beginning but definitely feeling the strain after a couple of hours. I really, really, really needed to go to the loo. It was good my digestive system was working well; not so good that I'd have to unclip from the rope and get myself an anchor in the snow just to the side of the now busy highway to camp two. I loved the colour of my Marmot down suit, along with its warmth and the fact it was a trouser and jacket rather than a boiler suit. However, it still meant I had to work around getting my layers down while keeping my harness on and exposing my bum to passing crowds during a very private bowel movement. Yet I had no choice. Phil was ahead of me at this point and had no idea his wife was making heads turn. This wasn't my most dignified moment but it made me feel much better.

Phil had pulled over for a break and to wait for me. We both felt the same thing: had we been in Scotland, we wouldn't go anywhere near a route with this many people on it. If all these people were going for the summit on the same day, we knew a proportion wouldn't make it; but even if only 50 per cent did that was a lot of people to be in the highest queue in the world. We agreed to go back to North Col and wait one more day.

When we got down, we made radio contact with Dickie and explained our decision. That night Chris and Seb had called in to say they were safely at camp two and intended to carry on to camp three next day as planned. We were now in two separate teams but that was fine. Seb and Chris had both shared TA army backgrounds and were probably well suited physically and mentally. Phil and I were suited, too, so the balance still worked.

Phil and I tried to entertain ourselves by making short video clips on his camera of how exciting life could be on Everest. He filmed me melting snow to make water so I tried to make it as exciting as possible by describing the process in the style of a Blue Peter presenter. There is a lot of just hanging around in tents; boring is the only word for it. A book was out due to its extra weight, an iPod was likely to not work and even break so it was down to good old chat. The benefit of this time was seeing so many people on their way down meaning there were lots of porters with nothing to do. I knew I had found the going tough so decided to make my life a little easier and a porter's life a little richer. I asked around and found a porter to carry my rucksack to camp two. That would make a difference to me and could be enough to help me summit. I think it was a good decision and so did the porter.

Next day proved another perfect day weather-wise and, more importantly, our strategic decision to hold back was shown to be right. There had been no fewer than 100 people on the rope the day before and now we only had about six people on the line with us. This didn't make the plod any easier. I don't want to sound repetitive but this really was high endurance at a slow pace over a short distance.

These felt like the longest hours of my life; I just needed to get to camp two. These were only a few hours in a whole lifetime. Anybody can be uncomfortable for a few hours; just get on with it and keep singing slow songs, Pauline. As I came over the brow of the wall, I could see our two tents. Phil would be in and getting a brew on by the time I got there. The big question for me was could I make another 20 meters? I made it to the tent and just collapsed into it: I could never remember feeling this exhausted.

Why had it taken so much out of me? Perhaps staying another night at the North Col had actually sapped me of energy. I didn't care; I was there and I could stop. I also knew we could get onto oxygen that night. Bring it on! We did our radio-in and it was always a joy to hear Dickie. He gave me the feeling he was there for us day or night. I couldn't have asked for a better voice to give me so much reassurance.

We were in camp early enough to see a flow of people coming down. They weren't all in good shape. It was easy to see the ones who were struggling as often there would be a Sherpa with them helping them with every step. I don't know if we will ever know what the Sherpa people really think of the range of people who come to climb. It is a big industry now and they gain great prestige from being on an Everest team so none would bad mouth the Everest Circus. Whatever they think, they only show the positives of support and encouragement. Rarely have I seen any evidence of intolerance or indifference. They are a very strong, noble and inspiring people.

The rest of the team was now heading for ABC or already there. Dickie and Ro were also getting ready to attempt the North Col together. That night, Seb and Chris were going for their summit bid. I wasn't with the team at BC or ABC but I am sure they were all equally as anxious to hear about their progress. They were the first ones from our team. We had the distraction of cooking, drinking and enjoying the first real taste of life through an oxygen mask. Our masks were Top Out Masks: with a small clear tube where you could see the sac of air going in and out as you breathed. It was easy to become fixated with it. The only reason it would stop inflating and deflating was if you stopped breathing. If it wasn't moving, the choice was simple: either worry or breathe. I slept like a dream that night; the best night's sleep I'd had in ages. I was worried I would feel claustrophobic in a mask, but actually I loved it.

We were up early and ready to go next morning. We were outside our tents and about to set off when we made our radio call. Dom was serious and explained that Chris and Seb had problems. They had made it to the summit but, on the way down, Chris had started to act strangely. As Seb was calling in to update them, Chris had gone off ahead out of his control. The next message they had from Seb was that he wasn't sure if he was going to be able to manage getting Chris down alone. Dom had made contact with Russell, who had given permission for them to use his tents at camp three as they were higher than

Phil just below Camp 3

ours and to use anything they needed. This was predictably generous. I asked what role we should play and Dom said to get to camp three as soon as we could. We could melt snow and be ready to help get him down.

Phil heard all this and, as I put the radio away, he calmly turned to me and said: "We are not now on a summit bid; we are on a rescue mission." It was exactly the right thing to say, as it clarified everything. We hadn't said the word rescue but that was what it was. We carried on walking up and up. The ground was now much more broken as we worked our way across ledges and over small rock steps. However, it already felt so much easier than yesterday. Oxygen was such a gift. Our minds were fixed on the hope Chris was ok: there was nothing else to think about. I tried not to major on the 'what ifs'. Instead I focused on the options we would have once we got to camp three. We would radio in, get their location and react accordingly.

We got to camp three and saw our two tents. We were absolutely elated to see Chris and Seb sitting there drinking. They looked completely shattered but managed to raise a smile when they saw us. The drop in altitude had made a huge difference to Chris, who was now talking normally, albeit with effort. They were fine and life was good again; their only concern being they had no food either at camp three or camp two. They needed to go to camp two as they hadn't brought their sleeping bags with them either and it would also do a great deal to help Chris recover properly. Even in their condition, it would only be a two-hour walk maximum – with no apparent risk over and above the fact they were on Mt Everest in the first place.

We were able to help with the food problem. We had five boil in the bags at camp two; they could have three and leave us with two. We had brought them just for this kind of situation so there was no problem. They could be warm, fed and lower within a couple of hours. We sat with them and Seb explained that on the way up Chris started to feel unwell just a couple of hundred meters from the summit; they had stopped and Seb saw he had run out of oxygen. Perhaps the oxygen supply had been knocked and was coming in at a higher flow than it should have, so he had run out earlier. They changed the oxygen tanks and decided he should take medication as, once the oxygen was flowing well again, he quickly felt much better. They made it to the summit but, on the way down, the effects of the medication must have worn off combined with the fact they were now exhausted having been on the go for more than 12 hours without food. Chris had started to behave irrationally and taken off ahead of Seb above the steps section. Seb had been understandably worried he would have an accident getting down the ladders on the two steps and had radioed down to Dom saying he might need help to get Chris down. Fortunately, that wasn't the case. We all agreed there was a dose of luck involved in the fact we were all sitting together celebrating. They walked off together back to camp two, knowing everything was about to be a lot easier and we would never be more than an hour or two away if they needed help.

Back at ABC, we had the success of Dickie and Ro to celebrate too. It was such a good moment to see them coming into ABC after successfully reaching the North Col, even if the only way I could witness it was on the DVD. They had been a huge part of the success of our bike journey by being the perfect team within a team. It was the icing on the cake to see them come back safely from the North Col, having reached their goal. Best of all, they did it together.

We arrived at camp three at about noon with the rest of the afternoon to devote to snoozing, drinking and eating. The side show was watching people of varied abilities going down; some slow, others really slow. Our view from the back opening of our tent was stunning. It overlooked the West Ridge, where the army team were doing their summit attempt, all the way around to views of the North Col where we had come from the day before.

The best incentive not to get out the wrong side of the tent was a sheer drop of about 3,000ft!

We were unbelievably lucky with the weather and feeling great. We were hungry, too, which was great as we needed the energy for our summit attempt. We had our energy gels and snacks for the day but wanted to get fuel in the tank over the day. Trying to sleep was hard as our minds were buzzing: Phil's all the more so as he always feels responsible for me on the mountain despite the fact we are a team. Knowing this is almost bad as I tend to rely on him too much to be the decision maker. It's easy to underestimate how many decisions you are constantly making going up this mountain – what to wear, how much to eat and drink, oxygen flow, kit, checks and so on. We were used to looking after ourselves in Scottish mountains facing the elements from all four seasons in one day. You have to go out in winter ready for the worst as there is a strong chance you will get it. The positive side was we were so used to looking after ourselves in extreme conditions as well as moving across broken ground in crampons. This meant we had plenty of head space to deal with what we weren't familiar with, namely oxygen tanks and altitude. We gave each other reassuring talks qualified by serious reminders there was no mountain rescue so there was no room for error. Why were we doing this again?

At about 9.30pm that night we were ready to go. We made our radio contact with ABC and agreed a check-in time for updates. We were both nervous. I could tell because we were both quiet. I wasn't quiet to give Phil his head space; I was quiet to give me mine. I turned to him as we stood outside our tent ready to take our first steps and said: "If I snap at you don't take it personally, I love you. I'm just scared!" I would love to write about a romantic look that flashed between us at that moment but I can't remember one. I just remember an "aye, me too" and we were off.

This is me starting out on our summit attempt from Camp 3

It was the perfect summit night: crystal clear skies and a huge-looking moon that appeared to hang next to the mountain to help us. I was never good at astrology despite admiring night skies but wanted to know why the moon was so big. Was it really just because we were so high? I refrained from asking Phil as I knew it was neither the time nor the place. We were on our own. We were at the bottom section of camp three so had to walk through the camp. There wasn't a lot of activity just a couple of pairs of headlamps ahead already walking. It wasn't long before we saw a couple of lights behind us too. We were well and truly on our way. It felt surreal.

Everything apart from the oxygen felt familiar. I was now even used to the oversized mountain boots and down outfits. I just had to stay focused on each step and Phil. We checked each other's oxygen regularly to make sure the flow rate hadn't been nudged. We also checked we were both still behaving and feeling normal. This was so reassuring; it was all going well. We checked we were both drinking and had regular energy gels. This would be a long day and we needed to stay on top of our body welfare the whole time.

I knew to expect two climbing steps where Sherpas had placed ladders but couldn't remember anything about a shear drop to the right of a ridge walk... was this the right way? Of course it was; we were on a fixed line. Get on with it, woman! It felt very precarious. Despite the night being almost as bright as day on one side of the mountain, the steep drop was so steep and long; all I could see was a dark space as the horizon of the slope fell away. As I took each step, I couldn't help but remind myself there was no mountain rescue.

We were on a fixed line - thin and already used by hundreds of people - yet, if I fell, the give in the line would let me go a long way and it would hurt. Just as I was filling myself with horrific potential incidents, my rope went tight. The tension caused my jumar to stop moving forward. I had been looking ahead not down at this point. I bent over to release the tension on the rope and had to catch my breath as I saw two feet sticking out from the upper section of the path. The rope had become snagged in the crampon of a motionless body: sitting there, back against the snow wall of a small cave-like recess to the left of the path, feet hanging just over into the path of the rope. I knew I would see bodies but wasn't expecting to see one so close. I knew he was dead; he was frozen stiff. I paused just to be sure and then saw a pair of famous green boots behind him. This was an Indian climber from previous years now so entrenched in ice, nobody would be able to cut him free without a disproportionate amount of effort. I didn't hang about; I just repeated to myself that we were doing all the right things.

Our next challenge was to climb a steep step that I would class a VDiff[16] in climbing terms. Normally this is easy but it was a challenge in big boots, crampons and at over 8,400m.

Doc at the bottom of the first step

I was very comfortable but very glad of the fixed line to help with some leverage. This day was turning into a proper mountaineering experience, not just a plod. I was almost enjoying it.

Next obstacle was the 'Second Step' consisting of a ladder up a steep rock face. I asked myself: is this really mountaineering? There was nothing simple about negotiating narrow metal steps at this altitude in big kit and in this environment. Different kit is needed for different mountaineering challenges; in this case we needed a ladder. The counter argument is: if we needed such artificial aids, should we have been there in the first place? Whatever the answer, the only way to get safely up was up a ladder and I wasn't about to say no.

I stood at the bottom of the ladder as Phil went up. I crossed my legs as I had hydrated a little too well. Girls will relate to the rocking motion we do when desperately wanting to stop ourselves passing water at an inconvenient time. If we rock long enough, the need to go can often subside for a short time and sometimes for quite a while. I rocked until the need stopped and took my first steps up the ladder. I had made it to the top and had one big step across onto the new ledge to go when my bladder exploded and the stretch was the last straw. I must have released what felt like two litres of urine into my suit and boots. How could something that bad feel so good?

Phil took my hand and helped me up over this big step. "Phil, I have just wet myself big time," I said. "Oh well," he replied and walked on. What could he do? There was neither scope, nor time to do anything. I was kicking myself for not stopping earlier but there never seemed to be a good spot. Now I was wet but, due to fantastic kit (thanks Marmot, Tiso and Scarpa), not cold. At no point did I feel remotely cold in my boot or in my suit. The sun was due up soon and, with a bit of luck, it would dry off soon. At least, I could get back to concentrating on walking rather than rocking.

After about seven hours, we came to the main snow face which meant we were back to a steady plod. I almost welcomed the plod as the intense concentration over the previous five hours had been relentless. The sun was starting to rise and the views were breathtaking. We could see the summit looking like it was an hour away until the fixed line cruelly took us around a bend and onto a very steep and precarious rock and snowy face. It was steep broken ground and felt dreadfully unstable.

Me on the final traverse

Then, yet again, a sinking feeling overwhelmed me. There was a separate line hanging from the fixed line with a body hanging from it. We had to physically step over the line to continue on our way. Why were we doing it? What had happened to him? Was he from this year? Questions raced through our head but we were about 40 minutes from the summit. We weren't going to turn back now.

As we pulled up over the final lip, I saw the true summit and knew it was only about 20 minutes away. I had already been on the radio to let the team know we were under an hour away. We were nearly there: not just Phil and I but the success of the whole Everestmax expedition was about to be achieved. I was representing the team; at no point did I feel this was my success. As a team, Everestmax was about to complete the last great overland challenge after nearly six months, eight countries and over 5,000 miles. I tried to think what to say on the radio when we got there but decided I was sure the moment would take me. My mind was suddenly filled with snap shots of the last six months: desert, snow, rain, borders, laughter, tears, illness, elation, cultures, scenery, food and constant stimulation. It was almost too much to take in that what we had been striving for was actually going to be accomplished. It had become so much a part of my daily life that, if I wasn't going slowly enough already, I'd gladly have slowed the whole thing down just to savour the moment. How could anything top this?

It was about 6am on May 18th 2006. The sky was blue, wind minimal, just perfect. Phil was just ahead and there were already about six people there. As I got to the true summit, I grabbed Phil and said: "We are on top of the world!' He hugged me back in a kind of robotic fashion and said: "We need to go soon." I had no intention of just arriving and going; I wasn't expecting violins and roses but wanted some form of reaction. I know it's not everybody's idea of romantic but not every married couple can claim to have summited Mt Everest together. I was determined to have a sense of such an amazing occasion.

I had carried the video up to film the moment we called our team at ABC. We had always talked about that moment being filmed on the summit and simultaneously receiving the call. Phil knew this but was convinced we didn't have time. I calmly communicated this was no time for a domestic and we needed to film it. I got the video out of my bag and the battery out of my pocket. Phil took the video and filmed as I made the call down. "ABC, this is Pauline, do you read me over?" Hearing Dom's voice seemed completely appropriate. I replied with a voice full of pride and emotion: "We have completed the longest climb on earth; we have done it guys... yee haa!" We could hear the cheers from the team. They had all got up early to be ready for the call. It was a great feeling to know we were all sharing it together just as planned. They passed the radio around to share the moment. Sarah said she wanted to speak to Phil. We swapped the radio for the camera but, just as I was getting it into focus, he said: "We are great, but we need to go now." That was the end of the team celebrations for now. We took a few photos and Phil took a complete 360 degree film from the summit. Time to go!

The first British married couple to summit Everest. Not everybody's idea of romantic

CHAPTER **EIGHTEEN**

The final team shot at BC before leaving. Ro, Doc, Sarah, Dickie, Nic, Dom, Nigel, Patrick, Jamie and Phil

Back Down to Earth

I KNEW Phil was right to keep the pressure up to go. It is common knowledge many of the problems and deaths happen on the way down. Phil reacted as if a stopwatch had been started as soon as we had got to the top. We had already changed our oxygen bottle and this one was to last us back down to camp three and, hopefully, camp two. He is a professional and knew our priorities. I was still milking in the wonder of being at the top of the world with my husband and having completed the longest climb in the world... I needed a few minutes but then I was with Phil all the way. No, it wasn't romantic, but it was safe and I wouldn't have wanted to be there with anybody else. It was perfect.

We walked and climbed down for hour after hour. There were still lots of people coming up. We were glad we left as early as we did the night before. Camp three was in sight when I suddenly knew something was wrong. I signalled to Phil my oxygen was out. As I lifted up my mask, he could see my lips were already going blue. We had no extra oxygen tank and had been checking the flow so we shouldn't have run out. Phil came back to meet me and, in no time at all, assessed I had somehow put a twist in my oxygen tube feeding the mask. All was good within seconds and I loved Phil even more! We could see camp three but, when I was losing my breath, it suddenly seemed a long way away!

About 100m before the first tents from camp three, I noticed Phil was walking a bit strangely. I suggested we have a seat. Then we got up again and not long afterwards his crampon came undone. I grabbed him and told him to sit down; he was acting very oddly as he swore at me and was reluctant to let me help him get his crampon back on. We were only 10 minutes from our tent complete with hot drinks and a sleeping bag to give Phil what he needed. He was now exhausted and his body and mind needed a break. We made it to the tent where he had a lay down, had something to eat and felt better almost instantly. We spent an hour just recharging and taking in what we had just done. We wanted to get down to camp two where it would be so much more comfortable and we could almost taste the boil in the bags.

As we walked down to camp two the weather took a turn for the worse – from a perfect day to a windy treacherous Everest nightmare. We were very glad we weren't any higher up. As we walked through the upper parts of camp two, I saw one tent completely shredded by the wind. I didn't know if it was from this season or a previous one; either way, it wasn't a welcoming sight. I picked up a stray can of hot dogs rolling next to it to have later. Even they were appealing to my taste buds.

We got into camp two. We went into one tent, took all our hardwear off and then moved into the next tent where our bags and food had been left. It was great to be down and felt almost comfortable. We were starting to feel we were nearing safety; we were beginning to relax but were still a long way from ABC so no guards were down. We started to melt snow and look for the two boil in the bags. We were so ready for some real food. Our last proper meal had been more than 18 hours ago before we had started out on our summit attempt. All we were able to eat since were energy gels and a cup of soup. Our appetites were back with vengeance.

We needed some solids so searched in both tents without finding any food. We had just had a big day on Mt Everest and all we wanted was a bag of food to chill out with. We dismissed as nonsense the possibility that Chris and Seb had eaten all five bags; even if they had been hungry, two each would have been lots so there was no way they would have eaten all five. We had told them we needed two. Surely not? There was only one way to find out whether we had any food for that night, have to wait until morning or carry on down to the North Col. I wasn't intending to go an inch further.

I did the radio check-in and it was Chris on the other end at ABC. I asked him about the food and could hear in his voice it had dawned on him that he and Seb had eaten the emergency rations: our rations! He was mortified. I didn't get annoyed as he sounded genuinely sorry. They must have been hypoxic and lost the ability to make good decisions. In that respect, we were lucky to have them at all. I didn't make a fuss on the radio other than making him feel bad with a sense of humour.

By next morning I was out of fuel. We had only eaten a tin of hot dogs and a chocolate bar since camp three and we had just climbed Everest; I felt like my body was eating itself. Their mistake, trivial at sea level, could have proved lethal had we got trapped at camp two through bad weather or been any weaker. We needed energy in the form of food to get back down. No climb is successful unless you actually get back down. I had to hide my anxiety on the radio for fear of the rest of the team hearing it. The very last thing they needed was someone else to worry about at the very moment they were trying to focus on their own ascent.

We were ready to go down as soon as possible so Phil went into the next tent to get our boots and hardwear. Unfortunately, we had managed to leave the zip open just one centimeter, enough for the wind to blow snow into the tent and almost fill it. I saw this and cried at the thought of digging it all out. I seriously had nothing left. Phil told me to go back and lie down while he cleared out the tent as he wasn't about to leave a snow-bound tent for the next team to come up to. He knew that when we got there we needed to just get in and collapse and that would be the same for the next climbers too.

I was so glad he had the energy and the selflessness to do this as I was running on empty. We left camp 2 with me still on oxygen as I thought I needed all the help I could get.

We eventually arrived at the North Col. I was so happy to be there. We stuck our heads into the tent and there was Dom and Jamie, with Sarah in the next. We all said our hellos and congratulations and the mood was great. I went in with Sarah as she needed a girl chat, apologising for the smell because my boots, socks and suit still had two litres of urine in them. She said she couldn't smell a thing. Perhaps because I'd drunk so much, the urine was more like water. Anyway, we both got some food down us and felt better straightaway.

Sarah updated me on all that had been happening on the mountain since we had gone. Radio communications hadn't kept us updated on all the sadness. Five people had died in the four days we had been on the mountain and one of them was our married French friend Jacque. That really shocked me and I cried instinctively. His body was the one hanging from a rope on the final traverse – thank God I hadn't recognised him at the time. We had only met a couple of times but he had made such a good impression and his poor wife was now a widow. It was all just too close to home. Sarah had also called for help when she saw a man in big trouble on his way up to the North Col. The Doc looked after him and the Everestmax team had co-ordinated his rescue with his reluctant team mates from Russia and given him one of our bottles of oxygen.

Each new story was enough to take the shine off our own euphoria; the Everest Circus was turning into the 'Everest

Graveyard' with our friends about to have their shot at the high ropes. We at least had gone up ignorant of all this – they would be climbing knowing all this horrible reality. This season was to see the death toll rise to 11 on Everest, the worst since the disaster of 1996 when eight alone died on May 11 and 15 in all perished during the spring climbing season.

Sarah was in a real quandary; she didn't know whether going for the summit was right due to her lack of experience and the fear of what would happen if she needed to come back down. She would then have felt guilty as we'd agreed nobody should do so alone. It was a huge decision for her. The only mountain she had done was Mt Blanc and, although incredibly able physically, I knew how useful I'd found it being completely familiar with equipment and moving across varieties of ground on crampons. I told her that, if she was my daughter, I would advise her to go to camp three and see how she felt then but to be happy to get that far. The final decision had to be hers and I could understand her dilemma. I was experienced and I had Phil; Sarah was inexperienced and had only done the North Col with Dom from her team. I trusted Sarah to make a sensible decision as she wasn't driven by ego or competitive spirit although she tended to beat herself up for not being good enough at things. This wasn't about her being good enough; it was whether she was ready both technically and mentally. They all got their gear to go and I took a team photo. As we said our goodbyes, I felt Chris Rouen's spirit as I took Jamie's shoulder and told him in my most zealous maternal, big sisterly way he wasn't to take any chances.

Phil and I ate our way through the evening and into the next morning. We packed up and made it down to ABC but about one hour from the camp saw Nic and Norbar (our Tibetan kitchen boy) coming our way. They had come to carry our bags; I am sure I saw a set of wings sprouting from them, or perhaps they just looked like angels. We walked back together and not having a pack on my back for the last hour actually made the final walk almost enjoyable.We got into the dining tent and a wave of complete relief came over me. I was at the beginning of a rollercoaster of emotions. I wanted to call home and needed to laugh and cry all at the same time. I got the satellite phone ready and called Robert's home. I knew Mum would be with them and we could finally let her know I had been on Mt Everest and was alive! The phone rang and it was Julia my sister-in-law. She sounded as excited as me. She passed me on to Mum and to Robert and I was doing exactly what I was feeling – crying, then laughing. It was so good to hear their voices but how could I explain what had just happened? I couldn't. They didn't need me to; they just needed to know I was safe and well. They vowed to open a bottle of champagne and have some cakes to celebrate. I didn't need to be with them, we could be together in spirit. That was all I needed right then.

The last hurdle of this epic journey was to have Dom, Jamie, Sarah, the Doc, Karma, Thering and Dorje back after a successful summit attempt or just back safely. It was my turn in the waiting room, at least that's what it felt like. We were waiting for news as there was very little we could actually do.

Nic decided he was going to come back after the North Col as he didn't feel good enough to make a full attempt. Nobody questioned him and he never blamed anybody. He just did what he thought best with utter dignity and minimum fuss. He was a crucial member of the Everestmax expedition and that expedition was a complete success. Multiple summits were a bonus but not a necessity.

I longed to go and see Caroline (Jaque's wife) but I wanted to go when I could be strong for her. I was just about ready now I had changed my clothes, had a semi-wash and just calmed down a bit. I was in the dining tent waiting to call my brother David to touch base and have another dose of family when, out of the blue, Caroline walked in. We said nothing: I just went up to her, flung my arms around her and we both burst into tears and stood there for several minutes. This was a wife on a mountain hugging another wife. We spent the next hour or two just talking and, believe it or not, laughing. It was amazing how such huge emotions can bring out such extreme feelings and behaviour.

We swung from tears to laughter. I'll never know why or how but it seemed to work for her and that was what counted. She had already asked Dom and the team to try and recover Jacque's wedding ring from around his neck and, if possible, the camera so she could at least have a last triumphant image of him when he had made it to the summit. It was a big ask but, if anyone would try, it would be our team.

I can't even attempt to do justice to the individual summit stories of Doc, Dom, Sarah, Jamie, Karma and Thering. At the time, it proved to be another long night for me as I couldn't relax until they were safe at the North Col. I will just say they all made it safely back. Sarah made it to camp three and set up a tea house for the rest of the team to get back to after they all made successful assents on May 21st.

I would like to mention Gerry Winkler who was also successful and summited Mt Everest on the May 20th 2006. He deserves so much credit. We met him in Kathmandu later and he came and found us to say congratulations. He was charming and great fun to be with.

The Everestmax expedition made lots of money for three superb charities and gave seven people the chance to have an experience of a lifetime and form friendships that will hopefully last forever. Phil was the icing on the cake for me.

I hope you have enjoyed sharing this amazing journey. I particularly hope I have been able to communicate the warmth and hospitality we experienced from people of all ages, religions and walks of life from across the world.

I hope you enjoy your journey – whatever and wherever it may be.

CHAPTER **NINETEEN**

The Everestmax team in a Tibetan tea house
the day before reaching Everest Base Camp

Stories From The Team

The team is the reason I enjoyed this expedition so much. We are all quite different characters but were able to bring out the best in each other. I asked them if they wanted to be part of this book; after all they are the reason I have a story to tell. The following short stories about our journey are from them.

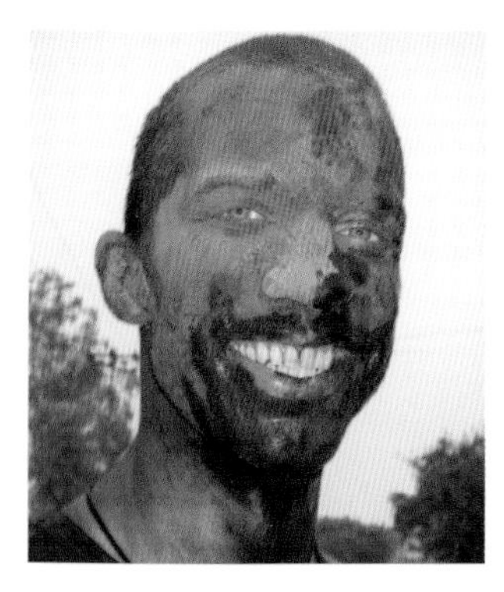

NIC CLARKE

A trip of a lifetime. Seven strangers with varying backgrounds left the UK heading for Jordan and lifelong friendships were quickly formed on the long roads to Tibet. Cycling through all weather conditions we were welcomed and accepted into all countries and communities to a far greater extent than we could ever have imagined or dreamt of. Homes offered to us for a night ranged from police cells, to kebab shops, to garages and army fortresses. And the cost? Always for free and always with a smile (did they know something we didn't? In the case of when our tent flooded on a flood plain, maybe!).

Of the many highlights of the six month trip, cycling the length of Iran was a truly memorable experience. Through the media, we only hear about the politics which rules Iran. Yet if you go past this, you will quickly find an amazing country full of wonderful people with stunning scenery that will remain in the heart forever.

From crossing the border into Iran and heading into the unknown, we were quickly accepted and welcomed into the lives of the Iranians. By cycling through the country, showing genuine interest and being full of enthusiasm, we quickly saw the warmth of the Iranians. Little did the locals know what a profound effect they were having on our lives and how humbling and inspiring it was meeting them.

When our van broke down and needed urgent repair, the engineers of Esfahan worked through several nights to construct the parts and repair the van. The cost? They refused to accept a penny. Where else would you find this generosity with such a giving and helpful attitude to life?

On Boxing Day 2003 the city of Bam was struck by an earthquake measuring more than six on the Richter Scale, killing over 25,000 people and destroying over 70 per cent of the city's buildings. Over two years later we cycled into the very same town not knowing what to expect. We were met with many buildings still flattened and locals working tirelessly to rebuild the city but mostly we saw an amazing spirit of great unity and one of sheer determination. Children, who had nothing apart from a stick and a ball (if they were lucky), played and laughed in the streets as the young should even though many had lost their parents, brothers and sisters, friends and other family.

Sitting at the old Citadel as the sun rose one morning, I was truly humbled and reduced to tears as I took in the surroundings and the devastation. It is vital we don't forget the areas that suffer from these natural disasters and continue to support them as they rebuild their lives and communities.

Iran is an amazing country I will never forget for all the right reasons. If I can show to others some of the wonderful qualities we saw and experienced first hand throughout Iran and to change people's perception of the country, I would be happy.

ROWEENA WRIGHT

Travelling through foreign countries at cycling speed is fantastic... especially when you are in a van! You go slowly enough to appreciate the small details but fast enough to see new cultures unfolding before you. For me, the way everything changed from day to day was fascinating and relentless in equal measure. Things would appear, become normal and just as you began to expect and rely on them they would disappear, never to be seen again.

As the support team, it was our job to make sure the cyclists had everything they needed. Basically, lots of tasty, nourishing food and somewhere comfortable to sleep at night; ideally with beds and a shower and loos that didn't smell too bad and a pizza restaurant near by!

It was a daily challenge explaining to baffled hotel owners, who often spoke no English, that we needed a room for the night for seven people, five of whom would be arriving on bicycles in about an hour - cold, wet, filthy, tired and hungry! A few well-practiced actions and some doodles on a sketch pad usually did the trick, all the while resisting the urge to say it again slowly and loudly in English! Throughout the trip people were incredibly helpful and generous but I do wonder how often they really understood exactly what was about to arrive and trail mud through their lobbies.

Buying food was equally complicated. Every day we'd be in a new town with no idea what kind of shops we would find or what they would sell. Without a fridge and with limited storage in the van, we had to shop every day, buying breakfast, lunch, tea, supper, snacks, hot drinks, cold drinks, treats, birthday cakes, water, plasters, sun cream, bike parts and all sorts of other essential bits and bobs that it might or might not be possible to find. The next day we'd do it all over again in a new town where you couldn't find that delicious thing you bought yesterday... the one everyone loved and wanted again. In fact, you never find it again as you are miles away and everything has changed.

It wasn't just the food. The landscape, weather, road conditions, population, language, religion, politics, attitudes, clothes, colours, facial features, hairstyles, wildlife, traffic, noise levels, drains, smells - in fact just about everything - kept changing all the way and we had to adapt accordingly.

Being British and liking our home comforts, Dom had the foresight to pack some English tea bags - about a thousand of them! It was just what we needed to get us going every morning. However, there were moments when our large mugs of milky English tea seemed a bit unadventurous. Tea and coffee seemed to oil the wheels of most transactions, from market stalls to border crossings, and each country had its own very individual ways of serving it.

In Jordan, smiling shopkeepers would produce trays of small glasses containing hot black tea. Of course, we would end up buying as much as possible from them – how could we not?

Miles from anywhere in the Syrian desert, a stallholder took out his battered thermos flask and poured us two small cups of thick, pungent, cardamom coffee. We offered him money but he refused. He was just sharing his coffee on a cold day. In Iran, they drank delicate glasses of strong black tea with sugar served in gift boxes - large amber crystals you put in your mouth and then sip the tea through it. Not great for your teeth but delicious.

We drank tea this way for a month and then in the space of an hour it changed... one hundred yards over the border from Iran and we were in Pakistan.

The customs officer welcomed us to his country with pretty china cups full of rich sweet tea that seemed to be made with condensed milk. This lasted for three weeks before it all changed again. Yes, another new country and a new way of serving tea. Further on, in the frozen, high altitude mountains of Tibet, we drank reviving milky tea churned in wooden barrels. If you weren't so lucky, you were given yak butter tea – an acquired taste, more like cheese soup than tea! By the time we arrived at Everest Base Camp, we were advised to drink lots of fluids as the thin, dry atmosphere was very dehydrating but not tea or coffee as they are diuretics! You would think we'd had enough by then but we missed it.

Coming back home to England, the land of tea and toast and Sunday papers, was perfect!

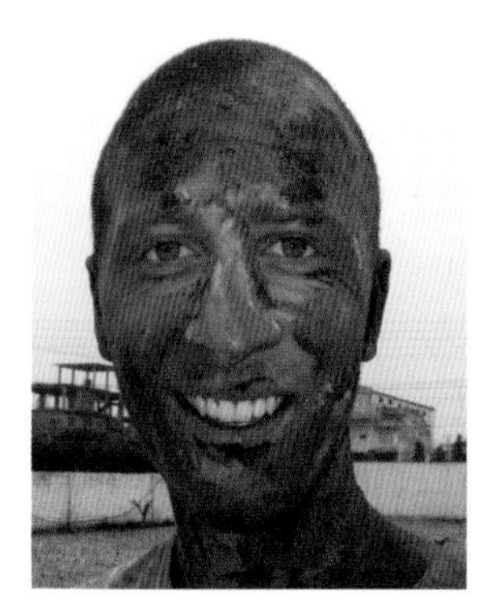

JAMIE ROUEN

The sun rose on the morning of the 21st May as Dom, Andrew and myself approached the bottom of the second step. This was the most welcome feeling as I had been desperately fighting the cold in my hands and feet since we had left our final camp the previous night.

We had been moving well as a team but I was beginning to slow. I was cold, my chest was painful and everywhere I looked was a sobering reminder of just how serious an environment we were climbing into. From the 3000m of Everest's north face disappearing below my feet; to the climber halfway up the second step, practically hanging from his harness and being pulled up by his Sherpas; to the two bodies we had climbed past previously whose time up here in the death zone had been too prolonged and had taken its most costly toll.

All this made me scared and I decided it was time for me to turn round. I removed my oxygen mask to speak to Dom and Andrew and told them how I was feeling. They both seemed strong and we all decided to give the second step a go and see how we felt when we get to the top. The sun was warming me and the brief rest we had, whilst we waited for the struggling climber above to free up the ropes, gave me new strength. The second step was awkward rather then technically difficult but the sunrise had seemed to bring with it a new sense of optimism and I desperately tried to suck in as much oxygen as I could whilst I climbed this section a step at a time.

I pulled myself over the final ledge at the top of the ladder and looked up at the route ahead. Only here, at this point high up on the exposed north ridge, did I finally realise that I actually had it in me to make it to the summit. Although there had been hundreds of unforgettable moments throughout the Everestmax journey - from all the good times we had on our bikes, cooking together and sharing a bottle of champagne on Christmas Day, experiencing that incredible feeling of team spirit as we finally cycled in to Base Camp - this moment, as I stood breathless at the top of the second step, has to be one of my most memorable. Although I was breathing harder than ever before and I was still extremely anxious about getting safely off the mountain, I finally realised I might actually make it. From the moment I left the

Dead Sea five months previously, I had never thought this would become reality, and here I was with what I thought and hoped was enough energy and will power to get me to the summit. This is a moment I will never forget and, after sipping some water, I set off again behind Dom and Andrew with a renewed sense of purpose. I was going to make it; I was going to complete the longest climb on earth.

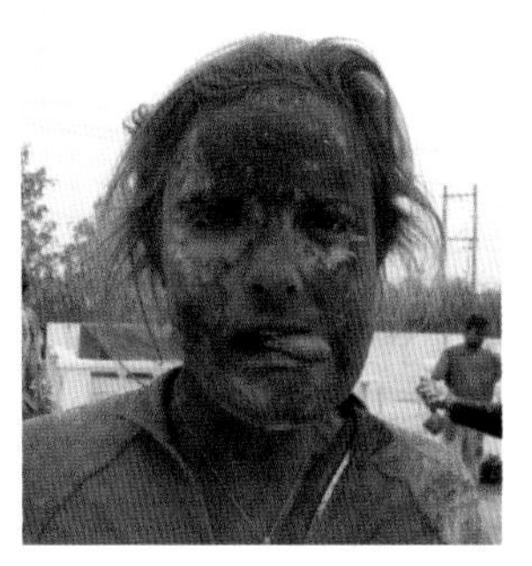

SARAH LYLE

Highs and lows were in abundance during the trip both physically and mentally but for me personally nothing beat cycling into the Himalaya. I kept a daily diary during the trip. It would not win The Man Booker Prize - the parish newsletter was my literary highlight - but I hope that the entry of 16th March, our first day in the Himalaya, will give some sense of how overwhelming and humbling it felt to have the privilege to be there.

16th March: Bhairahawa – Roadside café: Up to see Practical Action bicycle ambulance project at 9am. Really inspiring – great design being made by local people. ~150 bikes/yr, 7 people employed, ~£120/bike, in use for 4-5 yrs then come back in for repairs. Had a go at pulling one on the bike, felt good, most unstable when you set off. Weight limit = 100kg and supposedly for 2 people! Guys also making water pumps and grain sorters. Really good to see such a good use of money.

Breakfast/lunch at the hotel and then headed off. Road = flat, flat, flat. Lots of bikes, pedestrians and the odd motor bike. Soldiers in staggered file walking back to base looked tired.
20 km in and we hit the Himalaya – it was a dramatic change in gradient, immediate and just awesome cycling up into it. Lovely faces, really lush scenery, fantastic views, big drops. Grinning from ear to ear, just so happy to be here – very lucky girl.

Village stop for tea. Jamie, Nic and Pauline playing footy, Pauline did an overhead kick and sent the ball flying over a roof towards the valley floor – noooo! Thankfully it had got caught in the yard. Really enjoying the ride, lots of up but a nice gradient. Great downs and roads really quiet because of the Maoist strike. Can't predict where the road will go. Brilliant.

Final up was long with hairpins. Kids racing down the hill on a go kart dodging big tyres in the road – so dangerous!

Had booked into a hotel but it was 4 km off route. Ended up staying with a family at the junction where we should have turned off – perfect. They had a restaurant and shop downstairs and great room upstairs – big living room, sofas and beds around the edge, with plenty of space in the middle to kip. Perfect. Family came in to say hi – guessed Pauline as 32 and Dom as 55 – much laughter and a disgruntled Dom. Youngest daughter -20, really nice girl, big smile, showed us family photos, very good English, little baby boy running around with Mama close by.

Dinner = tasty, waitress tipped food on Jamie and then had a good giggle. Nic amazed by how quickly they refilled the dhalbat. Played a rolling quiz upstairs, star watched and then slept. Woken the next morning at 6.30 am to the sound of kids reading science books out loud, overseen by the family's daughter.

Wow. What a cracking day.

RICHARD WALTERS

Rather than highlight one single incident or magical moment, I thought I would reflect on the one thing that stood out to me throughout the trip; the people. Everestmax to me was a story of human endeavour not only for those trying to achieve 'The Longest Climb' but also for the warm-hearted lives we were lucky enough to meet and touch and the friendships forged.

Supporting the expedition was a real privilege. As the cyclists slogged on doggedly towards Everest, for Rowena and me every day was different and, although at one stage I thought I would love to have bragging rights, having cycled the monumental distance from Jordan to Everest, a summit bid was out of the question. The expedition and team had to maximise the chance for success and the best way I could help would be to keep the logistics under control. Sourcing victuals, crossing borders, finding hotels, pitching tents, filming and negotiating with police, customs and NGOs from country to country was a fascinating experience and opportunity to open the curtains to lives and cultures far away from our own.

We live our lives with opinion shaped by our politicians, peers and the media and so it was armed with these almost institutionalised thoughts we crossed new borders and met new challenges. We entered Iran the day after George Bush gave his 'Axis of evil' declaration on Iran; we entered Pakistan shortly after they had been made aware of the Danish cartoons depicting Mohammed, requiring us to organise a 24hr police guard and having to confront daily protests; and arrived in Nepal amid intensive Maoist strikes. Thankfully, despite the political lobbying and shenanigans, the lowest common denominator - the man on the street - remained true and virtuous and restored my faith in humanity.

Although there were many episodes of good will and warmth towards us and many tales of overcoming adversity amongst those we met, the one episode that stands out above all was the generosity of Ali, Modin and the team at Iran Khodro in Esfahan. Our van had suffered hugely in the minus 29 degrees celsius temperatures of Bostanabad. The diesel, hydraulics and pretty much everything froze and, naive to the precautions required having been in a desert only a few weeks earlier, Martha caught pneumonia, a condition she didn't properly recover from for the rest of the trip.

We soon discovered that the locals lit fires under their engines to keep them warm which is quite alien to our British mentality. So it was, having mended the gear stick that sheared off as the metal joint got too brittle in the cold, we set off out of the freezing bowl. A few days later, as we cleared the snow the van started to over heat. Having had a few dodgy vehicles in my time, I instantly recognised the smell. Filling her up with water every 20 minutes temporarily solved the issue but there was some major surgery required. When we reached the next garage, we were told the cylinder head gasket had blown and we would need to get to Esfahan.

We arranged a piggyback on the back of a lorry and were dropped on the edge of the city outside a non-descript line of shops. One, an industrial shelving supplier, happened to be owned by Ali, who said he would help us so our escort disappeared. Immediately he reached for his home made wine and poured four glasses. Muddling through with our few words of Farsi and their few words of English, Rowena and I were made completely at ease. On finishing our glasses he insisted on taking us out to lunch but reassured us that a mechanic would come round soon. Sure enough a mechanic turned up and took away the van with us following behind kindly being driven by Ali.

Sadly, it was the cylinder head gasket that had blown and, as this was the only Kia in the country, they would have to make their own replacement. It was going to take at least three days to mend the vehicle. Ali insisted that we stay with his family. He moved out of his bedroom to allow Rowena (my wife, as it saved any complications and awkward questions, and they obviously were able to predict the future as we are now married with a son) and I to use their room. They fed and watered us for two days before the cyclists arrived whereupon we joined them and moved to a hostel in the centre of the city.

A few days later we went to collect Martha. With lots of excitement, I took her for a test drive. I tried to put her in reverse and nothing happened. The gearbox had decided to fail! Back on the ramp they set back to work. A day later I was able to collect her and I feared for the bill. In the UK it would have cost us a few thousand pounds for all the time they had taken. Our bill was zero. "Thank you for visiting our country and thank you for raising money for the people of Bam." We were completely shocked and amazed by their generosity and will never forget them.

I am sure that when I limped back through the gates alone two days later with the same overheating issues they were annoyed to see me but they didn't show it. Ali and Modin sprung back into action and hosted me again whilst the garage sorted out the problem and didn't charge us for a second time. Life would be so much simpler without the media but unfortunately things are what they are and we will continue to be influenced by advertising and dialogue at every juncture. In the world of paranoia, what would you do if an Iranian knocked on your door asking for help?

DOMONIC FAULKNER

Dom has written a book called The Longest Climb, which if you would like to read about the story from a different perspective is worth the read.

EPILOGUE

All scrubbed up for the premiere of the film that Dom made.
It was a fantastic night at the RGS in London

THE EVERESTMAX experience has offered me so many opportunities since coming back. It seems in keeping with the ethos of the expedition that many of those opportunities have involved helping others by doing motivational presentations for various charities. Many have helped me as corporate talks have contributed to getting our bank balance back to normal.

This has been a story to inspire young, old and everyone in-between. I like to think the real message is in the story of the journey rather than, as has been suggested, 'if a middle aged woman can do an expedition like that, anything is possible!'

I think my personal favourite opportunity was to be the main speaker on 'Bike Night' at the Kendal Film Festival, the leader in the UK for outdoor festivals. I had only ever been in the audience and had often been in awe of the presenters and their tales of adventure. I had wondered what it would be like to deliver a presentation to such an experienced audience of amateur and professional activists. Well, I found out. I had a sell-out lecture of more than 500. I was bricking it; for want of a better expression. To me, this was the most intimidating audience ever. I have never had to rely on Dutch courage, but I happened to see Russell Brice in the VIP meeting area, who said hello by giving me a large glass of red wine about 15 minutes before show time. That did the trick nicely and I got out there and loved every moment. The audience was brilliant.

On a romantic note, Dickie and Ro did admit to romantic liaisons at Base Camp. They have subsequently got married and have a beautiful baby boy called Charlie. He will be the walking, talking legacy of the trip.

Phil and I went back to great jobs at Glenmore Lodge where I stayed until 2010. If there is one thing we both agree came from Everest, it's that our perspective on life has been tweaked. In Phil's words: "If you aren't badly ill, injured or dying, you can cope with anything." There is no time for worrying over trivia in our relatively short lives. Save that energy for what really counts.

Despite our differences of opinion on Everest, Dom and I walked away friends. We both agree we could have handled the situation and each other better. We still agree to differ on our chosen approaches, but that is fine. Respect is still intact and friendship is more important than ego, so we have moved on.

All of the Everestmax team are in good contact; not on a regular basis but, as anyone knows who has had good friends, it really doesn't matter how often you see each other. We continue to ridicule and support in equal amounts. Long may it last!

Thanks to the Everestmax Sponsors

Marin Bikes
Top Out
The Fine Art Society
Fluid Motivation
Polaris
NSSL Satcom-Solutions
PHD Mountain Software
Blackbrick Building Company
Catalyst
Wilfs
Sotherbys
Sign Studio
Khyam Outdoor Centre
Wombat Clothing
Commercial Group
Badger Rugby
Doughty Hanson & Co
Honda
Buff
Rab
Cotswold
Select Solar
Bloc
Moran's Eating House
Whatmore Plastics
Oxogen

Thanks to Phil & Pauline's Personal Sponsors

Tiso
Marmot
The North Face

Phil and I back in the Lakes enjoying climbing in the sunshine. (Photograph by Martyn Mills).

GLOSSARY

Kayaking

1. **Self-support:** When all you need for a multi-day trip is in the back of your boat for camping etc
2. **Shuttle:** When you need to get lifts from one end of the river to the other

Climbing/Mountaineering

3. **Ice axe arrest:** A method to stop a slide using an ice axe in the event of a slip on a snow slope.
4. **Crampons:** a close-fitting metal spike frame on a climber's boot that allows secure movement on hard snow and ice
5. **Rope up:** When mountaineers travel on potentially crevasse/glacial terrain, they are spaced apart by a section of rope as a form of protection if one should fall into a crevasse.
6. **Belay:** Belaying refers to a variety of techniques used in climbing to exert friction on a climbing rope so that if a climber falls they do not go far.
7. **Crevasse:** A deep, usually vertical, crack or split in a glacier, occurs as a result of the brittle ice flowing over a uneven surface beneath the ice. Crevasses can easily become covered by blown snow, even very wide ones. Great care must be taken when crossing ice and snowfields to avoid them.
8. **HVS:** A climbing grade, which means Hard Very Severe
9. **White out:** When you lose daylight visibility in heavy fog, snow, or rain
10. **Cerebral oedema:** This is a condition where there is an excess accumulation of water in the intracellular and/or extracellular spaces of the brain
11. **Pulmonary oedema:** This is a condition when there is fluid accumulation in the lungs. It leads to impaired gas exchange and may cause respiratory failure.
12. **Jumar:** A mechanical device, used to clip on a rope, which tightens when weight is applied, thus allowing the rope to be climbed.
13. **Fixed line:** A rope that is attached to the mountain using anchors at strategic points. A climber uses a jumar to clip onto the rope and uses it as a safety line to ascend and descend.
14. **MIA:** Mountain Instructor Award – summer multi-pitch rock climbing/mountaineering instructor
15. **MIC:** Mountain Instructor Certificate – winter climbing/mountaineering instructor
16. **VDiff:** A climbing grade, which means Very Difficult
17. **AMS:** Accute Mountain Sickness
18. **Hypoxia:** Hypoxia is a condition characterized by a lack of oxygen in the body's tissues. The hypoxia may encompass the general body, or a specific area, such as the brain.

    At high altitude, breathing "thin" air with reduced amounts of available oxygen, means that you inhale less oxygen than you need. When the condition first begins to develop, it can produce some signs that may not seem significant enough for a person to take seriously. This may include slight difficulty performing tasks that require coordination, trouble focusing, and bad judgment. In all cases, it can be dangerous or deadly, because without oxygen, the human body cannot function.

SOS TIBETAN CHILDREN'S
VILLAGE
Visit by Appointment Only

My publisher Mark Ramsden and I enjoying my 40th 'BACK TO SCHOOL' themed birthday party... it's amazing what you have to do to get a cheap deal!

THE CHARITIES

As we set off on our adventure we had decided to support three charities that had helped the countries we would be travelling through. Merlin, SOS Childrens Villages and Practical Action. As part of our route, we visited the two that are actually based there to see the 'good works' in action... having made our visits we left inspired by the dedication and ingenuity of those running the charities and were motivated to raise as much money as possible. 50% of the profits from this book will add to this figure.

SOS Children's Villages

SOS Children is the world's largest orphan charity, caring for children with no close family and is represented in over 123 countries worldwide.

www.soschildrensvillages.org.uk

SOS Childrens Villages Nepal.
A superb charity

Practical Action

Practical Action uses technology to challenge poverty, working with poor women and men around the world.

www.practicalaction.org

Practical Action bike ambulance